WILLIAMS-SONOMA

THE BAR GUIDE

TIME-LIFE BOOKS
Time-Life Books is a division of Time Life Inc.
Time Life is a trademark of Time Warner Inc. U.S.A.

TIME-LIFE CUSTOM PUBLISHING
Vice President and Publisher: Terry Newell
Vice President of Sales and Marketing: Neil Levin
Director of Financial Operations: J. Brian Birky
Director of Acquisitions and Editorial Resources: Jennifer L. Pearce

WILLIAMS-SONOMA
Founder and Vice-Chairman: Chuck Williams
Associate Book Buyer: Cecilia Michaelis

WELDON OWEN INC.
Chief Executive Officer: John Owen
Chief Operating Officer: Larry Partington
Vice President International Sales: Stuart Laurence
Vice President and Publisher: Roger S. Shaw

Series Editor: Janet Goldenberg
Contributing Editor: Norman Kolpas
Copy Editor: Gail Nelson
Indexer and Proofreader: Ken DellaPenta

Art Director: Diane Dempsey
Production Director: Stephanie Sherman
Production Manager: Lisa Cowart-Mayor
Design Assistant: William Erik Evans

The Williams-Sonoma Guides
conceived and produced by Weldon Owen Inc.
814 Montgomery Street, San Francisco, CA 94133

In collaboration with Williams-Sonoma
3250 Van Ness Avenue, San Francisco, CA 94109

Separations by Bright Arts Graphics (S) Pte. Ltd.
Printed in Singapore by Tien Wah Press (Pte.) Ltd.

A WELDON OWEN PRODUCTION

First printed in 1999.

10 9 8 7 6 5 4 3 2

Library of Congress Cataloging-in-Publication Data
The bar guide/ consulting editor, Ray Foley;
illustrations by Rodney Davidson
p. cm. -- (Williams-Sonoma guides)
Includes index.
ISBN 0-7370-0062-7 (hc.)
1. Bartending Handbook, manuals, etc. I. Foley, Ray.
II. Series.
TX951.B256 1999
641.8'74--dc21 99-33470
CIP

A NOTE ON WEIGHTS AND MEASURES

All recipes include customary U.S. and metric measurements. Metric conversions are based on a standard developed for these books and have been rounded off. Actual measurements may vary.

WILLIAMS-SONOMA

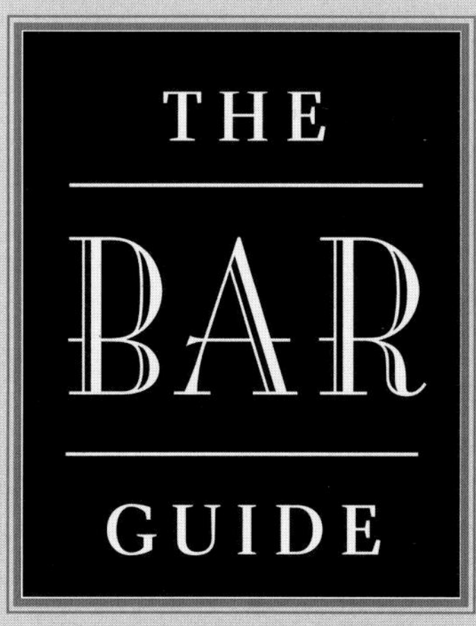

CONSULTING EDITOR / RAY FOLEY

ILLUSTRATOR / RODNEY DAVIDSON

CARTOGRAPHER / ANDREW THOMPSON

FOREWORD BY CHUCK WILLIAMS

CONTENTS

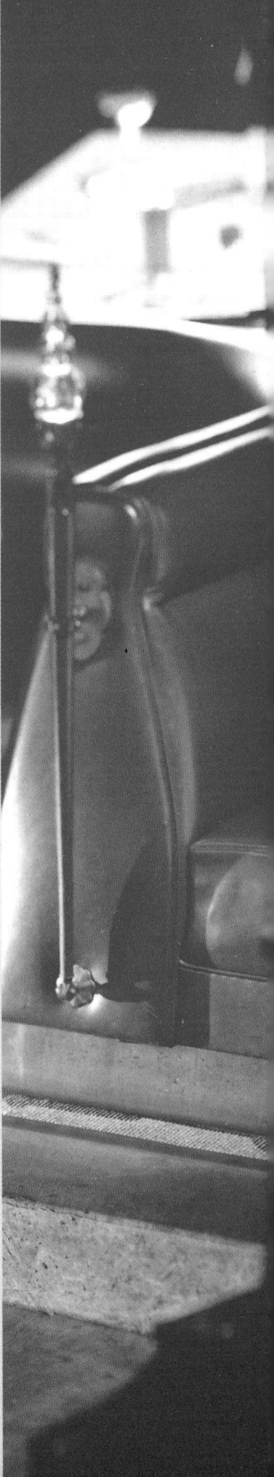

Foreword

"What'll It Be?"

Hardly more than a generation ago, you would hear those words in homes everywhere as good hosts offered their guests a drink. Today, cocktails are enjoying a new popularity—yet most people lack a basic knowledge of how to mix and serve them.

That's where this book comes in. We've designed it specifically to meet the needs of home bartenders.

The following pages explain everything you need to know about, from basic glassware, equipment, and ingredients to the fundamentals of mixology. You'll find an A-to-Z of recipes for more than 400 classic and contemporary cocktails and mixed drinks, along with indexes organized by drink type, main ingredient, and occasion.

We've tried to make the book interesting to read and beautiful to look at—the perfect cornerstone for your home bar. I hope you won't hesitate to reach for it the next time you turn to your own guests and ask, "What'll it be?"

BOMBAY
SAPPHIRE
Distilled
DRY GIN
BOTTLED AT THE DISTILLERY
MARTINI & ROSSI
MARTINI
France

CHAPTER 1

Stocking a Bar

If you want to offer your guests a range of cocktails and mixed drinks, you need a well-rounded selection of basic ingredients, tools, and glassware. These pages provide information on everything you'll require.

Drink Basics

Although experts differ on the definition of the cocktail, a common school of thought holds that any drink with two or more ingredients, shaken or stirred with ice and strained into a chilled cocktail glass, falls into the cocktail category. All other combinations are mixed drinks. Central to most cocktails or mixed drinks is an alcoholic beverage—often a distilled spirit such as gin or vodka. In this section you'll learn what spirits are, how they are made, and how to evaluate them.

COCKTAILS: A BRIEF HISTORY

People have been mixing various ingredients with wines, beers, and spirits since time immemorial, but cocktails and mixed drinks as we know them didn't appear in the United States or anywhere else until the early nineteenth century. This is not to say that no such drinks existed earlier—Colonial Americans very likely made Mint Juleps, for example.

But no one applied the word *cocktail*—originally used to describe a mixed-breed horse with a docked tail—to mixed beverages until the beginning of the nineteenth century. A New York newspaper of that time, the *Balance and Columbian Repository*, described a cocktail as "a stimulating liquor, composed of spirits of any kind, sugar, water, and bitters."

Many drinks now known as cocktails fall far from this early definition, and since their invention some two centuries ago, the range has grown to encompass Fizzes, Fixes, Slings, Sours, and myriad other mixed-drink categories. Today there are hundreds of standard recipes and thousands of variations, and more are invented every year.

A New York newspaper was among the first to describe the cocktail.

A NOTE ABOUT WHISK(E)Y

This book uses the spelling *whisk(e)y* where the text refers to both *whisky* (the Scottish or Canadian product) and *whiskey* (the Irish or American one). Where the text refers to a particular nation's whisky or whiskey, it uses the appropriate spelling.

FROM BEERS TO SPIRITS

Most cocktails and other mixed drinks have at their base a spirit such as vodka, whisk(e)y, gin, or rum. To understand spirits better, it is helpful to know they all start out the same way: as forms of wine or beer. Beer is typically made by allowing yeast to ferment the sugars in a "soup" of cooked grains, transforming them into alcohol and carbon dioxide. The precursor of whisk(e)y and many other distilled spirits is similar, except that different plant materials often take the place of grains. For example, the base for rum is fermented from sugarcane products, tequila is made from the agave plant, and vodka sometimes comes from beets or potatoes.

All liquor labels list the percentage of alcohol by volume, in this case 40 percent, the minimum permitted.

Similarly, wine—the starting point for brandy—results when yeast performs the same action on the juice of grapes or other fruits, though only rarely is the juice cooked before fermentation. Although these beerlike or winelike "soups" are not beers or wines in the commercial sense, they contain similar amounts of beverage alcohol—typically between 8 and 14 percent by volume.

Whatever their base, these fermented mixtures are then distilled to create spirits, which by law must contain at least 40 percent alcohol by volume. In the beverage world, distillation refers to the separation of alcohol from the other components of a fermented liquid. This is accomplished by heating (or sometimes freezing) the mixture so its nonalcoholic elements are left behind.

Alcohol evaporates at a lower temperature than water. Therefore, if you heat a fermented liquid, capture the first (alcoholic) vapors that rise from the liquid, and then condense them, the resulting liquid has a dramatically higher concentration of alcohol than the liquid from which it was distilled. Distill this product again, and its alcohol concentration rises even higher. In this way, spirits are made.

Spirits are the beverages that contain the highest concentration of alcohol. Following them in potency are liqueurs (sweetened and diluted forms of spirits) such as Drambuie and Bénédictine, fortified wines (wines with spirits added to them) such as port and sherry, aromatized wines (wines enhanced with spirits and flavorings) such as vermouth, sparkling and still wines, and finally, beers.

A Distillery at Work

IN THIS DISTILLING OPERATION for single-malt Scotch, barley grain is malted (sprouted), dried over a peat fire, and fermented with yeast before undergoing two distillations in pot stills. The new whisky is then aged in barrels.

EVALUATING SPIRITS AND LIQUEURS

A cocktail or mixed drink is only as good as the ingredients that go into it, and central to many is a spirit or liqueur. To appreciate fully the complexity of fine spirits and liqueurs, aficionados employ a tasting routine like the one used for wine.

Sherry copita

To evaluate these beverages, sit in a quiet, well-lighted room, preferably at a table with a clean white surface, and choose glasses conducive to the process. A sherry copita glass (left) is the professional taster's usual choice, though some people prefer brandy snifters and others rely on small tulip-shaped wineglasses (for

Proof and Percentage

PROOF DESCRIBES THE STRENGTH of alcoholic beverages. The scale used in the United States is based on 200 degrees, each degree equal to 0.5 percent alcohol by volume at 60°F (15°C). Thus, an 80-proof spirit is 40 percent alcohol by volume. The United Kingdom has its own wholly different scale, the Sikes, in which one degree of proof equals 0.57 percent alcohol by volume, also at 60°F (15°C). A bottle of bourbon that is 40 percent alcohol would be 65 proof on the Sikes scale.

The metric Gay-Lussac scale, based on the percentage of alcohol by volume, has become the benchmark measurement, probably due to its simplicity and the growth of the global marketplace. The current trend among many spirits manufacturers is to print on labels the percentage of alcohol by volume, instead of or in addition to the proof. This book uses the Gay-Lussac scale.

pictures of these vessels, see pages 41 and 43). The common denominator among them is that the rim has a smaller diameter than the base, thereby concentrating aromas at the top of the glass.

To begin the tasting, pour only about 1 tablespoon of the beverage into each glass. Observe it for color (here's where the white surface proves useful); this can range from clear in the case of gin or vodka, to pale amber or deep mahogany in the case of whisk(e)ys and brandies, to myriad hues—sometimes almost luminescent—in the case of liqueurs.

Swirl the liquid and bring the lip of the glass to your nose. Breathe in through your nose and mouth at the same time, trying to discern individual aromas. Take a small sip of the beverage, then swish it around to coat your mouth, trying to pick out component flavors of the drink (see Flavors and Aromas, page 16). Also notice how the beverage feels in your mouth: Does it seem to fill the mouth, even though you have taken just a small sip? If so, the beverage is full-bodied. Does it seem weak or watery? In that case, it is light- or thin-bodied (which is not necessarily bad). Is it somewhere in between? If so, it is medium-bodied. If the spirit is of high alcoholic strength, add a tablespoon of still mineral water and repeat the process. Dilution can open up a whole new spectrum of flavors and aromas.

Pour only a small amount into the tasting glass.

Next, swallow a little of the drink and observe whether it feels hot, warm, or astringent in your throat. Once again, try to detect individual flavors. Finally, note how long these flavors linger in the throat. If they disappear almost immediately, the drink has a short finish; if they stay with you for up to a minute or so, it has a medium finish; and if—as can be the case with some whisk(e)ys and brandies—the flavors remain detectable for a few minutes, the drink has a long finish.

Flavors and Aromas

A spirit's special characteristics arise from its ingredients, manufacture, and aging. Below are some representative flavor and aroma components of the major spirits.

Bourbon Almonds, apples, butterscotch, caramel, cloves, hazelnuts, leather, oranges, peaches, pears, plums, tobacco, vanilla, walnuts.

Cognac and other oak-aged grape brandies Almonds, dried flowers, hazelnuts, nutmeg, oak, oranges, pears, tangerines, vanilla, walnuts.

Gin Angelica root, citrus zest, coriander, juniper, lavender, orris, perfume, wildflowers.

Rum Allspice, apples, candy, cedar, chocolate, cinnamon, coffee, honey, molasses, nutmeg, oak, oranges, peaches, raisins, vanilla.

Scotch Apples, chocolate, citrus zest, grass, hay, heather, honey, iodine, leather, oak, oranges, prunes, raisins, smoke, tobacco, wildflowers.

Tequila Chives, citrus zest, grass, licorice, moss, nutmeg, pepper, pineapple, rosemary, tangerines, tarragon.

Vodka Baked bread, candy, caramel, citrus zest, grains, pepper, perfume, pine, spiciness.

Liquors for the Bar

Although you can make a home bar operational with just a single bottle of liquor, you need at least a basic assortment of spirits, liqueurs, wines, and beers to offer your guests a satisfying range of options. As your tastes and entertaining plans expand, you can gradually add to your collection. The question is, with so many varieties of liquor available, what do you buy first? Here are guidelines to help you prioritize your purchases.

BUYING LIQUORS

Few people deliberately set out to buy all the spirits, liqueurs, wines, and beers they'll ever need to stock an encyclopedic home bar. Instead, home bars evolve.

For instance, if you've recently discovered a tasty, inexpensive sparkling wine, you may be tempted to purchase a bottle of crème de cassis so you can serve Kir Royales. Or if Margaritas look to be the drink of the summer at your place, a bottle of premium triple sec may be in order. The point is that you can take your time—there's no reason to feel you should buy everything at once.

Keeping Liquors

UNOPENED BOTTLES of spirits and liqueurs last almost indefinitely. Once opened, however, they slowly deteriorate. Some connoisseurs insist that oxidation in an opened bottle of spirits causes it to decline in quality after six months. However, this decline is usually barely detectable until a year or more has passed.

Liqueur bottles need checking more frequently; any deterioration generally first becomes apparent three to six months after opening them.

To slow the deterioration of spirits or liqueurs, transfer unused portions into smaller bottles so the liquid fills the neck. Less contact with air helps liquors last longer.

Air makes liquor spoil faster.

Buying quality is always a good idea, but you needn't splurge on everything. By all means spring for a fine bottle when you want a superlative tasting experience. But when you're mixing punch for a party, a less-expensive bottling will do, since other ingredients mask the liquor's subtleties.

STOCKING UP

LIQUORS

Listed here are the essential and optional liquors for a home bar. For descriptions, see the A-to-Z Drinks Guide, beginning on page 76.

ESSENTIALS

Spirits Bourbon, blended Canadian whisky, gin, Irish whiskey, rum, Scotch, tequila, vodka.

Liqueurs Anisette, apricot brandy, Bénédictine, crème de cacao (white and dark), crème de cassis, crème de menthe, Irish cream liqueur, Kahlúa, maraschino, sambuca, Southern Comfort, triple sec.

Wines Dry white and red, sparkling, dry vermouth, sweet vermouth.

Beers Domestic lager, small selection of locally made microbrews.

EXTRAS

Spirits Select and unusual bottlings of brandy, gin, rum, tequila and mezcal, whisk(e)y, and vodka.

Liqueurs B&B, blackberry brandy, Chambord, Chartreuse, cherry brandy, Cointreau, crème de bananes, crème de noyaux, curaçao (white and blue), Drambuie, Frangelico, Galliano, Grand Marnier, Irish Mist, Jägermeister, Midori, ouzo, peach brandy, peach schnapps, pear brandy, peppermint schnapps, sloe gin, strawberry brandy, Tia Maria.

Wines Various bottlings of sherry, port, and Madeira; various wine varietals, such as Chardonnay, Pinot Noir, Merlot, Chablis, and Cabernet Sauvignon.

Beers Various bottlings of lambics, wheat beers, stouts, porters, and ales, domestic and/or imported.

Mixers and Modifiers

Liquor alone does not make a bar: Mixers such as fruit juices and sodas, and modifiers such as bitters, syrups, and sweeteners, are also indispensable. You'll find most of these at any well-stocked liquor, grocery, or specialty foods store. Some ingredients, such as the "simple syrup" many recipes call for, are easy to make at home and keep on hand. Others, such as citrus juices, are best squeezed fresh just prior to use.

BITTERS Several proprietary brands of alcohol-based infusions of herbs, spices, and aromatics used in very small quantities add nuance to many cocktails and mixed drinks. The ones most often called for are Angostura, orange, and Peychaud.

BOUILLON The Bloody Bull (page 104) and the Bullshot (page 128) use canned beef bouillon.

COCONUT CREAM Canned, sweetened cream of coconut (such as Coco López)

STOCKING UP

MIXERS AND MODIFIERS

The flavors of cocktails and mixed drinks come from many ingredients, some used only rarely or in small quantities. But omitting them from a recipe that requires them is a prescription for an inferior drinking experience. Below is a list of the basic mixers and modifiers you'll need, and a list of extras for occasional use.

ESSENTIALS

Mixers Bottled still mineral water, club soda or seltzer, cola, cranberry juice cocktail, fresh lemon juice, fresh lime juice, fresh orange juice, ginger ale, grapefruit juice, lemon-lime soda, pineapple juice, tomato juice, tonic water.

Modifiers Angostura bitters, canned coconut cream, grenadine, sweetened lime juice (such as Rose's), simple syrup (see recipe, page 23), sweet-and-sour mix (see recipe, page 22).

EXTRAS

Mixers Beef bouillon, ginger beer (spicier than ginger ale), heavy cream, light cream, milk.

Modifiers Eggs, Falernum syrup, orange bitters, orange flower water, orgeat syrup, Peychaud bitters, rose water.

adds coconut flavor to the Piña Colada (page 225) and other drinks.

DAIRY PRODUCTS The inclusion of milk makes sweetish mixtures more creamy and soothing. Whipped cream tops many coffee drinks and several mixed drinks. Melted butter graces hot buttered rum.

EGGS More than a few drink recipes call for raw eggs or egg whites. They add body and (in the case of shaken egg whites) frothiness. Unfortunately, in relatively rare cases contaminated eggs can cause salmonella poisoning, and you should decide for yourself whether this is a chance you want to take. To help reduce the risk, buy eggs from reputable vendors who keep them refrigerated at all times. At home, refrigerate them in the original carton and use them directly from the refrigerator. To be absolutely sure you won't fall prey to this form of food poisoning, either omit eggs from the recipe, avoid making such drinks, or buy pasteurized liquid egg substitutes. In most cases, omitting the eggs results in a textural difference rather than a loss of flavor. For eggnogs, store-bought pasteurized, unspiced eggnog is a viable alternative.

FLOWER WATERS Orange flower water and rose water—clear liquid flavorings distilled from bitter orange flowers and rose petals, respectively—add fragrant essences to a number of cocktails and mixed drinks.

SWEET-AND-SOUR MIX

This handy mixture can replace the fresh-citrus-juice-plus-simple-syrup combination many recipes call for. Simply substitute an equivalent measure of this mix, which keeps in the refrigerator for about ten days. (Note that doing so will alter the flavor of recipes calling solely for lemon juice or lime juice, since the mix contains both.)

Makes 1 cup (8 fl oz/250 ml)

- 3 fl oz (90 ml) fresh lime juice
- 3 fl oz (90 ml) fresh lemon juice
- 2 fl oz (60 ml) simple syrup (see recipe, opposite)

Pour all of the ingredients into a clean, resealable 12-fl-oz (355-ml) bottle. Shake well, seal, and refrigerate.

JUICES AND JUICE COCKTAILS Bottled, canned, or frozen juices and juice mixtures often used in cocktails include cranberry juice cocktail, grapefruit juice, pineapple juice, and tomato juice.

JUICES, FRESH Squeeze fresh orange, lemon, and lime juices from ripe fruit as needed (see Squeezing Citrus Juices, page 54).

MIXES Sweet-and-sour mix, based on citrus juice, sugar, and water, dilutes and flavors some drinks (see recipe, opposite). Prepared mixes for a number of drinks are available in stores, but fresh ingredients produce optimum flavor.

SODAS AND SELTZERS Club soda, cola, ginger ale, ginger beer, lemon-lime soda, seltzer, and tonic water are frequently used mixers that dilute or add other flavors to the base ingredients of a drink.

SWEETENERS, FLAVORED Sweet flavorings such as grenadine (based on pomegranates) and sweetened lime juice (such as Rose's) add flavor and sweetness to many cocktails and mixed drinks. Grenadine also contributes red coloring.

SYRUPS Orgeat syrup is a sweet, almond-flavored syrup used to flavor cocktails and mixed drinks. Falernum syrup, also used to flavor drinks, is made from a mixture of simple syrup, lime juice, almonds, ginger, and other spices. Simple syrup is a basic bar ingredient (see recipe, right).

SIMPLE SYRUP

Because it is difficult to dissolve sugar in cold liquid, bartenders use a sugar solution called simple syrup. It is easy to prepare and keeps two months or longer in the refrigerator.

Makes 1½ cups (12 fl oz/375 ml)

- 1 cup (8 fl oz/250 ml) water
- 1 cup (8 fl oz/250 ml) granulated sugar

Bring the water to a simmer in a saucepan set over medium-high heat. Add the sugar and stir until it completely dissolves. Remove the pan from the heat. Set aside to cool to room temperature. Pour the syrup into a clean 1-pint (500-ml) bottle, cap it, and refrigerate it until needed.

Garnishes and Accents

For many drinkers, a Martini wouldn't be a Martini without its gin-and-vermouth-soaked olive, nor would a Margarita seem quite so enticing without its rim of salt. Whether it contributes flavor or merely beauty, the garnish or accent often makes the drink. An ingredient can serve as a garnish, an accent, or both. For example, the pineapple spear in a Piña Colada is exclusively a garnish, since it doesn't contribute a new flavor; however, the grating of pungent nutmeg atop a Brandy Alexander is both an accent and a garnish, since it adds both taste and visual appeal.

Although certain garnishes and accents are traditional, there's no requirement that you stick to the tried and true. Many bartenders improvise these days by adding the likes of caperberries or tiny pickled tomatoes to Martinis, floating a slice of kiwi in a Champagne Cocktail, or hanging a crescent of papaya off the lip of a Tequila Sunrise. Nowadays, it seems, almost any ingredient is fair game as a cocktail garnish, so let your imagination and good sense be your guides.

A slice of jalapeño pepper accents a Cajun Martini.

Following is a list of the accents and garnishes commonly used in a professional cocktail bar. Unless you are planning a large gathering with a tended bar, you won't need all of them. But it helps to keep the essentials on hand. For instructions on how to make fresh garnishes, see Preparing Garnishes, page 50.

STOCKING UP

GARNISHES AND ACCENTS

Except for the fresh fruits and vegetables, many of these garnish and accent ingredients keep indefinitely in the pantry or refrigerator.

ESSENTIALS

Black pepper, coarse salt, cocktail onions, granulated sugar, horseradish, hot sauce (such as Tabasco), lemons, limes, maraschino cherries, olives, oranges, sugar cubes, table salt, Worcestershire sauce.

EXTRAS

Bananas, candies, celery, celery salt, cinnamon sticks, cloves, coffee beans, cucumbers, fresh mint, ground allspice, ground cinnamon, ground nutmeg (or whole nutmegs and a grater), pineapple, raspberries, strawberries.

Celery

Cocktail onions

Coffee beans

CANDIES Add cinnamon candy hearts to cinnamon schnapps, chocolate drops or shavings to chocolaty or creamy drinks, chocolate-filled candy sticks to sweet chocolate drinks, short peppermint sticks to Stingers (page 270) or crème de menthe drinks.

CELERY Use celery to garnish savory drinks such as the Bloody Mary (page 106) and its variations. (See Celery Ribs, page 54, for cutting instructions.)

COCKTAIL ONIONS Small, pickled pearl onions are a necessity for any bar that plans to serve a Gibson (page 159).

COCOA POWDER Sprinkle cocoa atop coffee drinks and some creamy drinks.

COFFEE BEANS Three beans are often dropped into sambuca or anisette, which is then flamed to release the coffee flavor.

CUCUMBERS A sliver of cucumber rind is essential for the Pimm's Cup (page 224).

FLOWERS Although many a drinker has exited many a Polynesian restaurant wearing a gardenia, flower garnishes are rarely used today. Occasionally you'll see orchids or the heads of daffodils afloat in punch bowls, but more frequently you'll find them frozen inside a block of ice. If you want to adorn drinks with flowers, wash them well, remove any anthers (the pollen-bearing portions of the stamens), and consider wrapping the stems and bases with florist's tape. Better yet, since some flowers may be toxic, put them in a small vase on the bar or cocktail table and omit them from the drink altogether.

Mint

HERBS Sprigs of fresh herbs, especially rosemary, thyme, or mint, can add great visual appeal to drinks such as the Mint Julep (page 214) or Gin and Tonic (page 164), and their aromas add an extra dimension to whatever drink they adorn. Keep the herbs refrigerated until use, and wash them thoroughly before adding them to a drink.

Citrus fruits

LEMONS, LIMES, AND ORANGES Used as garnishes and accents as well as sources of fresh juice, citrus fruits are indispensable at any bar (see Preparing Garnishes, page 50, and Squeezing Citrus Juices, page 54, for instructions).

Maraschino cherry

MARASCHINO CHERRIES Bright red and syrupy-sweet maraschino cherries, sold in jars, are essential to Manhattans, Old-Fashioneds, and Shirley Temples. Look for those with stems attached rather than the stemless type so you won't need a spoon to dispense them.

MISCELLANEOUS FRUITS AND VEGETABLES Some people think almost any ingredient is fair game as a cocktail garnish. Depending on what you plan to serve, you might want to have a stock of the following: pickled caperberries, okra, red-hot

Swizzle stick

chili peppers, or tomatoes for Martinis; peaches, bananas, pineapples, coconuts, berries, kiwifruit, or carambolas (starfruit) for fruit-based or fruit-flavored drinks.

NONEDIBLE DECORATIONS Plastic monkeys, dolphins, mermaids, and colorful swizzle sticks and paper parasols add a whimsical touch. Add them to any drink you think they might enhance.

Stuffed olives

OLIVES A jar of pimiento-stuffed green cocktail olives in brine is necessary to any bar serving Martinis (and the brine itself is the accent in a Dirty Martini, page 148). Olives of any size will do, but avoid unpitted ones—people are used to the pimiento-stuffed type. To personalize your Gin or Vodka Martinis, try marinating olives in herbs and vermouth according to the recipe opposite.

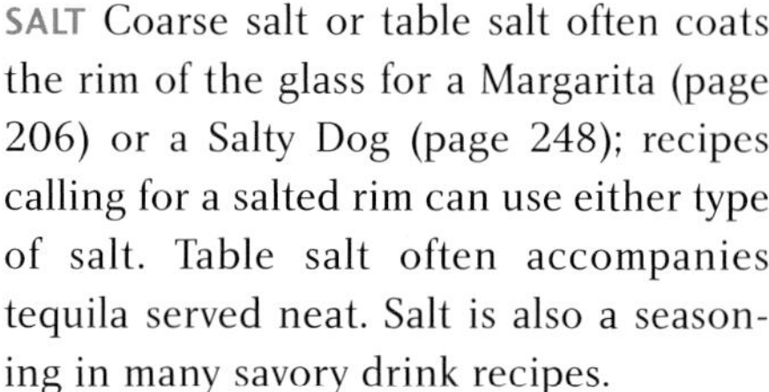

SALT Coarse salt or table salt often coats the rim of the glass for a Margarita (page 206) or a Salty Dog (page 248); recipes calling for a salted rim can use either type of salt. Table salt often accompanies tequila served neat. Salt is also a seasoning in many savory drink recipes.

SPICES AND SEASONINGS Cinnamon sticks and ground cinnamon accent coffee drinks and some creamy drinks. Cloves add flavor to mulled wines, hot toddies, or heated wine punches. Ground allspice adds dimension to creamy and coffee-based drinks. Grated nutmeg tops coffee drinks and some creamy drinks. Ground black pepper, horseradish, hot sauce (such as Tabasco), Worcestershire sauce, and on occasion celery salt, provide zip in Bloody Marys.

Sugar cubes

SUGAR Cubes are a necessity in Champagne drinks and Old-Fashioneds (page 219). Granulated, colored, or confectioners' sugar rims the glasses of sweet drinks.

Marinated Martini Olives

Makes 1 jar; keeps indefinitely if covered and refrigerated.

1 cup (8 fl oz/250 ml) dry vermouth
1 sprig fresh thyme
1 sprig fresh rosemary
3 fresh basil leaves
1 large jar (at least 2½ cups /20 fl oz/625 ml) of pimiento-stuffed green olives in brine

Combine the vermouth, thyme, rosemary, and basil in a saucepan made of stainless steel or other nonreactive material. Set over moderate heat. As soon as the mixture comes to a simmer, remove it from the heat, cover the pan, and allow the mixture to cool to room temperature, which takes about 1 hour. Strain the cooled marinade through a double thickness of dampened cheesecloth. Discard the solids.

Drain the brine from the jar of olives, leaving the olives in the jar. Reserve the brine. Pour the vermouth marinade over the olives. If necessary, add some of the reserved brine to cover all of the olives completely. Discard any remaining brine. Cover and refrigerate for at least a day before using.

Bar Tools and Supplies

Proper tools and supplies are as essential to the bartender as they are to the carpenter or surgeon. They make the work possible, professional, and most of all easy. Often several styles of a particular tool are available; you'll need hands-on experience to discover which works best for you. Pick up the tool in the store and pretend you are using it; think about how often it will be used and by whom. If your helpers find a particular corkscrew or other tool incomprehensible, you will be the one with the extra duty to perform.

BAR SPOON Long-handled, shallow-bowled spoon has a twisted shaft that functions like a screw, making the spoon travel up and down when rotated between the fingers. Use it for stirring and light-duty muddling (page 64).

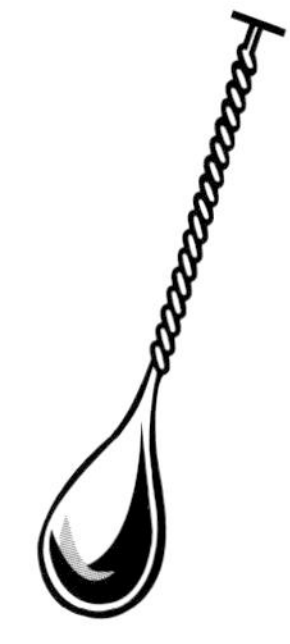
Bar spoon

BAR TOWELS Small, absorbent terrycloth towels aid in cleaning up spills; lint-free smooth towels are best for polishing glassware. Purchase enough of each to provide a ready supply of clean, dry towels.

BLENDER Electric appliance to blend thick mixtures, puree fruit, and break ice into fine particles for frozen drinks. A heavy-duty model with a strong motor is essential for bartending duty, since ice is a demanding ingredient that requires high, continuous power.

BOSTON SHAKER Two-piece device consists of a glass mixing vessel that is upended to fit snugly inside the top of a cone-shaped, flat-bottomed metal cup. Once you have shaken the mixture, you remove the glass portion and set a strainer over the lip of the metal portion to hold back the ice as you pour. Professional bartenders prefer the Boston shaker to the cocktail shaker because it is easier to wash and its glass portion can double as a mixing glass.

Boston shaker

BOTTLE OPENER Even in this day and age, not all crown-type bottle caps twist off. A strong tool to remove them is essential to every bar. (Also see Church Key, page 32.)

Bottle opener

Champagne keeper

CHAMPAGNE KEEPER Any of several devices that clamp tightly over the top of an opened bottle of sparkling wine to seal in the carbonation.

CHEESECLOTH Essential for straining spices from simmered punch mixtures, or for intercepting bits of cork when decanting vintage port (see page 231). Before using it to strain punch, fold this inexpensive lint-free cotton cloth into a double thickness and dampen it with fresh water.

Church key

CHURCH KEY OR BOTTLE-AND-CAN OPENER Dual-purpose tool has a bottle cap opener at one end and a pointed piercing tool at the other. Use it to open cans of liquid that lack a pull-open top.

Citrus reamer

CITRUS REAMER The device of choice when you require fresh citrus juice in small quantities. Whether made from glass, plastic, or stainless steel, a quality citrus reamer with a well-designed pouring spout is integral to a well-outfitted bar.

COCKTAIL NAPKINS OR COASTERS These provide resting places for glassware that prevent condensation from dripping onto the serving counter or other surface.

COCKTAIL PICKS Small plastic spears or toothpicklike wooden skewers are sometimes used to position garnishes in cocktails and make them easier for the drinker to eat or remove.

COCKTAIL SHAKER The alternative to a Boston shaker, a cocktail shaker is a metal vessel with a tight-fitting top and often a covered pouring spout with a built-in strainer mechanism. Pour well-shaken drinks directly from the spout into a glass, leaving the ice behind. Most cocktail shakers are more attractive than the plain, workaday Boston shaker, but they take longer to wash and are thus more popular with home bartenders than professionals.

Cocktail shaker

CUTTING BOARD AND PARING KNIFE Essential pair for peeling or cutting fruits for garnishes.

FOIL CUTTER This handy tool neatly cuts the foil around the neck of a wine bottle

Foil cutter

STOCKING UP

TOOLS AND SUPPLIES

You'll need the essentials below for the basic operations of bartending. The extras are handy for specialty drinks or large gatherings.

ESSENTIALS

Bar spoon, bar towels, Boston shaker and strainer (or cocktail shaker), church key or bottle-and-can opener, citrus reamer, cocktail napkins or coasters, corkscrew, cutting board, ice bucket, ice scoop or ice tongs, jigger, mixing glass, muddler, paring knife, sip sticks, straws, swizzle sticks.

EXTRAS

Blender, Champagne keeper, cheesecloth, cocktail picks, foil cutter, glass pitcher or carafe, grater, ice crusher, Martini pitcher and stirrer, measuring cups, measuring spoons, punch bowl or attractive large vessel with ladle, speed pourers.

for easy removal. Place the cutting edges astraddle the bottle's neck just below the lip, and turn the tool while pressing its sides together to slice through the foil.

GLASS PITCHER OR CARAFE Make one or more of these pouring vessels available at the bar to hold water or juices.

GRATER The tool of choice for obtaining small bits of citrus zest or grating whole nutmegs.

Ice bucket

ICE BUCKET Container for holding small amounts of cocktail ice or chilling individual bottles of wine. For making cocktails, the best choices are insulated and may have covers to keep the ice in top condition. For chilling wines, insulation and covers are not required.

ICE CRUSHER A motorized replacement for the old manual machine that breaks ice cubes into crushed ice. It is more efficient than a mallet or a manual ice crusher, but its noise is a drawback even if you're the only one around.

ICE SCOOP This metal tool is the quickest and most sanitary means of filling a glass or container with ice.

Ice tongs

ICE TONGS Smallish metal or plastic tongs for grasping and transporting ice cubes, usually one at a time, from an ice bucket to a glass. Tongs are less efficient than an ice scoop, but more precise.

Choosing a Corkscrew

THE BEST TOOL for removing a cork from a wine bottle is the one that makes it easiest for you.

Sommeliers and other restaurant personnel may prefer the *waiter's corkscrew*, but reluctant corks may prove challenging for this tool.

Waiter's corkscrew

The *screwpull* requires little effort from the user. You direct the nonstick-coated worm (screw) into the cork by turning the wingnut-shaped handle at the top; it pierces the cork and pulls it from the bottle with continuous turning. Thanks to the leverage supplied by supports on either side of the worm, no strength is required at all.

Screwpull

Those who don't want to pierce the cork prefer the *ah-so corkpuller*. It has no worm but instead two thin, flexible metal blades aligned to grasp the cork on two opposite sides. You work the blades into the bottle between the neck and the cork, then grasp the handle and twist the cork out. Though practice makes this tool easier to use, it's not a tool that everyone is willing or able to master.

Ah-so corkpuller

The *winged corkscrew* is a classic. As its worm turns down into the cork, its two winglike levers rise upward. With the worm fully entrenched, you lower the wings simultaneously and the device's gearlike mechanism causes the cork to ascend from the bottle.

Winged corkscrew

Jigger

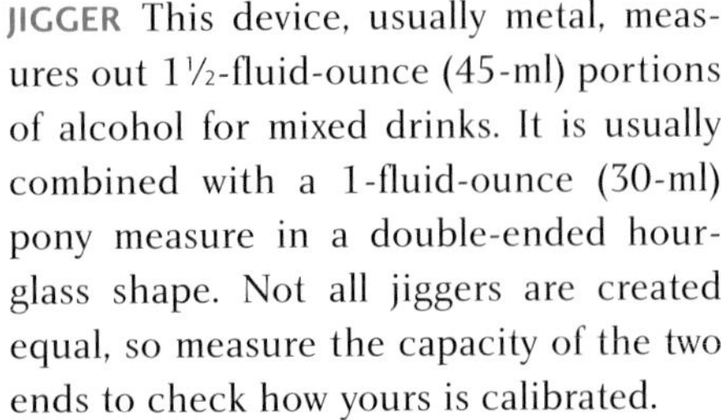

JIGGER This device, usually metal, measures out 1½-fluid-ounce (45-ml) portions of alcohol for mixed drinks. It is usually combined with a 1-fluid-ounce (30-ml) pony measure in a double-ended hourglass shape. Not all jiggers are created equal, so measure the capacity of the two ends to check how yours is calibrated.

MARTINI PITCHER AND STIRRER A set consisting of a pitcher and a long rod, both typically made of glass; the pitcher's pouring lip is designed to keep ice from escaping. The set is used to mix Martinis, but you don't really need one if you already have a mixing glass and a bar spoon.

Mixing glass

MEASURING CUPS AND SPOONS Very useful tools for precise measuring; the cups work well for punches and other large-yield recipes where measuring with a jigger would be too slow (for equivalences, see Bartending Measurements, page 55).

MIXING GLASS Tall glass, usually 2 to 2½ cups (16 to 20 fl oz/500 to 625 ml) in capacity, for mixing cocktails that are stirred, not shaken. A mixing glass may have a pouring spout to prevent ice from falling into the serving glass, or you can use it with a strainer. If you already own a Boston shaker, you have a mixing glass: Use the shaker's glass portion.

Muddler

MUDDLER A bat or pestle, usually made from wood and about 6 inches (15 cm) long, to crush and blend ingredients—

such as mint leaves, sugar cubes, or pieces of fruit—in a serving glass. The back of a spoon is sometimes used instead.

PUNCH BOWL A large bowl or other vessel, often decorative, that can hold a large quantity of punch; some bowls have matching cups. Use with a ladle.

SIP STICKS Short, very thin straws for stirring and sipping.

SPEED POURER Special top that fits into the neck of a bottle to facilitate easy, quick pouring; normally used with frequently poured ingredients.

STIRRERS AND SWIZZLE STICKS Plastic or glass rods for stirring; sometimes placed in a drink solely for visual appeal.

STRAINER, HAWTHORN A flat-topped device with a continuous coil of wire around its bottom face. The coil holds the strainer snugly across the mouth of a mixing glass or shaker.

STRAINER, PERFORATED This large, shallow, soupspoon-shaped strainer pierced with holes is an alternative to the Hawthorn design. Invert the device over a mixing glass or shaker and hold it in place with the index finger while straining.

STRAWS Stock several sizes to accommodate the different sizes and types of glassware. Also see Sip Sticks, above.

Speed pourer

Hawthorn strainer

Perforated strainer

Glassware

Graceful, good-looking glassware is available in a mind-boggling range of sizes and shapes. Classic handblown crystal is lovely, and you should choose it for your finest pre- or postdinner sipping. For day-to-day use, though, a better choice is machine-made glassware—slightly thicker or with a heavier base—that won't break the bank if it shatters on the floor. If you are entertaining large numbers outdoors, plastic is a safer bet than glass; you'll be surprised at how attractive modern plastics can be.

When buying, keep in mind that traditional, uncolored glassware is best for letting the drink shine through unimpeded. Go for simple styles of a well-known, widely available make so you can replace broken pieces easily. Save fanciful colored glassware for iced tea and soda. If you have a dishwasher, choose glasses that fit its interior. Washing dozens of glasses by hand is no fun for anyone.

The illustrations on pages 40–43 show the basic shapes and sizes of classic bar glassware. Use them as a guide, but remember that all glasses are not created equal: measure the capacity of your glasses before you use them. If necessary, feel free to substitute any glass of similar capacity for one of a specific style.

Clear glass is the best showcase for a drink.

STOCKING UP

ESSENTIAL GLASSWARE

Here is a basic assortment of glasses to keep at home for casual entertaining. For the full range of glassware, see pages 40–43.

FOR MIXED DRINKS AND COCKTAILS

4 to 6 cocktail (Martini) glasses, 4 to 6 highball glasses, 4 to 6 Collins glasses, 4 to 8 single or double Old-Fashioneds, 4 to 6 brandy snifters, 6 to 12 sherry copitas.

FOR WINE

4 to 6 red wine plus 4 to 6 white wine, or 8 to 12 all-purpose wine; 4 to 6 Champagne flutes or tulips.

FOR BEER

4 to 6 beer mugs or Pilsners.

STANDARD BAR GLASSES

Here and on the following pages are the glasses used to serve the cocktails and mixed drinks in this book. You probably won't need all of them unless you frequently offer guests a full bar.

FOR COCKTAILS AND MIXED DRINKS

Cocktail (also called Martini), 4 to 12 fl oz (125 to 375 ml)

Collins, 8 to 14 fl oz (250 to 430 ml)

Highball, 8 to 10 fl oz (250 to 310 ml)

Old-Fashioned (also called rocks; some versions have a short stem), 5 to 6 fl oz (150 to 180 ml)

Double Old-Fashioned, 8 to 10 fl oz (250 to 310 ml)

Sour, 4 to 6 fl oz (125 to 180 ml)

Zombie, 12 fl oz (375 ml) or more

FOR LIQUOR SERVED NEAT

Brandy snifter, 5 to 6 fl oz (160 to 180 ml) recommended—20 fl oz (625 ml) and larger capacities are available but not recommended because they expose too much surface area of the spirit to the air

Cordial, 1 to 3 fl oz (30 to 80 ml)

Pony, 1 to 3 fl oz (30 to 80 ml)

Pousse-Café, 3 to 4 fl oz (80 to 125 ml)

Sherry, 4 to 6 fl oz (125 to 180 ml)

Sherry copita, 4 to 6 fl oz (125 to 180 ml)

Shot, 1½ to 2 fl oz (45 to 60 ml)

Vodka, 1 to 2 fl oz (30 to 60 ml)

Cocktail
Collins
Highball
Old-Fashioned
Double Old-Fashioned
Sour
Zombie
Brandy snifter
Cordial
Pony
Pousse-Café
Sherry
Sherry copita
Shot
Vodka

FOR WINE

Champagne flute, 6 to 9 fl oz (180 to 280 ml)

Champagne saucer, 4 to 8 fl oz (125 to 250 ml)—not recommended because the wide surface area and short depth release carbonation too quickly

Champagne tulip, 6 to 9 fl oz (180 to 280 ml)

Wineglass, all-purpose, 8 to 14 fl oz (250 to 430 ml)

Wineglass, red (balloon), 8 to 14 fl oz (250 to 430 ml)

Wineglass, white, 8 to 14 fl oz (250 to 430 ml)

FOR BEER

Beer mug, 10 to 20 fl oz (310 to 625 ml)

Pilsner, 10 to 14 fl oz (310 to 430 ml)

SPECIALTY

Irish Coffee, 8 to 10 fl oz (250 to 310 ml)

Julep cup, 8 to 12 fl oz (250 to 375 ml)

Punch cup, 6 to 8 fl oz (180 to 250 ml)

Champagne flute
Champagne saucer
Champagne tulip
Wineglass, all-purpose
Wineglass, red (balloon)
Wineglass, white
Beer mug
Pilsner
Irish Coffee
Julep cup
Punch cup

CHAPTER 2

The Art of Mixing

Whether you're serving one guest or a crowd, mixing satisfying drinks that are pleasing to the eye is not a difficult feat. All it takes is mastery of a few simple techniques, and a bit of practice.

The Essentials of Preparation

A Screwdriver, which consists of just two ingredients—vodka and orange juice—is always a decent drink. But if you prepare a Screwdriver with freshly squeezed orange juice, using exactly the right ratio of vodka to juice, and if you serve the result in a fine glass, the Screwdriver can be a minor work of art.

Most cocktails and mixed drinks are more complicated than this one, yet the best of the best are surprisingly simple in structure—and remarkably easy to prepare.

Take the Martini: The classic recipe calls for just two ingredients—gin and dry vermouth—but the complex flavors of a good gin marry so well with the herbal notes in a fine dry vermouth that many deem this the perfect potion.

The Manhattan, a close runner-up to the Martini, is also a simple affair. Calling for just three ingredients—whisky, sweet vermouth, and bitters—the resulting cocktail, if proportioned carefully, can be a complex masterpiece.

One of the most important rules of mixology is that the quality of any drink relates directly to the quality of its ingredients. Although you might not want to use an expensive single-malt Scotch to make a Rob Roy, a high-quality blended Scotch renders a far better drink than an inexpensive, less-flavorful bottling.

Minuscule amounts of flavorings such as bitters, grenadine, or sweetened lime juice (known as modifiers in cocktail terminology) can also make a magnificent contribution. On the other hand, too much of these ingredients can be detrimental, upsetting a drink's delicate harmony. If you want a well-balanced result, follow the recipe precisely.

Martini

Manhattan

When it comes to certain ingredients, time is of the essence. For example, you should open carbonated mixers just before use to ensure they will not be flat. Fruit juices are best freshly squeezed. A wedge of lime, slice of lemon, or any other fruit garnish is more appealing freshly cut than prepared hours ahead.

So the lesson is clear: If you follow recipes precisely and remember that quality and freshness are paramount, not much can go wrong in your life as a mixologist.

MAKING OR BUYING ICE

HOW MUCH ICE DO YOU NEED?

A rule of thumb is to buy ½ pound (0.2 kg) of ice per person per hour of party time, plus enough to fill any container that will be used to keep beverages cold. Buy extra if the party location will be warm, since the ice will melt faster.

Good, flavorless, solid ice is imperative to making appetizing drinks. Without it, you can ruin an otherwise perfect cocktail. Just as professional tasters insist on using demineralized bottled water to dilute spirits, you should make the ice for your mixed drinks from still bottled water or filtered water.

If you use ice-cube trays, choose ones that produce ice cubes of a smaller size, such as ¾ inch (2 cm). The ice will freeze faster, chill liquids more quickly, and be far easier to mix with a bar spoon.

Many drink recipes call for crushed ice. To crush ice the hard way—by hand—place ice cubes on a clean, lint-free cloth and wrap the cloth tightly around the ice. Place the bundle on a sturdy cutting board and hit it repeatedly with a rubber mallet or sturdy rolling pin. You can also crush ice in an electric ice-crushing machine. Both options are time consuming and noisy, though, so you may want to buy your ice precrushed in bags from a supermarket or ice company.

Punches often call for blocks of ice. If you buy a block, make sure it isn't too big for your punch bowl. Ice companies can usually cut blocks to size if necessary. To make ice blocks yourself, fill large containers—empty juice cartons, milk jugs, ring molds, and the like—with filtered or still bottled water, and freeze the contents until solid, usually several days. A ring mold is ideal when you want to freeze an ingredient—say, raspberries—into the ice for a decorative floating chiller. You can arrange the fruit in the water or partially frozen ice. To release ice from any mold, rinse the mold briefly under warm water or wrap it inside a warm, moist towel for a few seconds.

PREPARING GLASSWARE

Chilling glasses, or coating their rims or interiors, is a prelude to mixing many drinks. Here are the best ways to accomplish these tasks.

CHILLING Glasses destined to contain Martinis, Manhattans, and other cocktails should always be prechilled. If you have empty space in the freezer, simply place an array of glasses inside it at least one hour before you will need them. If time or space is short, stand each glass in the sink and fill it with crushed ice (cubes will also suffice). Then fill the glass to the rim with cold water and let it chill while you prepare the drink in a mixing glass or shaker. At the last moment, pour out the ice and water and shake the glass to get rid of the last few drops.

Chilling

COATING RIMS Certain drinks, such as the Margarita (page 206) or Sidecar (page 261), are usually served with a coating around the rim. (Margaritas take salt;

Sidecars take sugar.) To coat a rim, choose a shallow container that is wider than the rim of the glass. Fill it 1/4 to 1/2 inch (6 to 12 mm) deep with the salt, sugar, cocoa powder, or other required coating material. Pour 1/4 to 1/2 inch (6 to 12 mm) of one of the cocktail's ingredients, such as the triple sec in a Margarita, into a similar container (the amount you use is in addition to, not part of, the quantity in the recipe). Dip the rim of the glass into the liquid, then into the coating ingredient. Shake off any excess.

Coating a rim

Alternatively, moisten the rim of the glass by fitting a wedge of citrus fruit onto the rim of the glass and sliding it around the rim while gently squeezing the fruit. Then dip the rim in the coating ingredient and shake off any excess.

If a recipe calls for a chilled and rimmed glass, rim it first, then stand it upright in the freezer for at least one hour.

COATING GLASSES Some drinks, such as the Pink Gin (page 226), call for coating the interior of the glass with bitters or spirits before adding the rest of the drink. Simply pour two to three dashes of the ingredient into the glass, then tilt and swirl the glass so the liquid touches the entire interior surface. Then shake out any liquid that hasn't adhered to the glass.

Coating a glass

PREPARING GARNISHES

Although the most immediate appeal of garnishes in drinks is visual, many also function as accents, contributing an extra flavor or aroma that makes them integral to the drinking experience. The orange wheels floating in a punch bowl, for example, are often eaten.

A sharp paring knife and a solid cutting board are requirements for making garnishes. Both must be completely clean. Also thoroughly wash and dry all fruits before cutting into them.

Here's how to prepare and place the most widely used garnishes.

Citrus wedges

CITRUS WEDGES Although many bartenders simply drop citrus wedges into drinks such as the Gin and Tonic, they are doing the drink and the drinker a disservice. Squeezing a wedge thoroughly before dropping it into the drink adds a discernible extra nuance.

To prepare fruit wedges from lemons, limes, or oranges, first cut off both ends of the rind, taking care not to expose the inner fruit. Next slice the fruit in half vertically, from stem end to blossom end, and cut each half into four to six equal wedges, depending on the size of the fruit. Don't skimp: Sizable wedges are pleasing to the palate and the eye.

Citrus twist

CITRUS TWISTS The colorful outer skins or "zests" of citrus fruits, the source of twists, contain the fruits' essential oils. Correctly employed, a twist releases those oils onto the top of the drink, adding an easily detected aroma and flavor.

Remove the stem end of a citrus fruit to give it an even base. Working from the top to the base, carefully cut 1/2 inch (12 mm) wide strips of outer skin, incorporating as little of the white inner pith as possible. To turn the resulting strip into a twist, hold it, pith side up, about 2 inches (5 cm) above the top of the drink, and twist the two ends in opposite directions, releasing the oils in a very fine mist. Finally, rub the outside of the twist around the rim of the glass and drop the twist in.

CITRUS WHEELS Although used mainly for visual effect, citrus wheels—particularly orange wheels—are often eaten and therefore become part of the drinking experience. You usually anchor wheels over the rim of a glass, but you can also float them in punches.

Citrus wheels

To create citrus wheels, remove both ends of the rind, exposing the inner fruit. Place the fruit on its side on a cutting board. Starting from one end, slice the fruit into wheels or rounds, each about 1/4 inch (6 mm) thick. One wheel at a time, cut through the rind up to the center of the fruit, creating a slit that will fit over the rim of the glass. (Omit this step if you will be floating the wheels.)

CITRUS SLICES Citrus slices are halved wheels—semicircular pieces of fruit usually placed on the rim of a glass.

Citrus slices

To prepare citrus slices, remove both ends of the rind and halve the fruit vertically, cutting from stem end to blossom end. Place each half, cut side down, on the cutting board and cut into slices, each about 1/4 inch (6 mm) wide. Next, cut into the slice from the center up to but not through the peel, creating a slit that will fit over the rim of the glass.

Citrus peel spiral

CITRUS PEEL SPIRALS These graceful spirals, usually from lemons, serve as a visual enhancement to drinks such as the Brandy Crusta (page 122), but they don't add much flavor because the essential oil–bearing outer skin is not squeezed.

To produce citrus spirals, make a cut 1/2 inch (12 mm) wide, well into one end of the fruit—you want to slice through the outer skin and some of the pith, yet not deeply enough to expose the inner fruit. Continue cutting, moving around the circumference of the fruit so the peel forms a continuous spiral.

To use the spiral, wind it tightly around your finger or place it on a clean surface and wind it into a tight, flat coil. Next, place it in a glass and let it unwind to line the interior (you may need to help it with your fingers). If an end of the spiral protrudes from the top of the glass, simply snip off the excess with scissors.

PINEAPPLE SPEARS Usually reserved for tropical drinks such as the Piña Colada (page 225) and the Planter's Punch (page 229), pineapple spears add visual appeal and are often consumed by the drinker.

To make pineapple spears, cut off the top and bottom of the pineapple and stand it on either end on a clean cutting board. Starting from the top, cut off the rind in long strips, making sure you cut deeply enough to remove every trace of it. Halve the pineapple lengthwise; halve each half lengthwise. Cut out the core from each quarter. Slice each quarter lengthwise into three to four long spears.

CELERY RIBS Used in drinks such as the Bloody Mary (page 106), celery adds visual appeal and is a treat for the palate.

To prepare celery ribs, place a bunch of celery on its side and cut off the entire base, leaving only the green portion of the ribs. Separate the ribs and wash them thoroughly in cold water. Cut each stalk to a length appropriate for your glassware, allowing 2 to 3 inches (5 to 7.5 cm) to extend over the top of the glass (do not cut away the leaves). Place the prepared ribs in a container, then add cold water and ice. Refrigerate until needed. The ribs with leaves attached are the most decorative ones; use these first.

JUICE YIELD PER FRUIT

Grapefruit, 6 fl oz (180 ml)

Lemon, 1½ fl oz (45 ml)

Lime, 1 fl oz (30 ml)

Orange, 2½ to 3 fl oz (80 to 90 ml)

SQUEEZING CITRUS JUICES

Freshly squeezed citrus juices make the difference between a merely good drink and a great one. A good citrus reamer (page 32) is the tool you need. Old-fashioned manual reamers made from pressed glass are as attractive and efficient as reamers made of stainless steel. For heavy-duty citrus squeezing, large lever-driven citrus reamers can save time and trouble. If you have an aversion to pulp or the odd stray seed, have a small sieve at hand to make straining easy.

Listed on the opposite page are approximate yields of medium-size citrus fruits. Actual yield may vary depending on fruit size, ripeness, and season. To maximize yield, roll the uncut fruit a few times against a countertop, pressing firmly. Then halve the fruit horizontally and press and twist each half against the reamer.

MEASURING AND POURING

You will notice that few professional bartenders ever use jiggers or other measuring devices when pouring spirits, and

Bartending Measurements

Unit	Equivalent measure	U.S. liquid measure	Metric units
Dash	1/8 teaspoon	1/48 fl oz	0.6 ml
Teaspoon	8 dashes	1/6 fl oz	5 ml
Tablespoon	3 teaspoons	1/2 fl oz	15 ml
Pony	2 tablespoons	1 fl oz	30 ml
Jigger	3 tablespoons	1 1/2 fl oz	45 ml
Gill	4 ponies	4 fl oz	120 ml
Cup	2 gills	8 fl oz	250 ml
Pint	2 cups	16 fl oz	500 ml
Quart	4 cups	32 fl oz	1 liter
Gallon	4 quarts	128 fl oz	4 liters

Note: Metric units have been rounded.

although some bars now use automated shot measurers, many others prefer free pouring. Being able to pour 1½ fl oz (45 ml) or any other measure of liquor accurately requires a little practice, but it's not hard to learn.

Take an empty liquor bottle, fill it with water, and fit it with a speed pourer (page 37). Next, take a jigger (page 36) or other measuring device and start pouring from the bottle while counting silently to yourself. Stop pouring when you have the desired amount.

If, for example, you reached the number three at the point when the measure filled to the top, then you know in future that at your counting speed, a count of three delivers the desired amount of liquid. Since people tend to count at different speeds, one person's count generally differs from another's. If you change to another speed pourer, check your counting again—different designs dispense at different rates.

Though some people use what is called the "two fingers" method of measuring (pouring to the level of your first two fingers held horizontally), it is not recommended. Variations in the size of the glass, and the size and shape of the ice in it, make this technique quite inexact.

A far more accurate approach for the beginner is to measure out ingredients with a jigger and measuring spoon or cup. Bartenders who measure industriously may lack the élan of free pourers, but they produce more uniform results.

PREMEASURING THE FILL LEVEL

If you can't get the hang of the counting method (right), use this shortcut to speed the preparation of highballs and other drinks mixed directly in the serving glass: Select one of the glasses you'll be using, fill it with ice, and pour in a measure of water. Note the water level in the glass. When you come to make real drinks, pour in the liquor to that point. This measuring method can be less accurate than counting, but it can save time when you're busy at the bar.

Mixing Techniques

In rough order of complexity, the five basic techniques for mixing drinks are building, stirring, shaking, layering, and blending. The larger the gathering or the less practiced the bartender, the wiser it is to rely on drinks at the simpler end of the spectrum. For instance, inexperienced bartenders should offer mainly built drinks, such as the Gin and Tonic and the Screwdriver, and perhaps some simple shaken or stirred cocktails such as the Whisky Sour or the Martini. Save layered drinks such as the Pousse-Café, blended drinks such as the Batida Abaci, and more complicated shaken drinks such as the Ramos Gin Fizz for the future, after you have mastered the basics.

BUILDING A DRINK

1. Fill the serving glass with ice.
2. Measure and pour in the ingredients.
3. If the garnish is a citrus wedge, squeeze it and then drop it into the drink.
4. Stir the drink briefly with a sip stick.
5. Add any other garnish.

BUILDING

A *built* drink is one you make by merely pouring all of the ingredients into the same glass you use for serving, then briefly stirring them together (about three times around the glass). Used for a highball—a drink with two ingredients, such as a Scotch and Soda (page 250)—this is the simplest technique for mixing a drink. Highballs are always a safe bet for entertaining, since they are comparatively quick and easy to prepare.

Combinations that contain fruit juices, such as the Screwdriver (page 256), require about twice as much stirring as drinks made with carbonated sodas, which you should stir only once or twice. The soda bubbles do the mixing for you; don't over-stir or you'll kill the carbonation.

Built drinks are usually served with a short, slim straw, commonly known as a sip stick (page 37), which the bartender has used for stirring. Although it enables the drinker to stir the drink after it has been served, there is no good reason to do this—unless it's perhaps to dilute the drink by mixing in melted ice. Nor, despite their name, are sip sticks much good for sipping, since their aperture is inconveniently small. Some people do like to sip through them, but most merely stir the drink once or twice with the sip stick and remove it from the glass. A few people like to hang onto their sip sticks to keep track of how many drinks they've had.

Swizzle sticks (page 37) are most commonly served with drinks such as the Rum

Swizzle (page 247); some bartenders also serve other drinks, such as the Tom Collins (page 282), with a swizzle stick, mainly as a visual accent.

Squeeze citrus wedges, if called for, into the glass before stirring and serving the drink. Add other garnishes, such as citrus wheels, maraschino cherries, or pineapple spears, to the glass after you have completely assembled the drink.

STIRRING

Martinis and most other clear cocktails—those containing no fruit juices, raw eggs, milk, or cream—should be stirred somewhat vigorously for 20 to 30 seconds in an ice-filled mixing glass or a Martini pitcher. This chills the drink, combines the ingredients, and dilutes the cocktail somewhat as the ice melts. Dilution from melted ice makes the drink more palatable by taking the harsh edge off the alcohol.

Most stirred drinks are mixed with a long bar spoon (page 31), usually in tandem with a mixing glass (page 36). Bar spoons typically have a twisted shaft designed to maximize mixing action; when used in a professional manner, the spoon plunges up and down while rotating.

To stir with this type of spoon, place your thumb on one side of the twisted shaft and two outstretched fingers of that hand on the other side. Slide your thumb back and forth, turning the shaft against your fingers. (Be sure to use small ice cubes when you employ this technique, since large cubes tend to lock together.)

STIRRING A DRINK

1. Fill a mixing glass two-thirds full of ice.
2. Measure and pour in the ingredients.
3. Stir the drink for 20 to 30 seconds.
4. Strain into a chilled or ice-filled glass.
5. Add the garnish.

STRAINING A DRINK

1. Fit a strainer (page 37) over the mouth of the mixing glass or lower (metal) part of the shaker.
2. Pour most of the liquid into the serving glass.
3. Twist the mixing glass or shaker with a clockwise motion while turning it upright as the last few drops flow out.

Cocktails are sometimes combined using a Martini stirrer, usually a long, straight glass rod that is part of a set consisting of the rod and a Martini pitcher (page 36). Ideally, the rod should be at least 4 inches (10 cm) taller than the pitcher so it offers a good grip.

If you serve the stirred cocktail over ice, or "on the rocks," always strain the drink into a glass filled with fresh ice cubes. If you serve the drink without ice, or "straight up," make sure the glass is thoroughly chilled (see Chilling, page 49).

SHAKING A DRINK

1. Fill a cocktail shaker or Boston shaker two-thirds full of ice.
2. Measure and pour in the ingredients.
3. Close the shaker and shake it vigorously up and down for 10 to 20 seconds.
4. Strain into a chilled or ice-filled glass.
5. Add the garnish.

SHAKING

All cocktails containing fruit juices, raw eggs, milk, or cream—drinks such as the Brandy Alexander (page 113) and the Bourbon Milk Punch (page 110)—should be shaken, not stirred, since these comparatively thick ingredients are difficult to blend with thinner liquids such as spirits. You can make shaken drinks in a standard cocktail shaker (page 33) or in a Boston shaker (page 31); also see Using a Boston Shaker, opposite. Whichever shaker you choose, fill it about two-thirds full of ice and then agitate it vigorously for 10 to 20 seconds, combining the ingredients and also chilling and slightly diluting them with melted ice. Then strain the drink into a chilled glass or over fresh ice.

LAYERING

Layered drinks, which have been around since at least the mid-nineteenth century, are made by pouring liquids in order of

Using a Boston Shaker

MOST PROFESSIONAL BARTENDERS prefer the Boston shaker to a cocktail shaker because the Boston shaker's two parts are easy to wash quickly. However, this type of shaker takes practice to use.

First, fill the glass portion two-thirds full of ice cubes or crushed ice. Next, pour in the ingredients. Invert the metal portion over the rim of the glass portion and tap it sharply on top to create a seal. This prevents liquids from leaking out as you shake. Now lift the shaker and quickly turn it upside-down so the metal portion is now on the bottom. Since the metal part has a wider rim than the glass, it will hold the glass in place should you accidentally lose your grip.

Next, place one pinkie finger on the top of the shaker and the other on the bottom, and spread your other fingers along its length. Intertwine your thumbs to lock your hands and the shaker together. Holding the shaker upright, bring it to approximately shoulder height and shake it vigorously up and down for about 15 seconds, or until ice cold.

To break apart a Boston shaker, hold the metal portion in one hand and use the heel of your other hand to strike its exterior at a point near the junction with the glass portion. This breaks the seal. Lift off the glass portion, set a strainer across the mouth of the metal portion, and strain the contents into the serving glass.

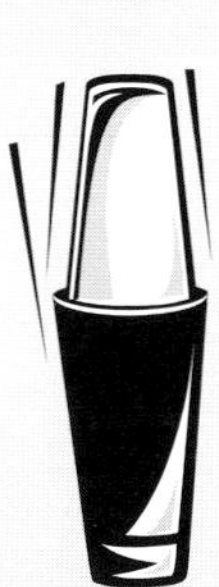

LAYERING A DRINK

1. Measure and pour in the densest ingredient.
2. Measure the next-densest ingredient and pour it in gently, over the back of a spoon, to create a new layer.
3. Repeat step 2 for each additional layer.

POURING ORDER FOR LAYERED DRINKS

(densest to least dense)

Syrups, such as grenadine
Crème de bananes
Crème de cassis
Crème de menthe
Crème de cacao
Apricot liqueur
Blue curaçao
Blackberry liqueur
Peach brandy
Triple sec
Rock and Rye
Kümmel
B&B
Sloe gin
Kirsch
Spirits, such as rum

density—from heavy to light—so they remain in distinct bands within the glass. Usually referred to as Pousse-Cafés (and served in a Pousse-Café glass, page 41), layered drinks test the bartender's skill. To layer a drink, pour the densest ingredient into the serving glass. Then pour each subsequent liquid very slowly over the back of a bar spoon held just above the previous layer so it cascades gently on top. Most Pousse-Café drinks consist of three to six layers.

Unfortunately, there is no foolproof way to guess which liquid will float on top of another, since similar products from different producers often have different densities. A rule of thumb is that liquids with more sugar tend to sink; those with more alcohol tend to float.

The list at the left provides general guidelines, but the best way to avoid unexpected results is to experiment before guests arrive, using the actual ingredients you'll be serving. If you'll be layering drinks frequently, you can purchase an inexpensive hydrometer (available from scientific-supply outlets) to measure the density of each ingredient exactly.

BLENDING

Blended drinks—a delightful frozen slush made typically with ice and juices, fresh fruit, and spirits—are labor intensive to prepare, so they are best served only at smaller gatherings.

Any electric blender used for making frozen drinks must have a powerful motor that can withstand continued use with ice. Several companies make blenders specifically for this purpose. Even with one of these, don't fill the container more than halfway—you can always make more batches. First, add the ice (smaller cubes break up more quickly) and the drink ingredients. Cover and blend at high speed. Most drinks require only 30 seconds or so. However, if lumps of ice remain, more blending is necessary.

BLENDING A DRINK

1. Add ice, liquids, and cut fruit to a blender.
2. Cover and blend at high speed until uniformly smooth, about 30 seconds.
3. Pour the drink into the glass.
4. Add the garnish.

ADDITIONAL TECHNIQUES

Some drinks require additional operations as adjuncts to the basic preparation techniques. These operations include flaming and muddling.

FLAMING A small number of drinks are served flaming, a process that burns off much of the alcohol in addition to putting on a show. If you choose to flame drinks, have a working fire extinguisher at the ready in the event of an accident.

Any drink you are going to set alight must contain enough alcohol to ignite. This is sometimes accomplished by floating a high-proof ingredient, such as an overproof 151-proof rum, on top of a drink by pouring it slowly over the back of a spoon. At other times, you'll flame glasses containing single, undiluted, ingredients, such as sambuca or Grand Marnier.

To flame a drink, make sure you are well away from other combustibles, including bottles of distilled spirits. Light a long wooden match and touch the flame to the

FLAMING A DRINK

1. Clear the area.
2. Measure and pour in the ingredients.
3. Touch a lighted wooden match to the top.
4. If flames have not gone out after 10 to 15 seconds, snuff them out with a saucer.
5. Advise drinkers to wait for their glasses to cool.

top of the drink. Although flamed drinks are rarely allowed to flame long enough to damage most glasses, don't use a treasured heirloom. Wait for the bluish flames to subside, usually 10 to 15 seconds; if they don't subside by themselves, extinguish them by placing a saucer atop the glass. Before serving flamed drinks, warn drinkers to wait until the rim is merely warm to the touch before imbibing.

When you're flaming entire pots of drinks, such as glogg, extreme caution is required. First make sure your stovetop is fitted with a clean exhaust system. Have a working fire extinguisher close at hand, and be prepared to stand well back as soon as you have ignited the liquid.

If you do not have the correct equipment for flaming, or if you're at all uncertain about how to flame a drink properly, do not attempt it.

MUDDLING Some drinks, including the Old-Fashioned (page 219), have solid ingredients—such as mint leaves, sugar cubes, or fruit—that you mash, or muddle, in the glass in which you serve them. In the case of a dry ingredient such as mint or sugar, you typically mash fruit or a liquid such as bitters with it to help carry its flavoring into the drink. Muddling requires a sturdy vessel, such as an Old-Fashioned glass.

Place the ingredients to muddle in the bottom of the glass and use a wooden drink muddler (page 36), a long-handled pestle, or the back of a sturdy spoon to press the ingredients together. Keep muddling until the items are truly melded together. Thoroughly crush mint leaves; crush sugar cubes and at least partially dissolve them in the liquid ingredients.

SERVING

Serve all drinks immediately after preparing them. Always place drinks on a cocktail napkin or coaster to catch any condensation from the glass. It's also a good idea to serve snacks with a drink; you'll find suggestions on pages 67 and 68.

REFILLS

After serving the first round of drinks, you will have a strong sense of what people will request next, since most drinkers stick with the same beverage. After making each drink, you should wash, rinse, and dry the mixing glass, bar spoon, or shaker, but don't fill the mixing vessel with ice again until you're ready to prepare the new round. Similarly, don't fill glasses with ice until just before the next set of drinks; otherwise they will be too watery.

Do make sure you have enough ingredients on hand to fulfill the next round of requests. Although fruit garnishes are best freshly cut, there's no harm in cutting a few extras if you anticipate needing them in the near future. In fact, if you are serving a large group, it is useful to have small bowls of garnishes precut on the bar top. Also have fresh glasses handy, since few people want to have their next drink served in the same glass.

MUDDLING SOLID INGREDIENTS

1. Place the ingredients at the bottom of a sturdy glass.
2. Crush the ingredients together by repeatedly pressing down on them with a muddler or the back of a strong spoon.

MAKING MULTIPLE DRINKS

Avoid the temptation to make more than two drinks at once, since the need to crowd extra ingredients into the mixing container inevitably displaces some ice. The result is an underchilled and insufficiently diluted drink.

Drinks and Food

Good drinks and fine food are classic, inseparable companions. At times, however, it can be difficult to know when to serve a certain beverage or what foods should accompany it. For example, should you offer sherry before or after dinner? What foods combine best with the smoky notes of Scotch? In this section you'll find general guidelines as well as specific recommendations. For more advice about when to serve particular beverages, see their respective entries in the A-to-Z Drinks Guide, beginning on page 76.

APERITIFS

Drinks served prior to a meal, known as aperitifs (from the French for "appetizers"), should be light and preferably dry. The idea is to stimulate the appetite without dulling the palate. Chilled dry sherries are a classic choice, as are proprietary aperitif spirits and fortified wines, such as Dubonnet, Campari, and Amer Picon.

Certainly, many people want a classic cocktail; think Martinis, Manhattans, and Rob Roys. Other good mixed drinks to offer before lunch or dinner, especially in warm weather, are tall drinks, such as Campari and Orange or Grapefruit Juice. Also good are highballs, such as Gin and Tonic or Scotch and Soda.

ACCOMPANIMENTS TO A MEAL

Wine is usually the best beverage to go with a meal. Although people these days often ignore the rule "red wine with meat, white wine with fish," a wise host serves fairly dry wines alongside savory courses, and reserves sweeter wines to serve with or after sweet desserts. Another useful approach for those not well versed in wines is to consult a knowledgeable wine dealer, describing the dishes you will be serving, the size of the gathering, and your approximate wine budget.

DIGESTIFS

After a meal, digestifs reign. This is the time to serve and savor the world's finest spirits, liqueurs, and dessert wines. Many people are enamored of spirits such as

PARTY SNACKS

Snacks at the bar for a cocktail party can consist of there-for-the-taking nibbles or hot or cold prepared foods. Nibbles might include popcorn, pretzels, potato chips, tortilla chips, mixed nuts, peanuts in their shells, spiced and roasted seeds, cheese crackers, and the like. If prepared food is the order of the day, consider Buffalo chicken wings, focaccia, individual pizzas, bruschetta, calamari with seafood sauce or tartar sauce, nachos, and quesadillas. Guests also won't ignore a selection of cheeses, or good old crudités—just make sure the accompanying dip is something special.

Cognac or brandy, single-malt Scotch, and boutique bottlings of bourbon; pour these in small quantities—about 1½ fl oz (45 ml) per glass—and serve them neat, at room temperature, in your very best glassware.

Others might crave something sweet: a liqueur such as Grand Marnier, Tia Maria, or Bénédictine; a fortified wine such as port, oloroso sherry, or Madeira; or a dessert wine such as Sauternes, Muscat, or late-harvest Zinfandel. Except for straight spirits, which are best served after the meal, you can offer any of these with dessert or even in place of it.

Foods to Pair with Spirits

Although it is not usual to serve anything but a simple snack, such as mixed nuts, alongside straight spirits, you should always offer hors d'oeuvres of some sort to accompany cocktails or mixed drinks. The chart below offers guidance on which foods go best with drinks based on various spirits.

Bourbon Savory tartlets, mushrooms, smoked ham and other meats, chutneys, stone fruits, fruit desserts.

Brandy Foie gras, rillettes, meat pâtés, earthy and well-aged cheeses.

Gin Salsa, highly flavored sausages, seafood with citrus sauces, duck pâtés.

Scotch All smoked foods (especially fish), beef carpaccio, cured sausages.

Tequila Salsa, smoked fish, chorizo, shrimp, scallops, Indian foods such as pappadams or samosas with dipping sauces.

Vodka Caviar, smoked salmon, oysters, shellfish.

Hosting a Cocktail Party

Whether the gathering is small and informal or large and lavish, preparing for a cocktail party can be demanding. If you want the event to run smoothly, you must decide what to serve, how much to buy, how to set up the bar, and who will tend it.

Stop and think for a minute: Is it a special occasion or a simple get-together? Are your guests friends or business associates? How large a crowd will there be? Once you've defined the affair, you'll have a better idea of what suits and what doesn't.

ADVANCE PLANNING

Time and money are significant factors when planning a party. If you decide to throw a bash at the last minute, you will probably have to make it a somewhat simple affair with a small range of drinks and simple or store-bought snacks. On the other hand, if the party won't take place for a few weeks, you have time to plan a schedule, buy everything you need, and perhaps make the hors d'oeuvres yourself.

Perhaps the most difficult challenge in party planning is deciding what beverages to serve. The easiest solution lies in knowing (or learning) the habits of those you've invited. If three-quarters of them drink vodka most of the time, buy extra vodka. And don't forget the needs of nondrinkers and designated drivers; the A-to-Z Drinks Guide (page 76) includes many alcohol-free recipes that use standard mixers and modifiers.

When you can't tell in advance what your guests will desire, try to limit your menu—say, by serving only wine or Champagne, or by offering only Martinis and Manhattans. A huge bowl of punch also satisfies many drinkers, and you can prepare it well ahead of time.

Setting a theme for your party—a Cinco de Mayo celebration, for instance, or a Saint Patrick's Day bash—is another way to narrow the options (see the index of drinks by occasion on page 327). If all else fails, you'll have to offer a wider selection; the list opposite will enable you to mix a range of drinks.

SEASONAL TREATS

For short periods each year, special bottlings of wine and beer become available. These can add a festive note to a party—or even provide an excuse for one. Look for Beaujolais Nouveau (the first Beaujolais of the new vintage) in mid-November, and special dark, spiced winter beers during the holidays.

Beverage List for a Full Bar

This list should enable you to offer a complete open bar for a three-hour party with 20 guests. If your liquor cabinet already contains opened bottles of the items marked with asterisks, there's no need to buy more if the bottles are at least half full.

1 750-ml bottle bourbon*

1 750-ml bottle blended Canadian whisky*

1 750-ml bottle blended Scotch*

2 750-ml bottles London Dry Gin

2 750-ml bottles vodka

1 or 2 750-ml bottles of liqueurs, such as amaretto, Bénédictine, Chartreuse, Chambord, Frangelico, Irish cream, or any other types your guests prefer

1 750-ml bottle dry vermouth*

1 750-ml bottle sweet vermouth*

4 to 6 750-ml bottles dry white wine

3 or 4 750-ml bottles dry red wine

24 12-fl-oz (355-ml) bottles beer

1 liter lemon-lime soda

2 liters cola

2 liters diet cola

6 12-fl-oz (355-ml) or smaller bottles ginger ale

12 12-fl-oz (355-ml) or smaller bottles tonic water

4 liters club soda

2 liters still mineral water

2 quarts (2 l) orange juice

1 quart (1 l) cranberry juice cocktail

1 quart (1 l) grapefruit juice

1 quart (1 l) tomato juice

20 to 30 pounds (10 to 15 kg) ice cubes or crushed ice

ESTIMATING QUANTITIES

A 750-ml bottle yields 17 shots of liquor or 5 glasses of wine.

A 1-liter bottle provides 22 shots, or mixer for about 12 highballs.

Five pounds (2.5 kg) of medium-size ice cubes fills about 24 10-fl-oz (310-ml) glasses.

PARTY GLASSES

Figure on using one to one-and-a-half glasses per person per hour, and do your best to keep the drink selection simple so that you'll need fewer kinds of glasses. If you'll be renting glassware, the rental company may be able to help define your needs based on current drinking trends in your area.

The next job is to determine how much to buy. A good rule of thumb is that the vast majority of guests consume no more than one drink per hour. So if you multiply the number of expected guests by the number of hours the party is scheduled to last, you'll have an approximate idea of how many drinks you will serve.

A SELF-SERVICE BAR

The best kind of self-service bar offers drinks that require little effort from guests, such as punches, wines, beers, soft drinks, and perhaps simple mixed drinks such as highballs. Otherwise, guests may be reticent about helping themselves.

If you'll be serving only punch, it's wise to prepare one alcohol-free punch (see the list on page 321) and another—such as Sangria (page 249)—that contains some alcohol but not too much. Display the punches in attractive punch bowls, and tell guests which contains alcohol.

You can judge how much to prepare by figuring that in the course of a three-hour party, 20 guests could potentially consume about 60 cups of punch at 6 fl oz (180 ml) each. Therefore, if you make a total of three gallons (384 fl oz/12 l), there will be enough for everyone. Display punch cups around the bowl and provide a ladle so guests can serve themselves.

If you are also serving wine, make sure to prechill the white wine and keep it on ice. Before the guests arrive, open two bottles each of red and white wine and replace the corks loosely. If you decide to offer beer, make sure it is well chilled and display one or two bottle openers where guests can easily spot them. Also make cocktail napkins readily available.

Although guests may be serving themselves, that doesn't relieve you of all duties. Take time now and then to clear the room of empty glasses and used napkins, and to replenish ice and other supplies that are running low.

A TENDED BAR

If you choose to set up a tended bar, the wisest option is to hire a professional bartender to serve your guests—otherwise you won't have time to mingle. You can often find a bartender by asking at your favorite bar or restaurant for a staff member who will be off duty on the night of your party. Professional caterers (listed in the phone book) may also be able to supply a bartender for the evening.

Many bartenders will set up the bar for you prior to the party; you'll need to have the proper items on hand so the bartender can prepare the work space in a professional manner. In addition to the beverages and mixers, you'll need garnishes, supplies, glassware, and equipment—see the list on page 74. If you don't have an actual bar in your home, you'll need to set up two tables: one against a wall for bottles, extra glassware, and miscellanea, and another for preparing and serving drinks. The tables should be about 3 feet (0.9 m) high, 2 feet (0.6 m) wide, and 5 to 6 feet (1.5 to 1.8 m) long. If you

ECONOMY VERSUS CONVENIENCE

Large-size bottles of liquors or mixers are often more economical than standard sizes. However, their greater bulk and weight can make them unwieldy at a crowded bar. You may want to avoid them.

Vodka and Tonic

THE MOST POPULAR DRINKS

(according to U.S. bartenders)

1. Vodka and Tonic
2. Scotch and Water
3. Martini
4. Screwdriver
5. Cosmopolitan

Supplies for a Full Bar

Apart from the beverages you need for a cocktail party (see page 71), there are many other items to have on hand. This assortment assumes that most people will request fairly standard drinks. If you have reason to expect otherwise, adjust the list accordingly.

FLAVORINGS AND GARNISHES

1 bottle Angostura bitters

1 jar green cocktail olives

1 jar cocktail onions

1 bottle grenadine

1 jar horseradish

lemons, for garnishes

lemons, to squeeze for juice

limes, for garnishes

limes, to squeeze for juice

1 bottle sweetened lime juice, such as Rose's

1 jar maraschino cherries

oranges, for garnishes

pepper

salt

sugar, granulated

sugar cubes

Tabasco sauce

Worcestershire sauce

EQUIPMENT

bar spoon

bar towels

bottle opener

bowls and glasses to hold garnishes and straws

church key

cocktail napkins

cocktail shaker or Boston shaker

cocktail strainer (if using a Boston shaker)

corkscrew

cutting board

1 or more ice buckets

2 large ice-filled coolers to keep beers and wines cold

ice tongs or ice scoop

jigger

1 or 2 mixing glasses

1 paring knife

sip sticks

straws

1 trash container

1 tub or tray to hold used glassware and implements

don't possess such tables, look into renting trestle tables from a party supplier.

Ideally, a sink should be easily accessible for washing glassware and bar implements. For this reason, many people set up the bar in the kitchen. If no sink is available, make sure that there are always enough clean glasses at hand, and that the bartender has clean tools available.

Under the tables, store ice in coolers you can use to keep wine or beer chilled. You should also provide a garbage receptacle for bottle caps and the like. You might also want to cover the serving table with a cloth long enough to hang over the front, almost to the floor, so as to hide these items from guests.

The serving table should have a selection of glassware, cocktail napkins, a cocktail shaker, sip sticks, straws, and fruit garnishes (see the list, opposite). Place a premade supply of about 20 of each garnish in small bowls for the bartender's use. When you hire a bartender, discuss whether he or she will arrive early enough to prepare the garnishes, or whether you will make them in advance. Place straws and sip sticks in glasses tall enough to keep them upright, but at least 2 inches (5 cm) shorter than the straws or sip sticks to allow easy grasping.

People commonly deposit empty glasses, used napkins, and the like on any available surface. You may want to hire a waiter in addition to the bartender to help clear these away at a large party. This person can also take orders for drinks.

PARTY POINTERS

❖ Set a starting and ending time, and include it on invitations. This discourages overindulgence and keeps your liquor bill within limits. Two to three hours is a good time span.

❖ Always serve food. Alcohol takes effect more slowly in people who have eaten, and food diverts attention from drinking.

❖ Have alcohol-free drinks on hand for drivers and abstainers.

❖ Never serve anyone too many drinks—intoxicated guests are a liability to you, themselves, and other guests.

❖ Remember that neither coffee nor tea sobers people up—only time can do that.

CHAPTER 3

A-to-Z Drinks Guide

Here you'll find recipes for more than 400 classic and contemporary mixed drinks, along with descriptions of the major spirits, liqueurs, beers, and wines. The symbol ⊘ denotes nonalcoholic drinks.

ABC

A complex drink that's as easy to make as ABC.

2 fl oz (60 ml) Scotch
1 tablespoon apricot brandy
1 tablespoon sweet vermouth

Pour all of the ingredients into a mixing glass two-thirds full of ice cubes. Stir well. Strain into a chilled cocktail glass.

ACAPULCO COCKTAIL

This is a refreshing drink suitable for preprandial sipping.

2 fl oz (60 ml) light rum
1 tablespoon triple sec
1 tablespoon fresh lime juice
1 tablespoon simple syrup (page 23)

Pour all of the ingredients into a shaker two-thirds full of ice cubes. Shake well. Strain into a chilled cocktail glass.

Absinthe Substitutes

AT THE TURN OF THE twentieth century, it was believed that the wormwood (a bitter herb) in the green liqueur called absinthe might be responsible for causing the insanity that afflicted some who drank it. Beginning in 1905, several nations officially banned absinthe, and substitutes such as Pernod (page 223) and Ricard appeared on the market. Sweeter than true absinthe, they still bear its intense aniseed flavor and are essential to many drinks.

ADONIS COCKTAIL

The orange bitters in this drink highlights the complex herbal notes of the vermouth.

3 tablespoons dry sherry
2 tablespoons sweet vermouth
Dash of orange bitters

Pour all of the ingredients into a mixing glass two-thirds full of ice cubes. Stir well. Strain into a chilled cocktail glass.

AFFINITY COCKTAIL

A variation on the Perfect Rob Roy (page 237), this is a warming drink, best sipped by a roaring fire.

2 fl oz (60 ml) Scotch
1 tablespoon sweet vermouth
1 tablespoon dry vermouth
2 dashes orange bitters

Pour all of the ingredients into a mixing glass two-thirds full of ice cubes. Stir well. Strain into a chilled cocktail glass.

ALABAMA SLAMMER

This relatively new drink has become popular among those who enjoy sweeter potions.

2 tablespoons amaretto
2 tablespoons Southern Comfort
2 tablespoons sloe gin
1 teaspoon fresh lemon juice

Pour all of the ingredients into a shaker two-thirds full of ice cubes. Shake well. Strain into an ice-filled double Old-Fashioned glass.

ALEXANDER

The original recipe that inspired the better-known Brandy Alexander (page 113).

2 fl oz (60 ml) gin
3 tablespoons white crème de cacao
2 tablespoons light cream
Ground or freshly grated nutmeg, for garnish

Pour the gin, crème de cacao, and cream into a shaker two-thirds full of ice cubes. Shake well. Strain into a chilled cocktail glass. Sprinkle with nutmeg to taste.

ALGONQUIN

This drink is named for New York's Algonquin Hotel, where in the 1920s and 1930s an infamous group of artists, including writer Dorothy Parker, held court at the so-called Algonquin Round Table.

2 fl oz (60 ml) Canadian whisky
1 tablespoon dry vermouth
2 tablespoons pineapple juice

Pour all of the ingredients into a shaker two-thirds full of ice cubes. Shake well. Strain into a chilled cocktail glass.

AMARETTO SOUR

For those with a sweet tooth, here is a sweet, nutty version of the Sour.

2 fl oz (60 ml) amaretto
2 tablespoons fresh lemon juice
1 tablespoon simple syrup (page 23)
1 maraschino cherry, for garnish

Pour the amaretto, lemon juice, and simple syrup into a shaker two-thirds full of ice cubes. Shake well. Strain into a chilled Sour glass. Garnish with the cherry.

Amaretto

21–28% alcohol by volume

GOOD BOTTLINGS of this almond-flavored liqueur, usually made in Italy, actually gain their nutty flavor from apricot kernels rather than almonds.

The legend behind the creation of the world's first amaretto involves a sixteenth-century artist, Bernardino Luini, who was commissioned to restore two frescos in the chapel of Santa Maria delle Grazie in the small town of Saronno, near Milan. It is said that the model who posed for Luini when he executed a fresco of the Madonna rewarded him by concocting a love potion made from apricot pits. She named it amaretto. Although you might be tempted to believe the word has its roots in *amore* (love), it actually means "something small and bitter."

Disaronno Amaretto is made in Italy according to a 200-year-old recipe.

In 1800, Carlo Dominico Reina patented a recipe for amaretto and began to produce and market the product locally. Reina's descendants started commercial production of Disaronno Amaretto in Italy about half a century ago. Other liqueur producers make amaretto as well.

Amaretto can be sipped neat as an after-dinner drink, but it is most often used as a base or flavoring element in cocktails and mixed drinks. Should you have trouble locating the almond-flavored crème de noyaux some recipes call for (see Liqueurs, page 198), you can use amaretto in its stead.

Amer Picon

21% alcohol by volume

THIS FRENCH BITTER APERITIF bears orange notes with a bitter herbal backdrop. Amer Picon is usually served with club soda, but it also makes a perfect foil for orange juice, especially with the addition of a few dashes of grenadine to counteract its bitterness. It is also the featured ingredient in the Amer Picon Cocktail (see below).

AMER PICON COCKTAIL

2 fl oz (60 ml) Amer Picon
2 tablespoons fresh lime juice
Dash of grenadine

Pour all of the ingredients into a mixing glass two-thirds full of ice cubes. Stir well. Strain into a chilled cocktail glass.

AMERICANO

It is said that this drink was created in Italy during the late nineteenth century and dubbed the Americano because at that time many Europeans considered mixed drinks to be American in style. Some experts claim that the Negroni (page 218) is a variation on the Americano.

3 tablespoons Campari
3 tablespoons sweet vermouth
1 orange slice, for garnish

Pour the Campari and vermouth into an Old-Fashioned glass filled with ice cubes. Stir well. Add the garnish.

ANGEL'S TIP

The modest refer to this drink by the euphemistic "tip" instead of its more risqué true name, which presumably refers to the delicate mound of whipped cream on top.

2 fl oz (60 ml) dark crème de cacao
1 teaspoon whipped cream
½ maraschino cherry, for garnish

Pour the crème de cacao into a small Pousse-Café glass. Top with the whipped cream. Place the half cherry on top of the whipped cream.

Apple Brandy

40–50% alcohol by volume

UNLIKE APPLEJACK (page 84), which is a blended product, pure apple brandy is made solely from apples, much like Calvados (page 116).

The hard cider made from fermenting an apple mash is distilled twice in pot stills, and the resultant spirit is aged in oak for up to seven years.

You can freely substitute apple brandy for applejack in any mixed drink or cocktail.

American apple brandy is also commonly called applejack, as this old label shows.

⊘ APPLE-CRANBERRY PUNCH

Makes 10 6-fl-oz (180-ml) servings.

1 quart (32 fl oz/1 l) unsweetened nonalcoholic apple cider
1 quart (32 fl oz/1 l) cranberry juice cocktail
5 whole cloves
2 small (3-inch/7.6-cm) cinnamon sticks
1 teaspoon ground or freshly grated nutmeg
1 large block of ice, for serving
10 orange wheels, for garnish

Pour the apple cider and cranberry juice into a large pot made of stainless steel or other nonreactive material. Set over high heat. Add the cloves, cinnamon sticks, and nutmeg and bring the mixture to a boil. Reduce the heat to low, cover, and simmer for 20 minutes.

Strain the mixture through a double layer of dampened cheesecloth. Set the liquid aside to cool to room temperature, about 1½ hours. Cover and refrigerate for at least 2 hours or up to 5 days.

Place the block of ice into a punch bowl. Add the chilled punch. Add the garnish. Serve in punch cups.

Applejack

40% alcohol by volume

ALTHOUGH AMERICANS generally use this term interchangeably with apple brandy (page 83), applejack is a blend of distilled cider and neutral spirits. Apple brandy, on the other hand, is made from fermented and distilled apples alone. Most applejack is aged in oak casks for four to eight years before bottling. It is an integral part of many mixed drinks, especially the Jack Rose (page 185).

Applejack Cobbler

THIS IS THE CLASSIC representative of the Cobbler family, whose members are typically composed of a base spirit (or wine) and simple syrup, poured into a wineglass filled with crushed ice and garnished with fresh fruit.

Thin slices of tart apple make an ideal garnish. Arrange them on top of the ice as though you were preparing a pie.

2½ fl oz (75 ml) applejack
1 tablespoon simple syrup (page 23)
1 lemon wedge, for garnish

Pour the applejack and simple syrup into a wineglass filled with crushed ice. Stir briefly. Add the garnish.

SEE ALSO *Bourbon Cobbler, Brandy Cobbler, Champagne Cobbler, Gin Cobbler, Irish Cobbler, Rum Cobbler, Scotch Cobbler.*

APPLEJACK COLLINS

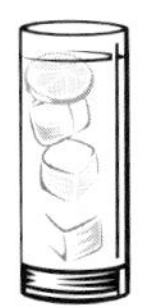

2 fl oz (60 ml) applejack
1 tablespoon fresh lemon juice
1 tablespoon simple syrup (page 23)
5 to 6 fl oz (150 to 180 ml) club soda
1 orange wheel, for garnish

Pour the applejack, lemon juice, and simple syrup into a shaker two-thirds full of ice cubes. Shake well. Strain into an ice-filled Collins glass. Add the club soda. Stir briefly. Add the orange wheel.

APPLEJACK COOLER

The ginger ale marries well with the applejack in this drink, but you can also try it with lemon-lime soda for a change of pace.

2½ fl oz (75 ml) applejack
6 to 7 fl oz (180 to 210 ml) ginger ale
1 lemon twist, for garnish

Pour the applejack and ginger ale into an ice-filled Collins glass. Stir briefly. Add the lemon twist.

APPLEJACK FIZZ

2 fl oz (60 ml) applejack
2 tablespoons fresh lemon juice
1 tablespoon simple syrup (page 23)
5 to 6 fl oz (150 to 180 ml) club soda
1 lemon wedge, for garnish

Pour the applejack, lemon juice, and simple syrup into a shaker two-thirds full of ice cubes. Shake well. Strain into a chilled wineglass. Add the club soda. Stir briefly. Add the lemon wedge.

APPLEJACK RICKEY

2½ fl oz (75 ml) applejack
2 tablespoons fresh lime juice
5 to 6 fl oz (150 to 180 ml) club soda
1 lime wedge, for garnish

Pour the applejack and lime juice into an ice-filled highball glass. Add the club soda. Stir briefly. Garnish with the lime wedge.

APPLEJACK SANGAREE

The ingredient that makes this drink so special is the cherry brandy, which brings all the other flavors into harmony.

2 fl oz (60 ml) applejack
1 tablespoon ruby port
1 tablespoon cherry brandy
Ground or freshly grated nutmeg, for garnish

Pour the applejack, port, and cherry brandy into a mixing glass two-thirds full of ice cubes. Stir well. Strain into a chilled wineglass. Sprinkle with nutmeg.

APPLEJACK SLING

2½ fl oz (75 ml) applejack
1 tablespoon simple syrup (page 23)
1 tablespoon fresh lemon juice
5 to 6 fl oz (150 to 180 ml) club soda
1 lemon wedge, for garnish

Pour the applejack, simple syrup, and lemon juice into a shaker two-thirds full of ice cubes. Shake well. Strain into an ice-filled Collins glass. Pour in the club soda. Stir briefly. Add the lemon wedge.

APPLEJACK SMASH

6 fresh mint leaves
1½ tablespoons simple syrup (page 23)
2½ fl oz (75 ml) applejack
1 mint sprig, for garnish

Place the mint leaves in the bottom of an Old-Fashioned glass. Add the simple syrup and muddle well (see technique, page 64). Fill the glass with crushed ice. Pour in the applejack. Stir briefly. Garnish with the mint sprig.

APPLEJACK SWIZZLE

2 fl oz (60 ml) applejack
1 tablespoon fresh lemon juice
1 tablespoon cherry brandy
5 to 6 fl oz (150 to 180 ml) ginger ale
1 lemon wheel, for garnish

Pour the applejack, lemon juice, and cherry brandy into a shaker two-thirds full of ice cubes. Shake well. Strain the mixture into an ice-filled Collins glass. Pour in the ginger ale. Stir briefly. Add the lemon wheel and a swizzle stick.

APRICOT COOLER

2½ fl oz (75 ml) apricot brandy
6 to 7 fl oz (180 to 210 ml) lemon-lime soda
1 lemon twist, for garnish

Pour the apricot brandy and lemon-lime soda into an ice-filled Collins glass. Stir briefly. Add the garnish.

APRICOT FIZZ

2 fl oz (60 ml) apricot brandy
2 tablespoons fresh lemon juice
1 tablespoon simple syrup (page 23)
5 to 6 fl oz (150 to 180 ml) club soda
1 orange wheel, for garnish

Pour the apricot brandy, lemon juice, and simple syrup into a shaker two-thirds full of ice cubes. Shake well. Strain into a chilled wineglass. Pour in the club soda. Stir briefly. Add the orange wheel.

APRICOT RICKEY

2½ fl oz (75 ml) apricot brandy
2 tablespoons fresh lime juice
5 to 6 fl oz (150 to 180 ml) club soda
1 lime wedge, for garnish

Pour the apricot brandy and lime juice into an ice-filled highball glass. Pour in the club soda. Stir briefly. Garnish with the lime wedge.

APRICOT SOUR

2 fl oz (60 ml) apricot brandy
1½ tablespoons fresh lemon juice
1 tablespoon simple syrup (page 23)
1 orange wheel, for garnish
1 maraschino cherry, for garnish

Pour the apricot brandy, lemon juice, and simple syrup into a shaker two-thirds full of ice cubes. Shake well. Strain into a chilled Sour glass. Add the garnishes.

GOLF BAG SHAKER

Silver-plated 1926 shaker takes the form of a golf bag, with a golf ball finial on top.

ARTILLERY PUNCH

No one is sure how this potent mixture got its weapons-related name, but it certainly packs a wallop, or if you prefer, a punch.

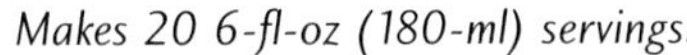

Makes 20 6-fl-oz (180-ml) servings.

1 750-ml bottle blended Canadian whisky
1 750-ml bottle ruby port
1 quart (32 fl oz/1 l) chilled strong tea
2 cups (16 fl oz/500 ml) fresh orange juice
1 cup (8 fl oz/250 ml) fresh lemon juice
3 fl oz (90 ml) brandy
2 fl oz (60 ml) Bénédictine
1 large block of ice
20 lemon wheels, for garnish

Pour all of the liquid ingredients into a large pan or bowl made of stainless steel or other nonreactive material. Stir well, cover, and refrigerate for at least 4 hours.

Place the large block of ice in the center of a large punch bowl. Pour in the punch. Add the garnish. Serve in punch cups, transferring a lemon wheel to each cup.

AUTUMNAL PUNCH

The perfect punch for an early-autumn "falling leaves" party.

Makes 18 6-fl-oz (180-ml) servings.

1 750-ml bottle dry red wine
2 750-ml bottles dry white wine
3 fl oz (90 ml) sweet vermouth
3 fl oz (90 ml) dry vermouth
1 cup (8 fl oz/250 ml) applejack
1 cup (8 fl oz/250 ml) citrus vodka
1 cup (8 fl oz/250 ml) cranberry juice cocktail
2 fl oz (60 ml) simple syrup (page 23)
1 large block of ice
9 orange and 9 lemon wheels, for garnish

Pour all of the liquids into a large pan or bowl made of stainless steel or other nonreactive material. Stir well, cover, and refrigerate for at least 4 hours.

Place the block of ice in the center of a large punch bowl. Pour in the punch. Add the garnish. Serve in punch cups, transferring a wheel of fruit to each cup.

Bacardi Cocktail

DURING THIS DRINK'S heyday in the 1930s, it came to the attention of the Bacardi family that bars were making its eponymous cocktail with rums other than Bacardi's own. Family members took the matter to the New York Supreme Court, which ruled in 1936 that the Bacardi Cocktail was not a Bacardi Cocktail unless made with Bacardi rum. After falling into neglect for a number of years, the drink made quite a comeback in the swinging seventies.

The Bacardi Cocktail is essentially a Daiquiri sweetened with grenadine rather than simple syrup. Despite that, it is a drink unto itself, a happy marriage of the peppery rum with the tart lime juice and sweet grenadine.

2 fl oz (60 ml) Bacardi light rum
2 tablespoons fresh lime juice
1 tablespoon grenadine

Pour all of the ingredients into a shaker two-thirds full of ice cubes. Shake well. Strain into a chilled cocktail glass.

BALTIMORE BRACER COCKTAIL

2 fl oz (60 ml) brandy

1½ tablespoons anisette

1 egg white (see caution, page 22)

Pour all of the ingredients into a shaker two-thirds full of ice cubes. Shake very well. Strain into a chilled cocktail glass.

BAMBOO COCKTAIL

2 fl oz (60 ml) cream sherry

2 tablespoons sweet vermouth

2 tablespoons fresh lemon juice

1 tablespoon simple syrup (page 23)

Pour all of the ingredients into a shaker two-thirds full of ice cubes. Shake well. Strain into a chilled cocktail glass.

BANANA RUM MARTINI

The marriage of dark rum and crème de bananes makes a very sophisticated dark Martini. If it's too sweet for your taste, use a little less of the banana liqueur.

2 fl oz (60 ml) dark rum

1 tablespoon crème de bananes

Pour both of the ingredients into a mixing glass two-thirds full of ice cubes. Stir well. Strain into a chilled cocktail glass.

BARON COCKTAIL

The Grand Marnier in this cocktail is a substitution for the orange bitters prevalent in all Martinis until the standard recipe changed in the 1950s.

2 fl oz (60 ml) gin
1 tablespoon sweet vermouth
1 tablespoon dry vermouth
1 ½ teaspoons Grand Marnier

Pour all of the ingredients into a mixing glass two-thirds full of ice cubes. Stir well. Strain into a chilled cocktail glass.

BATIDA ABACI

Make this blended drink with fresh pineapple chunks to get the finest end product. In a pinch, you can use canned pineapple packed in its own juice—not in sweetened syrup.

2 fl oz (60 ml) cachaça or other light rum
½ cup (4 fl oz/120 ml) pineapple chunks

Put the ingredients in a blender containing 1 cup (8 fl oz/250 ml) of ice cubes. Blend well. Pour into a chilled wineglass.

BAY BREEZE

The Bay Breeze is a distant cousin of the Sea Breeze (page 256).

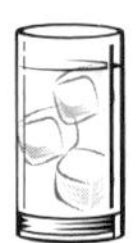

2 fl oz (60 ml) light rum
3 fl oz (90 ml) cranberry juice cocktail
2 tablespoons pineapple juice

Pour all of the ingredients into a highball glass filled with ice cubes. Stir briefly.

BEADLESTONE COCKTAIL

This variation on the Rob Roy (page 237) calls for a relatively large quantity of vermouth and results in a much lighter cocktail, very suitable for serving at parties.

3 tablespoons Scotch
2 tablespoons dry vermouth

Pour the Scotch and vermouth into a mixing glass two-thirds full of ice cubes. Stir well. Strain into a chilled cocktail glass.

BEAUTY SPOT COCKTAIL

The name derives from the drop of grenadine that floats on top and resembles a beauty spot. It is an ideal cocktail for warm-weather consumption.

2 fl oz (60 ml) gin
1 tablespoon white crème de cacao
1 egg white (see caution, page 22)
Dash of grenadine

Pour the gin and crème de cacao into a shaker two-thirds full of ice cubes. Add the egg white. Shake very well. Strain into a chilled cocktail glass. Add the grenadine by simply pouring it into the center of the drink.

Beer

4–16% alcohol by volume

Beer is a hopped, fermented liquid made from grains. Barley is usually the predominant grain, but some classic brews use wheat, and some others are made with grains such as rice. A beer is referred to as ale when made with a yeast that ferments at a warm temperature at the top of the beer. Lagers use a bottom-fermenting yeast that works best at lower temperatures, and they are aged, or lagered, for longer periods than ales. Ales are generally more robust than lagers and slightly less carbonated.

An old California beer first made in 1861, Acme was revived as a handcrafted brew in the 1980s.

ANCHOR BEER

San Francisco's Anchor Brewing Company was a pioneer in the production of "handcrafted" beers, which now emanate from small breweries throughout North America.

HOW BEER IS MADE

Beer production involves cooking a mash of malted (sprouted) grains and hops, adding yeast, fermenting the mixture, and then straining the liquid from the grains. This liquid then goes into storage tanks to mellow briefly before it is carbonated and packaged. Of course, it's not quite that simple, and many brewers employ their own idiosyncratic techniques to add character and nuance to their brews.

STYLES OF ALE

The following styles of ale are widely available in the United States and Canada.

AMBER ALE Originally from Great Britain, amber ale comes in many styles. Most have a heavier body than lager, with a medium alcohol content, pale to deep amber color, and medium to heavy hops flavor.

CREAM ALE Peculiar to the northeastern United States, this mixture of ale and lager is light-bodied and low in alcohol.

INDIA PALE ALE IPA (as beer lovers refer to it) is more or less a bottled version of British bitter (an amber ale). Gold in color, it is quite dry with plenty of hops.

SCOTCH ALE Native to Scotland, this ale is generally on the sweet side, coppery to deep brown in color, lightly hopped, and quite high in alcohol content.

TRAPPIST ALE Made in Belgian and Dutch monasteries by the Trappist order of monks, this ale is typically strong, amber to dark in color, and often has a fruity, spicy richness that is quite far from most people's impression of beer.

BARLEY WINE Very high in alcohol content (up to 12 percent by volume), this British style of beer usually comes in 6-fl-oz (180-ml) bottles. It is thick in texture, sherrylike, and immensely warming.

OLD ALE A specialty of Great Britain, old ale is either matured in casks after fermentation for longer periods than most other beers, or removed from the casks after a short time and matured in the bottle through the addition of extra yeast just prior to sealing. Admired for its sherrylike qualities, old ale is usually dark, sweetish, and very soothing.

PORTER The forerunner of stout, porter originated in Great Britain. It tends to have a lighter body but is still dark brown to black in color, with medium hops and medium to high alcohol content.

STOUT This distinctively British ale is made in three styles, all of them almost black in color and high in hops and alcohol, with full, rich body. *Irish stout* is generally very dark and bitter, with a creamy head and distinct flavors of burnt barley. *Milk stout* is sweetened with lactose for a somewhat milder flavor than Irish stout. *Imperial stout,* originally concocted for the Russian czars, is very strong and very dry.

WHEAT BEER Bavaria was the birthplace of wheat beer, which contains wheat as well as malted barley. Although it is sometimes placed in a separate category, it is actually an ale because it is top-fermented. Wheat beer goes by numerous names, among them *white beer, Weizenbier,* and *Weiss Bier.* It is generally a light straw color, lightly

VINTAGE LABELS

Before the advent of national brands, the United States was home to myriad small breweries with colorful names—a tradition modern brewmasters are reviving.

MATCHBOOK ADS

Vintage matchbook covers advertise American light lagers, a variety of Pilsner that has long been the most popular style of beer in the United States.

hopped, and slightly citrusy and tart. *Hefe-Weizen* is a wheat beer that undergoes a second fermentation in the bottle.

LAMBICS Unlike other beers, lambics in their true form are fermented by wild, airborne yeasts rather than by cultivated strains. Although often placed in their own category, these specialties of Belgium are top-fermented and are thus classified as ales. *Faro lambics* are somewhat sweet, pale to reddish gold in color, and very refreshing. *Gueuze lambics* are a blend of young and old lambics, rather winy, fruity, and complex. *Kriek lambics* are blended with cherries. They can be slightly sweet but are better described as fruity and tart. *Framboise lambics* are similar to krieks, but are made with raspberries.

STYLES OF LAGER

The style of beer we know as lager originated in mainland Europe. All of the following types of lager are readily available in the United States and Canada.

AMERICAN LIGHT LAGER Beers in this Pilsner style are the best sellers in the United States. They are very light in color and flavor—some unkindly say insipid—but are refreshing in hot weather.

BOCK Ranging from amber to deep brown and generally full-bodied and malty, bocks have a generous dose of hops and medium to high alcohol content. *Dopplebock* (double bock) is strong and full-bodied, with a hint of sweetness. *Eisbock* (ice bock) is first frozen, and then some ice is removed, raising the alcohol content. It can be quite sweet and malty. *Maibock* (May bock), made in the spring, is usually slightly sweet with some malty tones. Similar, slightly darker *Märzen* is typically made in March and aged over the summer for consumption during Oktoberfest.

RAUCHBIER "Smoked beer" in German, this is made from malted barley dried over wood or peat fires. Warm and spicy, it can be reminiscent of bacon or Scotch.

MALT LIQUOR These are high-alcohol lagers with up to 14 percent by volume. In some U.S. states, high-alcohol beers such as barley wine are labeled as malt liquors.

PILSNER Created in Pilsen, Czechoslovakia, this style of beer was the model for American light lager. Most Pilsners are pale in color, crisp and dry in flavor, with medium to high hops content.

REGIONAL BEERS

Local pride is evident in these vintage American beer labels.

Serving Beer

LIGHTER BEERS, such as Pilsners, light American lagers, and wheat beers, should be served at 45°F to 48°F (7°C to 9°C). Heavier styles, such as amber ales and stouts, are ideally served at 50° to 55°F (10°C to 13°C). When serving from a bottle or can, pour the beer slowly down the center (not the side) of a tilted glass, creating a tall, foamy head. The object is to rid the beer of some carbonation and release the bouquet. When dispensing from a keg, pull the tap, let a few drops of beer or foam pass through, and slide a tilted glass under the stream. Most beer can be served in beer mugs, large wineglasses, metal tankards, and even 16-fl-oz (500-ml) mixing glasses, but Pilsner is served in a Pilsner glass.

Bellini

CREATED IN 1948 by Harry Cipriani at Harry's Bar in Venice, Italy, this sophisticated drink was named for the fifteenth-century Venetian artist Jacopo Bellini, a painter Cipriani much admired. Apparently, the wonderful faint pink hue of the Bellini reminded him of a similar shade in one of Bellini's paintings. The components are fairly simple, but when combined they make an intricate, stylish drink.

If white peaches are out of season, don't hesitate to make this with yellow ones—it won't be quite the same in color, but it will retain its marvelous balance and flavor.

Makes 4 drinks.

1 ripe white peach, pitted but not peeled, cut into 1-inch (2.5-cm) cubes
1 teaspoon fresh lemon juice
1 teaspoon simple syrup (page 23)
2 cups (16 fl oz/500 ml) Prosecco (an Italian sparkling wine), Champagne, sparkling wine, or nonalcoholic sparkling wine

Put the cubed peach flesh, lemon juice, and simple syrup in a blender. Blend well. Divide the peach puree among 4 chilled Champagne flutes. Gently pour in the sparkling wine. Stir gently to combine.

SEE ALSO *Faux Bellini.*

BERMUDA ROSE COCKTAIL

2½ fl oz (75 ml) gin

1 tablespoon apricot brandy

Dash of grenadine

Pour all of the ingredients into a mixing glass two-thirds full of ice cubes. Stir well. Strain into a chilled cocktail glass.

BETWEEN THE SHEETS

The origins of its somewhat risqué name are lost to history, but this drink remains a classic.

3 tablespoons brandy

1 tablespoon light rum

1 tablespoon triple sec

1 tablespoon fresh lemon juice

1½ teaspoons simple syrup (page 23)

Pour all of the ingredients into a shaker two-thirds full of ice cubes. Shake well. Strain into a chilled cocktail glass.

B-52

A fairly new concoction, this is a Pousse-Café–style layered drink made for sipping. However, some people down it as a shooter, in one big gulp.

1½ tablespoons coffee liqueur (such as Kahlúa)

1½ tablespoons Irish cream liqueur

1½ tablespoons Grand Marnier

Pour the ingredients, in the order given, over the back of a spoon into a Pousse-Café glass, floating one on top of the other (see technique, page 60).

BISHOP PUNCH

This drink dates from Dickensian England, although the recipe has changed down through the years. A nonalcoholic version of the recipe uses alcohol-free red wine.

2 tablespoons fresh lemon juice
2 tablespoons fresh orange juice
1½ teaspoons simple syrup (page 23)
4 fl oz (120 ml) red wine
1 orange slice, for garnish

Pour the citrus juices and simple syrup into a shaker two-thirds full of ice cubes. Shake well. Strain into a chilled wineglass. Pour in the wine. Stir briefly. Add the orange slice.

BLACK RUSSIAN

Since it first caught on during the 1960s and 1970s, the Black Russian has retained a loyal group of fans. Feel free to use less coffee liqueur if you desire a drier drink.

2 fl oz (60 ml) vodka
3 tablespoons coffee liqueur (such as Kahlúa)

Pour the vodka and coffee liqueur into an ice-filled Old-Fashioned glass. Stir briefly.

BLACK VELVET

An unlikely but elegant mixture, the Black Velvet is even more delightful when the Champagne is a sweeter bottling, such as doux or sec.

1 cup (8 fl oz/250 ml) chilled Irish stout
1 cup (8 fl oz/250 ml) chilled Champagne or sparkling wine

Carefully pour the stout and Champagne into a chilled 16-fl-oz (500-ml) beer glass.

BLACKTHORN

2 fl oz (60 ml) sloe gin
1 ½ tablespoons sweet vermouth
1 lemon twist, for garnish

Pour the sloe gin and vermouth into a mixing glass two-thirds full of ice cubes. Stir well. Strain into a chilled cocktail glass. Garnish with the lemon twist.

BLARNEY STONE

A wonderful if somewhat strong drink with which to celebrate Saint Patrick's Day.

2 fl oz (60 ml) Irish whiskey
1 teaspoon curaçao
1 teaspoon absinthe substitute (such as Pernod or Ricard)
1 lemon twist, for garnish

Pour the whiskey, curaçao, and absinthe substitute into a mixing glass two-thirds full of ice cubes. Stir well. Strain into a chilled cocktail glass. Add the garnish.

BLOOD-AND-SAND

The unusual mixture of ingredients comes together in a sweet drink with some smoky notes from the Scotch.

2 fl oz (60 ml) blended Scotch whisky
2 tablespoons fresh orange juice
1 tablespoon cherry brandy
1 tablespoon sweet vermouth

Pour the ingredients into a shaker two-thirds full of ice cubes. Shake well. Strain into a chilled cocktail glass.

BLOODHOUND COCKTAIL

2 fl oz (60 ml) gin
1 tablespoon dry vermouth
1 tablespoon sweet vermouth
2 teaspoons strawberry puree or liqueur

Pour all of the ingredients into a shaker two-thirds full of ice cubes. Shake well. Strain into a chilled cocktail glass.

BLOODY BULL

A marriage of the Bloody Mary and the Bullshot, this drink is ideal for brunch or any daytime party.

2 fl oz (60 ml) vodka
2 fl oz (60 ml) tomato juice
2 fl oz (60 ml) beef bouillon
2 teaspoons fresh lemon juice
Pinch of ground black pepper
Pinch of celery salt
3 dashes Worcestershire sauce
Dash of hot sauce
1 lemon wedge, for garnish

Pour the vodka, tomato juice, beef bouillon, and lemon juice into a shaker two-thirds full of ice cubes. Add the pepper, celery salt, Worcestershire sauce, and hot sauce. Shake well. Strain into an ice-filled highball glass. Add the lemon wedge.

BLOODY CAESAR

This variation on the Bloody Mary uses clam-tomato juice in place of tomato juice.

2 fl oz (60 ml) vodka
4 fl oz (120 ml) clam-tomato juice
2 teaspoons fresh lemon juice
Pinch of ground black pepper
Pinch of celery salt
Dash of hot sauce (optional)
1 lemon wedge, for garnish

Pour the vodka, clam-tomato juice, and lemon juice into a shaker two-thirds full of ice cubes. Add the pepper, celery salt, and hot sauce. Shake well. Strain into an ice-filled highball glass. Garnish with the lemon wedge.

BLOODY MARY—See page 106.

BLUE BLAZER

A pyrotechnical showstopper, the Blue Blazer dates from the nineteenth century. If you attempt it, be very careful—and have a fire extinguisher on hand just in case. Please read about flaming, page 63.

2 fl oz (60 ml) Scotch whisky
3 tablespoons hot water
1 tablespoon simple syrup (page 23)
1 lemon twist, for garnish

Pour the Scotch and hot water into an Irish Coffee glass or a metal tankard and ignite it carefully with a match. Pour the flaming liquid with care into a second Irish Coffee glass or metal tankard and repeat this process, pouring it back and forth between the glasses three or four times. Add the simple syrup. Stir briefly. Garnish with the lemon twist.

Bloody Mary

BARTENDER FERNAND PETIOT reportedly created this classic in the 1920s at Harry's New York Bar in Paris. He brought the recipe to New York after Prohibition ended. It was there that Americans became enamored of the drink. Over the years it has changed greatly, and everyone seems to have a favorite recipe calling for an extra pinch of one seasoning or another. This recipe is basic, but well balanced.

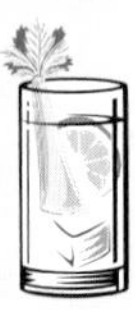

2 fl oz (60 ml) vodka
4 fl oz (120 ml) tomato juice
1 tablespoon lime juice
¼ teaspoon black pepper
Generous pinch of salt
¼ teaspoon ground cumin
2 dashes Worcestershire sauce
2 dashes hot sauce
1 lime wedge and 1 celery stalk, for garnish

Pour the vodka, tomato juice, and lime juice into a shaker two-thirds full of ice cubes. Add the pepper, salt, cumin, Worcestershire sauce, and hot sauce. Shake well. Strain into an ice-filled highball glass. Add the garnishes.

SEE ALSO *Bloody Bull, Bloody Caesar, Gin Bloody Mary, Tequila Mary, and the nonalcoholic Virgin Caesar and Virgin Mary.*

BOBBY BURNS

Named for the immortal Scottish poet Robert Burns, this whisky drink is a variation on the Rob Roy. If you like the somewhat medicinal flavor of Bénédictine, you're sure to enjoy this cocktail—whether you're a Scot or not.

2 fl oz (60 ml) blended Scotch whisky
2 tablespoons sweet vermouth
2 teaspoons Bénédictine

Pour all of the ingredients into a mixing glass two-thirds full of ice cubes. Stir well. Strain into a chilled cocktail glass.

BOCCE BALL

Named in honor of the Italian game of lawn bowls, this drink fittingly features an Italian-style liqueur (see Amaretto, page 81).

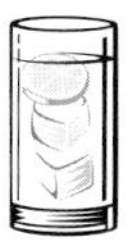

2 fl oz (60 ml) amaretto
4 fl oz (120 ml) fresh orange juice
1 orange wheel, for garnish

Pour the amaretto and orange juice into an ice-filled highball glass. Stir briefly. Add the orange wheel.

BOLERO

2 fl oz (60 ml) dark rum
1 tablespoon sweet vermouth
1 tablespoon applejack

Pour all of the ingredients into a mixing glass two-thirds full of ice cubes. Stir well. Strain into a chilled cocktail glass.

BOMBAY COCKTAIL

You might be tempted to add more than the two dashes of absinthe substitute this cocktail calls for, but beware—the anise flavor can take over the whole drink.

3 tablespoons brandy
1 tablespoon sweet vermouth
1 tablespoon dry vermouth
1 tablespoon curaçao
2 dashes absinthe substitute (such as Pernod or Ricard)

Pour all of the ingredients into a mixing glass two-thirds full of ice cubes. Stir well. Strain into a chilled cocktail glass.

BOURBON—See Whisk(e)y, page 301.

BOURBON AND BRANCH

A favorite drink of Southern gentlemen—and ladies, too. Alter the proportions however you wish.

2½ fl oz (75 ml) bourbon
4 to 5 fl oz (120 to 150 ml) still spring water

Pour the bourbon and water into an ice-filled highball glass. Stir briefly.

BOURBON BUCK

1 lemon wedge
2 fl oz (60 ml) bourbon
5 fl oz (150 ml) ginger ale

Squeeze the lemon wedge into a highball glass and drop it into the glass. Fill the glass with ice cubes. Add the bourbon and ginger ale. Stir briefly.

BOURBON COBBLER

2½ fl oz (75 ml) bourbon
1 tablespoon simple syrup (page 23)
1 lemon wedge, for garnish

Pour the bourbon and simple syrup into a wineglass filled with crushed ice. Stir briefly. Add the garnish.

BOURBON COLLINS—See John Collins, page 187.

BOURBON CRUSTA

Granulated sugar, to coat rim of glass
Lemon peel spiral (see technique, page 53)
2 fl oz (60 ml) bourbon
1 tablespoon maraschino liqueur
1 tablespoon fresh lemon juice

Coat the rim of a Sour glass with sugar (see technique, page 49). Place the lemon peel spiral in the glass so that it uncoils to almost fill the interior. Pour the bourbon, maraschino liqueur, and lemon juice into a shaker two-thirds full of crushed ice. Shake well. Strain into the glass.

BOURBON FIX

2½ fl oz (75 ml) bourbon
2 tablespoons fresh lemon juice
1 tablespoon pineapple juice
1 pineapple spear, for garnish

Pour the bourbon, lemon juice, and pineapple juice into a shaker two-thirds full of crushed ice. Shake well. Strain into a highball glass filled with crushed ice. Garnish with the pineapple spear.

BOURBON FIZZ

2 fl oz (60 ml) bourbon
2 tablespoons fresh lemon juice
1 tablespoon simple syrup (page 23)
5 to 6 fl oz (150 to 180 ml) club soda
1 orange wheel, for garnish

Pour the bourbon, lemon juice, and simple syrup into a shaker two-thirds full of ice cubes. Shake well. Strain into a chilled wineglass. Add the club soda. Stir briefly. Add the orange wheel.

BOURBON FLIP

2½ fl oz (75 ml) bourbon
1½ tablespoons simple syrup (page 23)
1 egg (see caution, page 22)
Ground or freshly grated nutmeg, for garnish

Pour the bourbon and simple syrup into a shaker two-thirds full of ice cubes. Add the egg. Shake very well. Strain into a chilled wineglass. Sprinkle with nutmeg.

BOURBON MILK PUNCH

This punch, created in New Orleans, is made in individual portions.

2 fl oz (60 ml) bourbon
1 tablespoon dark crème de cacao
4 fl oz (120 ml) milk
Dash of vanilla extract
¼ teaspoon ground cinnamon
Ground or freshly grated nutmeg, for garnish

Pour the bourbon, crème de cacao, milk, and vanilla extract into a shaker two-thirds full of ice cubes. Add the cinnamon. Shake well. Strain into an ice-filled Old-Fashioned glass. Sprinkle the nutmeg on top.

BOURBON OLD-FASHIONED

1 sugar cube
3 dashes Angostura bitters
1 orange slice
1 lemon wedge
1 maraschino cherry
2½ fl oz (75 ml) bourbon

Put the sugar cube, bitters, orange slice, lemon wedge, and maraschino cherry in a double Old-Fashioned glass and muddle well (see technique, page 64). Fill the glass with ice cubes. Add the bourbon. Stir well.

BOURBON SLING

2½ fl oz (75 ml) bourbon
1 tablespoon Southern Comfort
1 tablespoon fresh lemon juice
5 to 6 fl oz (150 to 180 ml) club soda
1 lemon wedge, for garnish

Pour the bourbon, Southern Comfort, and lemon juice into a shaker two-thirds full of ice cubes. Shake well. Strain the drink into an ice-filled Collins glass. Add the club soda. Stir briefly. Garnish with the lemon wedge.

BOURBON SMASH

6 fresh mint leaves
1½ tablespoons simple syrup (page 23)
2½ fl oz (75 ml) bourbon
1 mint sprig, for garnish

Place the mint leaves in the bottom of an Old-Fashioned glass. Add the simple syrup and muddle well (see technique, page 64). Fill the glass with crushed ice. Add the bourbon. Stir briefly. Garnish with the mint sprig.

BOURBON SOUR

2 fl oz (60 ml) bourbon
1½ tablespoons fresh lemon juice
1 tablespoon simple syrup (page 23)
1 orange wheel, for garnish
1 maraschino cherry, for garnish

Pour the bourbon, lemon juice, and simple syrup into a shaker two-thirds full of ice cubes. Shake well. Strain the drink into a chilled Sour glass. Add the garnishes.

BOURBON SWIZZLE

You can sweeten this Swizzle by replacing the apricot brandy with Southern Comfort.

2 fl oz (60 ml) bourbon
1 tablespoon fresh lemon juice
1 tablespoon apricot brandy
5 to 6 fl oz (150 to 180 ml) ginger ale
1 lemon wheel, for garnish

Pour the bourbon, lemon juice, and apricot brandy into a shaker two-thirds full of ice cubes. Shake well. Strain the mixture into an ice-filled Collins glass. Add the ginger ale. Stir briefly. Add the garnish and a swizzle stick.

Three now-forgotten brands of bourbon

BRANDIED EGGNOG

If you wish, you can substitute 5 cups (40 fl oz/1.25 l) of store-bought unspiced, pasteurized eggnog for the raw eggs and milk.

Makes 8 6-fl-oz (180-ml) servings.

4 eggs (see caution, page 22)
6 fl oz (180 ml) brandy
2 fl oz (60 ml) Grand Marnier
1 teaspoon vanilla extract
½ teaspoon ground cinnamon
½ teaspoon ground allspice
3¾ cups (30 fl oz/940 ml) milk
Ground or freshly grated nutmeg, for garnish

Break the eggs into a large bowl and whisk thoroughly until frothy. Add the brandy, Grand Marnier, vanilla extract, cinnamon, and allspice. Whisk to combine. Slowly add the milk, whisking all the time, until the eggnog is thoroughly mixed. Ladle or pour into Irish Coffee glasses, adding a sprinkle of nutmeg to each serving.

BRANDY—See page 114.

BRANDY ALEXANDER

It's hard to imagine, but the original Alexander (page 80) was made with gin.

2 fl oz (60 ml) brandy
1 tablespoon dark crème de cacao
2 tablespoons heavy cream
Ground or freshly grated nutmeg, for garnish

Pour the brandy, crème de cacao, and heavy cream into a shaker two-thirds full of ice cubes. Shake well. Strain into a chilled cocktail glass and sprinkle with nutmeg.

Brandy

Usually 40–50% alcohol by volume

Brandy is made by distilling fermented fruit juice, and although grape brandies such as Cognac and Armagnac are the best known types, there are many other delicious varieties. Herewith, a brief survey of brandies from around the world.

The brandy regions of France

HOW BRANDY IS MADE

All brandies are produced in essentially the same way: A mash of grapes or other fruit undergoes fermentation to become a wine that is then distilled and often aged before bottling. Old-fashioned pot stills, known in France as *alembiques,* are thought to produce better results than the more modern and cost-efficient column stills—but it's actually the combined skills of the distiller and the cellar master, who oversees the aging process, that determine the quality of the final product.

FRANCE

The brandies of France, in particular Cognac, set the standard against which other brandies are judged. Other famous brandies from France include Armagnac and Calvados.

COGNAC In order to be labeled Cognac, a French brandy must be made from grapes grown in the Cognac district of the Charente and Charente-Maritime departments (see map, left). The Cognac area is divided into six subregions: Grande Champagne, Petite Champagne, Borderies, Fins Bois, Bons Bois, and Bois Ordinaires. The Grande and Petite Champagne areas are said to produce the finest Cognacs.

By law, Cognac must be made from white grapes only, specifically 90 percent from Ugni Blanc, Folle Blanche, and/or Colombard grapes, all of which produce a rather thin, acidic wine that is perfect for distillation. The remaining 10 percent of

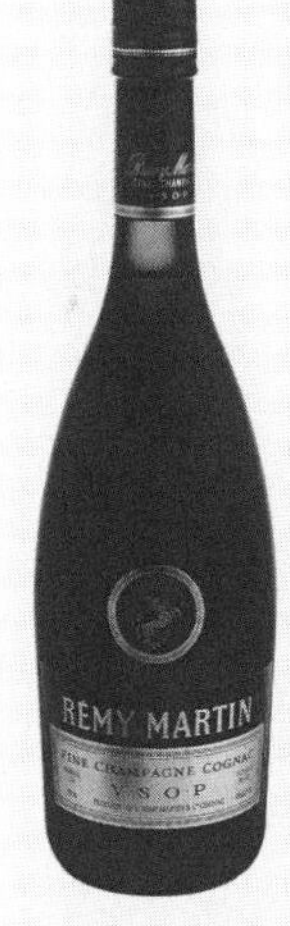

COGNAC

French Cognacs, such as Rémy Martin, are typically distilled in small pot stills and aged in casks made of Limousin oak, which imparts a vanilla flavor.

the Cognac may legally include other types of white grapes.

Cognacs are usually aged in casks made of Limousin oak; any aged for fewer than two years cannot be exported to the United States. However, vintage labeling is rare, since the blending process usually includes brandies of different ages to produce each brand's consistent style. The best Cognacs are dry, austere spirits with hints of fruit, but some of the bolder, sweeter, fruitier bottlings can be very pleasant also.

ARMAGNAC Produced in the Gascony area (department of Gers), Armagnac is made from grapes grown in three subregions: Ténarèze, which produces a light brandy; Haut-Armagnac, whose brandy is usually used for blending; and Bas-Armagnac, which produces the finest Armagnac. Bottlings labeled simply Armagnac contain a blend of brandies from all three regions. Armagnac must be made from white grapes, largely Ugni Blanc, Colombard, and/or Folle Blanche. It is aged in black oak casks.

Unlike Cognacs, Armagnacs are produced in many vintages. The best are well-balanced brandies with a dry fruitiness and a sharp, nutty character.

CALVADOS Fermented apple cider is the base for this brandy made in a delineated region of Calvados (a department in northern Normandy). Pears are often added to provide a balanced flavor. Well-aged bottlings of Calvados can be found in the market, and vintage-dated Calvados

AGE DESIGNATIONS FOR COGNACS

Cognacs labeled with these letter codes have been aged as least as long as indicated—often far longer.

VS (Very Special*): 2.5 years

VSOP (Very Special* Old Pale) or VO (Very Old): 4.5 years

XO (Extra Old) or Napoléon: 6 years

**or Very Superior*

is also available. The finest bottlings, called Calvados du pays d'Auge, are distilled, like Cognacs, in pot stills and bear flavorful apple notes that lie under an austere blanket of dry spiciness.

SPAIN

Brandy de Jerez, made from either Airén or Palomino grapes, is produced in the Jerez district of Spain, otherwise famous for sherry. This brandy is usually sweeter than most grape brandies and bears caramel notes that make it a good choice as an accompaniment to desserts such as ice cream or chocolate. Brandy de Jerez is aged similarly to sherry, using the solera method, which involves periodically taking young brandy from one barrel and mixing it with older brandies. Bottlings of brandy de Jerez that bear the word *solera* contain brandy that has been aged for about a year, *solera reserva* bottlings have usually matured for at least two years, and *solera gran reserva* brandies are normally over seven years old.

UNITED STATES

American brandies were once dismissed as mediocre at best, and some of the less-expensive bottlings are still good enough only for cooking or inferior cocktails. However, California now boasts a few distilleries—including Germain-Robin, Carneros, and Jepson—that use traditional French-style Cognac stills to make highly flavorful, top-notch brandies. Part of their secret is that American brandy

MOST POPULAR BRANDY DRINKS

(according to U.S. bartenders)

1. Stinger, page 270
2. Sidecar, page 261
3. Keoki Coffee, page 190
4. Brandy Alexander, page 113
5. Café Brûlot, page 129

COGNAC FANS

Liquor distributors gave these away to advertise French Cognac in the 1920s.

distillers can use whatever grapes they choose—Pinot Noir, Chenin Blanc, Palomino, Sémillon, Chardonnay, Meunier, and Muscat grapes, among them—to produce bold, forthright products. Law limits French brandy producers, by contrast, to certain inferior-quality varietals. Although these boutique bottlings of American brandies can be prohibitively expensive for making cocktails, they are fine sipping spirits.

GREEK BRANDY

Greek Metaxa brandy is made from a blend of grape-based spirits and Muscat wine, aged in oak casks and flavored with botanicals.

OTHER COUNTRIES

Greece produces a decent brandy under the Metaxa label. Similarly, several brandies from Cyprus, Italy, Israel, Australia, South America, and South Africa are quite passable for use in cocktails and mixed drinks, although many of them are a little too sweet to be considered fine products.

EAUX-DE-VIE AND OTHER FRUIT BRANDIES

All brandies are fruit brandies, but the term *fruit* is used to differentiate brandies made from grape juice, normally referred to simply as brandies, from those made with other fruits or from the leftovers of the winemaking process.

A few fruit brandies, especially European bottlings, are aged in wood like the finest Cognacs and are sipped and savored with the best. Calvados is an example. But brandies in the less-exalted category called *eau-de-vie* (water of life) or *alcool blanc* (white alcohol) are usually clear, unaged spirits, best served chilled. The flavors of the base fruit are detectable, but often only slightly. Those made from grape pomace, the leftovers of pressing the grapes for winemaking, are known as *marc* in France and *grappa* in Italy. Other popular categories include *kirsch* or *Kirschwasser,* made from cherries; *framboise,* made from raspberries; *fraise,* made from strawberries; and *mirabelle,* made from yellow plums. Assorted other bottlings usually bear the name of the fruit from which they were made: eau-de-vie de poire, for example, is an eau-de-vie made from pears.

Beware: Many bottlings labeled as peach, cherry, or blackberry brandy are actually liqueurs (page 195) containing only a small percentage of spirits distilled from fruit. The rest consists of neutral spirits flavored with fruit essence and a sweetener.

EAU-DE-VIE

The pear in this eau-de-vie actually grew inside the empty bottle, which was secured to the tree when the fruit was small.

Serving Brandy

AGED GRAPE BRANDIES, such as Cognac and Armagnac, should be served in a smallish snifter or a sherry copita glass (page 41). Pour 1½ fl oz (45 ml) into each glass.

Never heat these brandies artificially—say, by holding the glass over a candle—as this will produce an intense aroma that isn't true to the spirit. They should be served at room temperature and warmed only by cupping your hand around the base of the glass.

Serve eau-de-vie, marc, and grappa at room temperature or chilled, straight from the freezer.

BRANDY BLAZER

As with all flaming drinks, exercise caution and keep a fire extinguisher at hand. Please read about flaming, page 63.

1 orange wheel
1 lemon wedge
1 maraschino cherry
2 fl oz (60 ml) brandy
1 tablespoon simple syrup (page 23)
1 lemon twist, for garnish

Put the orange wheel, lemon wedge, and maraschino cherry in a mixing glass and muddle well (see technique, page 64). Add the brandy and simple syrup. Stir briefly. Carefully ignite the mixture with a match. Stir with a bar spoon until the flame is extinguished. Strain into an Irish Coffee glass. Add the lemon twist.

BRANDY BUCK

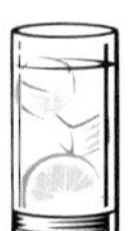

1 lemon wedge
2 fl oz (60 ml) brandy
5 fl oz (150 ml) ginger ale

Squeeze the lemon wedge into a highball glass and drop it into the glass. Fill the glass with ice cubes. Add the brandy and ginger ale. Stir briefly.

BRANDY COBBLER

2½ fl oz (75 ml) brandy
1 tablespoon simple syrup (page 23)
1 lemon twist, for garnish

Pour the brandy and simple syrup into a wineglass filled with crushed ice. Stir briefly. Add the garnish.

BRANDY COLLINS

Requested only rarely these days, the Brandy Collins is in fact a flavorful, refreshing drink. Ginger ale can replace the club soda if you wish.

2 fl oz (60 ml) brandy
1 tablespoon fresh lemon juice
1 tablespoon simple syrup (page 23)
5 to 6 fl oz (150 to 180 ml) club soda
1 lemon wedge, for garnish

Pour the brandy, lemon juice, and simple syrup into a shaker two-thirds full of ice cubes. Shake well. Strain into an ice-filled Collins glass. Add the club soda. Stir briefly. Add the lemon wedge.

BRANDY COOLER

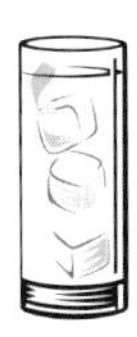

2½ fl oz (75 ml) brandy
6 to 7 fl oz (180 to 210 ml) club soda
1 lemon twist, for garnish

Pour the brandy and club soda into an ice-filled Collins glass. Stir briefly. Add the lemon twist.

BRANDY CRUSTA—See page 122.

BRANDY DAISY

2½ fl oz (75 ml) brandy
2 tablespoons fresh lemon juice
1 tablespoon grenadine
1 lemon twist, for garnish

Pour the brandy, lemon juice, and grenadine into a shaker two-thirds full of crushed ice. Shake well. Strain into a highball glass filled with crushed ice. Garnish with the lemon twist.

Brandy Crusta

THE BRANDY CRUSTA is considered to be the original Crusta, a drink that combines a base spirit with lemon juice and maraschino liqueur (page 199). Like the other members of the Crusta category, the Brandy Crusta is served straight up in a sugar-rimmed Sour glass lined with a spiral of lemon peel.

Granulated sugar, to coat rim of glass
Lemon peel spiral (see technique, page 53)
2 fl oz (60 ml) brandy
1 tablespoon maraschino liqueur
1 tablespoon fresh lemon juice

Coat the rim of a Sour glass with sugar (see technique, page 49). Place the lemon peel spiral into the glass so that it uncoils to almost fill the interior.

Pour the brandy, maraschino liqueur, and lemon juice into a shaker two-thirds full of crushed ice. Shake well. Strain into the glass.

SEE ALSO *Bourbon Crusta, Gin Crusta, Irish Crusta, Rum Crusta, Scotch Crusta, Whisky Crusta.*

BRANDY FIX

2½ fl oz (75 ml) brandy
2 tablespoons fresh lemon juice
1 tablespoon pineapple juice
1 pineapple spear, for garnish

Pour the brandy, lemon juice, and pineapple juice into a shaker two-thirds full of crushed ice. Shake well. Strain into a highball glass filled with crushed ice. Add the pineapple spear.

BRANDY FIZZ

2 fl oz (60 ml) brandy
2 tablespoons fresh lemon juice
1 tablespoon simple syrup (page 23)
5 to 6 fl oz (150 to 180 ml) club soda
1 lemon twist, for garnish

Pour the brandy, lemon juice, and simple syrup into a shaker two-thirds full of ice cubes. Shake well. Strain into a chilled wineglass. Pour in the club soda. Stir briefly. Garnish with the lemon twist.

LIGHTHOUSE SHAKER

This 1929 silver-plated shaker is a facsimile of Boston Harbor Light, built in 1783.

Brandy Flip

DATING FROM THE eighteenth century, the Brandy Flip was probably the first Flip to gain popularity. Like other true Flips, it contains a base spirit, a wine or beer, a raw egg, and simple syrup. These are shaken together into a thick, creamy drink and served straight up in a wineglass or beer glass with a garnish of nutmeg.

2½ fl oz (75 ml) brandy
1½ tablespoons simple syrup (page 23)
1 egg (see caution, page 22)
Ground or freshly grated nutmeg, for garnish

Pour the brandy and simple syrup into a shaker two-thirds full of ice cubes. Add the egg. Shake very well. Strain into a chilled wineglass. Sprinkle with nutmeg.

SEE ALSO *Bourbon Flip, Gin Flip, Port Wine Flip, Rum Flip, Scotch Flip, Sherry Flip, Whisky Flip.*

BRANDY JULEP

Few people these days think of making juleps with brandy, but Brandy Juleps were a big favorite in Colonial days.

2 tablespoons simple syrup (page 23)
3 fl oz (90 ml) brandy
3 large mint sprigs, for garnish

Pour the simple syrup into a Julep cup filled with crushed ice. Stir well. Add the brandy. Stir until a film of ice forms on the cup's exterior. Add the mint sprigs.

BRANDY SANGAREE

2 fl oz (60 ml) brandy
1 tablespoon ruby port
1 tablespoon Grand Marnier
Ground or freshly grated nutmeg, for garnish

Pour the brandy, port, and Grand Marnier into a mixing glass two-thirds full of ice cubes. Stir well. Strain into a chilled small wineglass. Sprinkle with nutmeg.

BRANDY SLING

2½ fl oz (75 ml) brandy
1 tablespoon Grand Marnier
1 tablespoon fresh lemon juice
5 to 6 fl oz (150 to 180 ml) club soda
1 lemon wedge, for garnish

Pour the brandy, Grand Marnier, and lemon juice into a shaker two-thirds full of ice cubes. Shake well. Strain the drink into an ice-filled Collins glass. Add the club soda. Stir briefly. Garnish with the lemon wedge.

BRANDY SMASH—See page 126.

BRANDY SOUR

2 fl oz (60 ml) brandy
1½ tablespoons fresh lemon juice
1 tablespoon simple syrup (page 23)
1 orange wheel, for garnish
1 maraschino cherry, for garnish

Pour the brandy, lemon juice, and simple syrup into a shaker two-thirds full of ice cubes. Shake well. Strain the drink into a chilled Sour glass. Add the garnishes.

Brandy Smash

POUR A BASE SPIRIT over sweetened and mashed mint leaves, add crushed ice, and you have a Smash. The Brandy Smash is the predominant member of the family.

6 fresh mint leaves
1½ tablespoons simple syrup (page 23)
2½ fl oz (75 ml) brandy
1 mint sprig, for garnish

Put the mint leaves in the bottom of an Old-Fashioned glass. Add the simple syrup and muddle well (see technique, page 64). Fill the glass with crushed ice. Pour in the brandy. Stir briefly. Garnish with the mint sprig.

SEE ALSO *Applejack Smash, Bourbon Smash, Irish Smash, Rum Smash, Scotch Smash.*

BRANDY SWIZZLE

2 fl oz (60 ml) brandy
1 tablespoon fresh lemon juice
1 tablespoon cherry brandy
5 to 6 fl oz (150 to 180 ml) ginger ale
1 lemon wheel, for garnish

Pour the brandy, lemon juice, and cherry brandy into a shaker two-thirds full of ice cubes. Shake well. Strain the mixture into an ice-filled Collins glass. Pour in the ginger ale. Stir briefly. Add the garnish and a swizzle stick.

BRAVE BULL

2 fl oz (60 ml) white tequila
1 tablespoon coffee liqueur (such as Kahlúa)

Pour the tequila and coffee liqueur into an ice-filled Old-Fashioned glass. Stir briefly.

Bronx Cocktail

SOMETIME BEFORE PROHIBITION, bartender Johnnie Solon created this drink at New York's Waldorf-Astoria Hotel. He reportedly invented it at a customer's request and needed a name whereby the customer could order it regularly. Solon had recently visited the Bronx Zoo, where he had his first glimpse of exotic animals. Since he had heard that some people saw strange animals when they over-indulged, he named his creation the Bronx Cocktail.

2 fl oz (60 ml) gin
2 tablespoons fresh orange juice
2 teaspoons dry vermouth
2 teaspoons sweet vermouth

Pour all of the ingredients into a shaker two-thirds full of ice cubes. Shake well. Strain into a chilled cocktail glass.

BRONX COCKTAIL (DRY)

2 fl oz (60 ml) gin
2 tablespoons fresh orange juice
1 tablespoon dry vermouth

Pour all of the ingredients into a shaker two-thirds full of ice cubes. Shake well. Strain into a chilled cocktail glass.

⦸ BROOKE SHIELDS

A contemporary variation on the Shirley Temple (page 263).

2 tablespoons fresh orange juice
1 tablespoon fresh lemon juice
1 teaspoon fresh lime juice
6 fl oz (180 ml) ginger ale
Dash of grenadine
1 maraschino cherry, for garnish

Pour the orange, lemon, and lime juices into a shaker two-thirds full of ice cubes. Shake well. Strain into an ice-filled Collins glass. Add the ginger ale and grenadine. Stir briefly. Add the cherry.

BULLSHOT

To warm up on a cold night, try pouring the same ingredients into an Irish Coffee glass and microwaving on high for 30 seconds or until hot.

2 fl oz (60 ml) vodka
4 fl oz (120 ml) beef bouillon
2 teaspoons fresh lemon juice
Pinch of ground black pepper
Pinch of celery salt
3 dashes Worcestershire sauce
Dash of hot sauce
1 lemon wedge, for garnish

Pour the vodka, beef bouillon, and lemon juice into a shaker two-thirds full of ice cubes. Add the pepper, celery salt, Worcestershire sauce, and hot sauce. Shake well. Strain into an ice-filled highball glass. Add the lemon wedge.

CABARET

2 fl oz (60 ml) gin
1 tablespoon dry vermouth
1 teaspoon Bénédictine
1 lemon twist, for garnish

Pour the gin, vermouth, and Bénédictine into a mixing glass two-thirds full of ice cubes. Stir well. Strain into a chilled cocktail glass. Add the lemon twist.

CAFÉ BRÛLOT

This flamboyant drink from New Orleans is often made in a copper brûlot pot atop a candle or Sterno flame. You can prepare this version on the stovetop. Please read the cautions about flaming, page 63.

Makes 2 7-fl-oz (210-ml) drinks.

3 lemon twists
3 orange twists
4 whole cloves
1 cinnamon stick (about 2 inches/5 cm long)
3 tablespoons brandy
2 tablespoons curaçao
1½ cups (12 fl oz/375 ml) strong, hot coffee

Place the citrus twists, cloves, cinnamon stick, brandy, and curaçao in a large saucepan made of stainless steel or other nonreactive material. Cook over medium-low heat until warm. Carefully ignite the liquid with a match and allow it to flame for about 10 seconds. Pour in the hot coffee and stir well until the flames subside. Divide the mixture between two Irish Coffee glasses.

CAIPIRINHA

The national drink of Brazil is made with a rum known as cachaça. If you can't find cachaça, use an inexpensive light rum.

½ lime, cut into 4 to 6 wedges
1 tablespoon simple syrup (page 23)
2 fl oz (60 ml) cachaça

Put the lime wedges and simple syrup in an Old-Fashioned glass and muddle well to release all of the juice from the limes (see technique, page 64). Fill the glass with crushed ice. Add the cachaça. Stir thoroughly.

CAJUN MARTINI

2½ fl oz (75 ml) pepper vodka
1 tablespoon dry vermouth
1 slice fresh jalapeño pepper, for garnish

Pour the vodka and vermouth into a mixing glass two-thirds full of ice cubes. Stir well. Strain into a chilled cocktail glass. Add the pepper slice.

CAMPARI AND GRAPEFRUIT JUICE

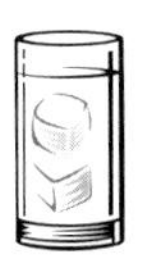

2 fl oz (60 ml) Campari
4 fl oz (120 ml) fresh grapefruit juice

Pour the ingredients into an ice-filled highball glass. Stir briefly.

CAMPARI AND ORANGE JUICE

2 fl oz (60 ml) Campari
4 fl oz (120 ml) fresh orange juice

Pour the ingredients into an ice-filled highball glass. Stir briefly.

CAMPARI SPECIAL

- 2 fl oz (60 ml) Campari
- 2 tablespoons Grand Marnier
- 1 orange twist, for garnish

Pour the Campari and Grand Marnier into a mixing glass two-thirds full of ice cubes. Stir well. Strain into a chilled cocktail glass. Add the orange twist.

Campari

24% alcohol by volume

ALTHOUGH LEGALLY DEFINED AS a liqueur in the United States, Campari is in fact a form of aperitif bitters—spirits flavored with an assortment of herbs, fruits, spices, and other botanicals. Because of its bitterness, Campari is widely considered an acquired taste. Indeed, in Milan, the city where restaurateur Gaspare Campari introduced the beverage in 1860, it is often said that you must drink Campari three times before you enjoy it.

Campari is usually combined with orange or grapefruit juice or a splash of soda. It is also a wonderfully complex addition to cocktails and mixed drinks. Sometimes small quantities of it replace bitters such as Angostura, and although their flavors bear no resemblance, they produce similar effects in cocktails, adding a complex, spicy bitterness while melding the other ingredients.

CANADIAN WHISKY—See Whisk(e)y, page 302.

CAPE CODDER

2½ fl oz (75 ml) vodka
4 to 6 fl oz (120 to 180 ml) cranberry juice cocktail
1 lime wedge, for garnish

Pour the vodka and cranberry juice into an ice-filled highball glass. Stir briefly. Add the lime wedge.

CARDINAL PUNCH

Makes 20 6-fl-oz (180-ml) servings.

4 fl oz (120 ml) dark rum
4 fl oz (120 ml) fresh lemon juice
3 fl oz (90 ml) simple syrup (page 23)
2 750-ml bottles dry red wine
1 750-ml bottle Champagne or sparkling wine
1 cup (8 fl oz/250 ml) sweet vermouth
1 cup (8 fl oz/250 ml) brandy
1 large block of ice
Orange wheels, for garnish

Pour 2 fl oz (60 ml) of the rum, all of the lemon juice, and all of the simple syrup into a shaker two-thirds full of ice cubes. Shake well. Strain into a large punch bowl. Pour in the wines, vermouth, brandy, and the rest of the rum. Stir well. Add the ice and let chill, stirring from time to time, for at least 30 minutes. Ladle into punch cups. Garnish each serving with an orange wheel.

CARUSO

2 fl oz (60 ml) gin
1 tablespoon dry vermouth
1 teaspoon green crème de menthe

Pour the ingredients into a mixing glass two-thirds full of ice cubes. Stir well. Strain into a chilled cocktail glass.

CASABLANCA

2½ fl oz (75 ml) light rum
1 tablespoon triple sec
1 teaspoon cherry brandy
1 tablespoon fresh lime juice

Pour all of the ingredients into a shaker two-thirds full of ice cubes. Shake well. Strain into a chilled cocktail glass.

CHAMPAGNE & SPARKLING WINE—See page 134.

CHAMPAGNE COBBLER

Not a true Cobbler, since it calls for liqueur instead of simple syrup.

4 fl oz (120 ml) Champagne or sparkling wine
2 tablespoons Grand Marnier
1 orange slice, for garnish

Pour the Champagne and Grand Marnier into a wineglass filled with crushed ice. Stir briefly. Add the orange slice.

CHAMPAGNE COCKTAIL—See page 136.

CHAMPAGNE FIZZ

2 tablespoons gin
2 tablespoons lemon juice
2 teaspoons simple syrup (page 23)
4 fl oz (120 ml) chilled Champagne or sparkling wine

Pour the gin, lemon juice, and simple syrup into a shaker two-thirds full of ice cubes. Shake well. Strain into a chilled Champagne flute. Gently add the Champagne.

Champagne & Sparkling Wine

Usually about 12% alcohol by volume

All winemaking countries produce some type of effervescent wine, but true Champagne originated in France in the early eighteenth century. European law limits the use of the term to bottlings from the Champagne region that are produced using the Méthode Champenoise, *or Champagne method. Wine aficionados everywhere usually refer to all other Champagne-style beverages as sparkling wines.*

French Champagne advertisement from the 1920s

Blanc de Blancs is Champagne made from Chardonnay (white) grapes, whereas *Blanc de Noirs* is made from Pinot Noir and/or Pinot Meunier (red) grapes. Vintage Champagnes contain only wines from the year noted on the label. They are chosen as vintages when the winemaker deems a particular year's Champagne to be exceptional.

Connoisseurs often judge the quality of Champagne by the bubbles. Look for many continuous streams of small bubbles. Most people find the dry to very dry *Brut* most desirable, but there are styles ranging in sweetness from bone-dry *Extra Brut* to very sweet *Doux* (see list, right).

CHAMPAGNES FROM DRY TO SWEET

EXTRA BRUT
(bone dry)

BRUT
(dry to very dry)

EXTRA SEC
(medium dry)

SEC
(dry)

DEMI SEC
(sweet)

DOUX
(very sweet)

Serving Champagne

ICE THE CHAMPAGNE to about 45°F (7°C)—slightly warmer than most refrigerators. Pointing the bottle away from everyone, carefully remove the foil covering the neck and then loosen the cage by untwisting the wire. With the bottle at a 45-degree angle pointing away from you and anyone else, grasp the cork firmly with one hand and hold the base of the bottle with the other. Hold the cork steady as you gently twist the bottle, letting the pressure inside slowly push the cork out.

Carefully pour the Champagne into Champagne flutes, adding small amounts to each glass and allowing the foam to subside before adding more. If you swirl the wine to release the aroma, do it gently; you don't want rough treatment to extinguish the bubbles.

Champagne Cocktail

THIS IS ONE OF the world's oldest cocktails, dating back to at least 1862. The pale pinkish color is appealing, and the flavor of the bitters heightens the cocktail's taste while masking any deficiencies in a less-expensive sparkling wine.

1 sugar cube
2 to 3 dashes Angostura bitters
5 fl oz (150 ml) Champagne or sparkling wine
1 lemon twist, for garnish

Put the sugar cube and the bitters into a Champagne flute. Carefully add the Champagne. Add the garnish.

SEE ALSO *French Champagne Cocktail, Irish Champagne Cocktail, Kentucky Champagne Cocktail, Royal Champagne Cocktail, Thames Champagne Cocktail.*

CHAMPAGNE JULEP

3 mint leaves
2 teaspoons simple syrup (page 23)
2 tablespoons bourbon
4 fl oz (120 ml) chilled Champagne

Put the mint leaves, simple syrup, and bourbon in a mixing glass and muddle well (see technique, page 64). Strain the mixture into a chilled Champagne flute. Carefully pour in the Champagne.

CHAMPAGNE PUNCH

There's nothing quite like a Champagne punch to make a special occasion sparkle. The hazelnut liqueur in this recipe makes it a sure crowd-pleaser.

Makes 20 6-fl-oz (180-ml) servings.

1 large block of ice
4 fl oz (120 ml) chilled brandy
4 fl oz (120 ml) chilled hazelnut liqueur (such as Frangelico)
4 fl oz (120 ml) chilled triple sec
3 750-ml bottles chilled Champagne or sparkling wine
16 to 20 fl oz (500 to 625 ml) chilled club soda
1 orange, cut into wheels, for garnish
1 lemon, cut into wheels, for garnish
1 apple, cored, seeded, and cut into thin slices, for garnish

Place the ice in the center of a large punch bowl. Add the brandy, hazelnut liqueur, triple sec, Champagne or sparkling wine, and club soda. Stir briefly. Float the garnishes on top. Serve in punch cups, dispensing a slice of any garnish into each cup.

⃠ CHARGER

The two dashes of Angostura bitters do add a trace of alcohol, so avoid this drink if you must abstain from alcohol completely.

1 cup (8 fl oz/250 ml) club soda
2 dashes Angostura bitters
1 lime wedge, for garnish

Pour the club soda and bitters into an ice-filled Collins glass. Stir briefly. Add the lime wedge.

CHERRY BRANDY RICKEY

Although less popular than its cousin the Gin Rickey (page 170), this drink is very flavorful and refreshing.

2½ fl oz (75 ml) cherry brandy
2 tablespoons fresh lime juice
6 to 8 fl oz (180 to 250 ml) club soda
1 lime wedge, for garnish

Pour the cherry brandy and lime juice into an ice-filled highball glass. Pour in the club soda. Stir briefly. Garnish with the lime wedge.

CHI-CHI

For those not fond of rum, here's a vodka-based variation on the classic Piña Colada (page 225).

2½ fl oz (75 ml) vodka
6 fl oz (180 ml) pineapple juice
2 fl oz (60 ml) coconut cream (such as Coco López)
1 pineapple spear, for garnish

Pour the vodka, pineapple juice, and coconut cream into a blender two-thirds full of ice cubes; blend thoroughly. Pour the mixture into a large wineglass. Add the pineapple spear.

CHOCOLATE MARTINI

This drink has caught on in a big way. It's the cocktail of choice for many who want something sweet but not cloying.

2 fl oz (60 ml) vodka
2 tablespoons white crème de cacao

Pour the ingredients into a mixing glass two-thirds full of ice cubes. Stir well. Strain into a chilled cocktail glass.

⊘ CHOIRBOY

3 fl oz (90 ml) alcohol-free red wine
2 tablespoons fresh lemon juice
2 tablespoons fresh pineapple juice
1 pineapple spear, for garnish

Pour the wine and fruit juices into a shaker two-thirds full of ice cubes. Shake well. Strain into a chilled wineglass. Add the pineapple spear.

CLARIDGE COCKTAIL

2 fl oz (60 ml) gin
1 tablespoon dry vermouth
1 tablespoon apricot brandy

Pour all of the ingredients into a mixing glass two-thirds full of ice cubes. Stir well. Strain into a chilled cocktail glass.

CLASSIC COCKTAIL

This is essentially a Sidecar (page 261) with maraschino liqueur added.

Granulated sugar, to coat rim of glass
3 tablespoons brandy
1 tablespoon triple sec
1 tablespoon maraschino liqueur
1 tablespoon fresh lemon juice

Coat the rim of a cocktail glass with sugar (see technique, page 49) and chill it. Pour the remaining ingredients into a shaker two-thirds full of ice cubes. Shake well. Strain into the glass.

CONTINENTAL

Measure carefully: Too much crème de menthe can be overpowering.

2 fl oz (60 ml) light rum
2 teaspoons green crème de menthe
1 tablespoon fresh lime juice
1 teaspoon simple syrup (page 23)
1 lemon twist, for garnish

Pour the rum, crème de menthe, lime juice, and simple syrup into a shaker two-thirds full of ice cubes. Shake well. Strain into a chilled cocktail glass. Add the garnish.

COOPERSTOWN COCKTAIL

The mint sprig adds an extra dimension to this drink as you sip it.

3 tablespoons gin
1 tablespoon sweet vermouth
1 tablespoon dry vermouth
1 mint sprig, for garnish

Pour the gin and both vermouths into a mixing glass two-thirds full of ice cubes. Stir well. Strain into a chilled cocktail glass. Add the mint sprig.

CORNELL COCKTAIL

Named for the Ivy League college, this is a frothy drink, thanks to the egg white.

2 fl oz (60 ml) gin
1 tablespoon maraschino liqueur
2 teaspoons fresh lemon juice
1 egg white (see caution, page 22)

Pour all of the ingredients into a shaker two-thirds full of ice cubes. Shake well. Strain into a chilled cocktail glass.

CORONATION

2 tablespoons gin
2 tablespoons dry vermouth
1 tablespoon Dubonnet Blanc

Pour all of the ingredients into a mixing glass two-thirds full of ice cubes. Stir well. Strain into a chilled cocktail glass.

Corpse Reviver Number 1

THE DRINKS IN THIS series with a macabre name were popular in Victorian England as pick-me-ups, usually for those suffering from a hangover. They have nothing in common except that all are strong cocktails. Crosby Gaige, a bon vivant of the 1930s, once said that one Corpse Reviver would revive any self-respecting corpse, but that four taken in swift succession would return the corpse to a reclining position.

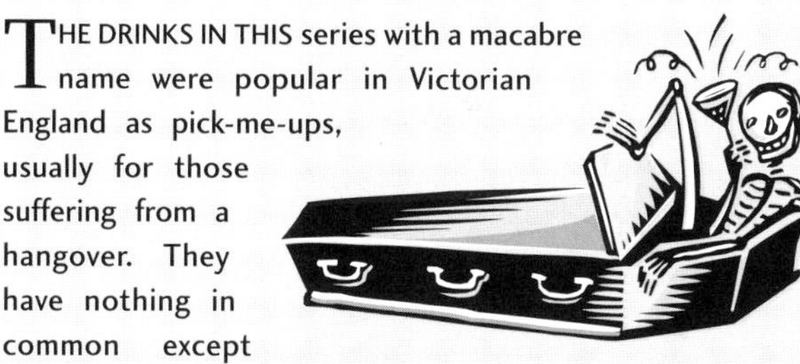

3 tablespoons brandy
1½ teaspoons sweet vermouth
1½ teaspoons applejack

Pour all of the ingredients into a mixing glass two-thirds full of ice cubes. Stir well. Strain into a chilled cocktail glass.

CORPSE REVIVER NUMBER 2

3 tablespoons triple sec
2 tablespoons dry vermouth
1 tablespoon fresh lemon juice
2 dashes absinthe substitute (such as Pernod or Ricard)

Pour all of the ingredients into a shaker two-thirds full of ice cubes. Shake well. Strain into a chilled cocktail glass.

CORPSE REVIVER NUMBER 3

2 tablespoons Cognac
2 tablespoons Campari
2 tablespoons triple sec
1 tablespoon fresh lemon juice

Pour all of the ingredients into a shaker two-thirds full of ice cubes. Shake well. Strain into a chilled cocktail glass.

CORPSE REVIVER NUMBER 4

This layered drink may be sipped, Pousse-Café style, or consumed in one go as a shooter. Be careful—it's strong stuff.

1 ½ tablespoons hazelnut liqueur (such as Frangelico)
1 ½ tablespoons maraschino liqueur
1 ½ tablespoons green Chartreuse

Pour the ingredients, in the order given, over the back of a spoon into a Pousse-Café glass, floating one on top of the other (see technique, page 60).

Cosmopolitan

IF ANY ONE DRINK can be credited for the resurgence of the cocktail in recent years, it's the Cosmopolitan, which appeared in bars across the country in the mid-1990s. No one seems to know who created it, and there has been much debate as to whether it first appeared in San Francisco or New York. But no matter who first put these ingredients together, there's no doubt this is the most popular new drink to come along since the Martini.

The best thing about the Cosmopolitan is that it is extremely well constructed. Although it's a far cry from the Martini, the balance of flavors that comes from mixing the tart lime juice, the semisweet cranberry juice cocktail, and the sweet triple sec, and the extra dimension the citrus-flavored vodka adds, is sensational.

2 fl oz (60 ml) citrus vodka
1 tablespoon triple sec
1 tablespoon cranberry juice cocktail
1 tablespoon fresh lime juice

Pour all of the ingredients into a shaker two-thirds full of ice cubes. Shake well. Strain into a chilled cocktail glass.

Crème de Menthe Frappé

FRAPPÉS CONSIST OF a base liqueur or spirit poured over crushed ice and served in either a saucer Champagne glass or a Sour glass. This one, the most popular, features crème de menthe (page 198).

2 fl oz (60 ml) green crème de menthe
3 slim straws or sip sticks, each cut to about 3 inches (7.5 cm) long

Fill a chilled Champagne saucer or Sour glass with crushed ice until it forms a dome that rises in the center of the glass. Drizzle the crème de menthe into the glass. Add the straws.

SEE ALSO *Pernod Frappé*.

CREOLE

This variation on the Bullshot (page 128) is a little spicier and more complex, since it is made with rum instead of vodka.

2 fl oz (60 ml) light rum
2 fl oz (60 ml) beef bouillon
1 tablespoon fresh lemon juice
2 dashes hot sauce
Pinch of salt
Pinch of ground black pepper

Pour the rum, bouillon, and lemon juice into a shaker two-thirds full of ice cubes. Add the hot sauce, salt, and pepper. Shake well. Strain into an ice-filled Old-Fashioned glass.

CUBA LIBRE

Fresh lime juice is what makes the difference between a true Cuba Libre and a mere rum and cola with a lime wedge.

2½ fl oz (75 ml) light rum
2 tablespoons fresh lime juice
6 fl oz (180 ml) cola
1 lime wedge, for garnish

Pour the rum and lime juice into a shaker two-thirds full of ice cubes. Shake well. Strain into an ice-filled Collins glass. Add the cola. Stir briefly. Add the lime wedge.

CUBAN COCKTAIL

3 tablespoons light rum
1 tablespoon fresh lime juice
1 tablespoon simple syrup (page 23)

Pour all of the ingredients into a shaker two-thirds full of ice cubes. Shake well. Strain into a chilled cocktail glass.

CURTIS COCKTAIL

Orange bitters is the ingredient that gives the Curtis its sharp, tangy, refreshing bite.

3 tablespoons gin
1 tablespoon triple sec
1 tablespoon sweet vermouth
Dash of orange bitters

Pour all of the ingredients into a mixing glass two-thirds full of ice cubes. Stir well. Strain into a chilled cocktail glass.

Daiquiri

LEGEND HAS IT THAT Teddy Roosevelt and his Rough Riders were among the first to sample this drink when they landed on Daiquirí Beach, Cuba, during the Spanish-American War. Americans in the area had recently created the drink, perhaps thinking that its combination of lime juice and the light local rum—with a little sugar to help the medicine go down—would ward off malaria.

Be that as it may, it was Ernest Hemingway who really popularized the drink when he consistently ordered double Daiquiris at La Floridita bar in Havana, where he became known as Papa Dobles (Father Doubles).

2 fl oz (60 ml) light rum
2 tablespoons fresh lime juice
1 tablespoon simple syrup (page 23)
1 lime wedge, for garnish

Pour the rum, lime juice, and simple syrup into a shaker two-thirds full of ice cubes. Shake well. Strain into a double Old-Fashioned glass filled with crushed ice. Add the lime wedge.

SEE ALSO *Frozen Banana Daiquiri, Frozen Daiquiri, Frozen Peach Daiquiri, Frozen Strawberry Daiquiri, and the nonalcoholic Virgin Banana Daiquiri, Virgin Peach Daiquiri, and Virgin Strawberry Daiquiri.*

DEBONAIR COCKTAIL

One of the few drinks that calls for single-malt Scotch (page 299), the Debonair varies with the Scotch you use. For example, an Islay single malt would impart more pungency than a Highlands single malt.

2 fl oz (60 ml) single-malt Scotch
2 tablespoons Canton ginger liqueur
1 lemon twist, for garnish

Pour the Scotch and ginger liqueur into a mixing glass two-thirds full of ice cubes. Stir well. Strain into a chilled cocktail glass. Add the lemon twist.

DEMPSEY COCKTAIL

It's the absinthe substitute that brings the gin and applejack together in this cocktail named for boxer Jack Dempsey.

3 tablespoons gin
1 tablespoon applejack
½ teaspoon absinthe substitute (such as Pernod or Ricard)
½ teaspoon grenadine

Pour all of the ingredients into a mixing glass two-thirds full of ice cubes. Stir well. Strain into a chilled cocktail glass.

DIPLOMAT

3 tablespoons dry vermouth
2 tablespoons sweet vermouth
½ teaspoon maraschino liqueur
2 dashes Angostura bitters
1 lemon wedge, for garnish

Pour both vermouths, the maraschino liqueur, and the bitters into a mixing glass two-thirds full of ice cubes. Stir well. Strain into a chilled cocktail glass. Add the garnish.

DIRTY MARTINI

Olive juice creates the drink's "dirty" appearance. Feel free to alter the ratio of gin to vermouth—or to use vodka instead of gin.

2½ fl oz (75 ml) gin
1½ teaspoons dry vermouth
1 teaspoon olive juice (from a jar of green cocktail olives)
1 green cocktail olive, for garnish

Pour the gin, vermouth, and olive juice into a mixing glass two-thirds full of ice cubes. Stir well. Strain into a chilled cocktail glass. Add the olive.

DUBONNET COCKTAIL

2 fl oz (60 ml) Dubonnet Rouge
1 tablespoon gin
2 dashes Angostura bitters
1 lemon twist, for garnish

Pour the Dubonnet, gin, and bitters into a mixing glass two-thirds full of ice cubes. Stir well. Strain into a chilled cocktail glass. Add the lemon twist.

DUBONNET MANHATTAN

2 fl oz (60 ml) bourbon
1 tablespoon Dubonnet Rouge
2 dashes orange bitters
1 orange wheel, for garnish

Pour the bourbon, Dubonnet, and bitters into a mixing glass two-thirds full of ice cubes. Stir well. Strain into a chilled cocktail glass. Garnish with the orange wheel.

Dubonnet

17% alcohol by volume

AN APERITIF WINE available in red (Dubonnet Rouge) and white (Dubonnet Blanc) bottlings, Dubonnet is often used as a substitute for vermouth in cocktails and mixed drinks. Since it is more complex than most vermouths and has a heavier body, it can add an extra dimension to many drinks. A dry gin Martini made with Dubonnet Blanc is especially fine.

EGGNOG—See page 150.

EL PRESIDENTE

2½ fl oz (75 ml) light rum
2 tablespoons fresh lime juice
2 tablespoons pineapple juice
Dash of grenadine

Pour all of the ingredients into a shaker two-thirds full of ice cubes. Shake well. Strain into an ice-filled Old-Fashioned glass.

EVERYBODY'S IRISH

2 fl oz (60 ml) Irish whiskey
1 tablespoon green Chartreuse
1 teaspoon green crème de menthe

Pour all of the ingredients into a mixing glass two-thirds full of ice cubes. Stir well. Strain into a chilled cocktail glass.

⦸ Eggnog

THE FAMOUS NINETEENTH-CENTURY mixologist Jerry Thomas wrote: "Egg Nogg is a beverage of American origin, but it has a popularity that is cosmopolitan." Eggnogs are popular not only in the United States, but in many European countries, too. One of the beauties of this nonalcoholic recipe is that if some guests want to spike it, they can just add a tot of rum or whiskey to their glasses and stir briskly for a few seconds. Everyone else can enjoy their holiday cheer unspiked.

If you are hesitant to use the raw eggs this recipe calls for, just substitute 5 cups (40 fl oz/1.25 l) of store-bought unspiced, pasteurized eggnog for the eggs and milk.

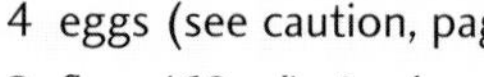

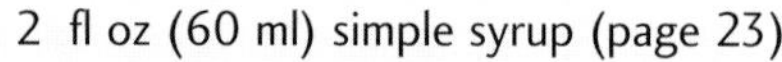

Makes 6 6-fl-oz (180-ml) servings.

4 eggs (see caution, page 22)
2 fl oz (60 ml) simple syrup (page 23)
1 teaspoon vanilla extract
½ teaspoon ground cinnamon
½ teaspoon ground allspice
3 cups (24 fl oz/750 ml) milk
Ground or freshly grated nutmeg, for garnish

Break the eggs into a large bowl and whisk until frothy. Add the simple syrup, vanilla extract, cinnamon, and allspice. Whisk to combine. Slowly add the milk, whisking all the time, until thoroughly blended. Serve in Irish Coffee glasses or punch cups. Sprinkle nutmeg on each serving.

SEE ALSO *Brandied Eggnog, Irish Eggnog, Tom and Jerry.*

FALLEN ANGEL

2 fl oz (60 ml) gin
1 teaspoon white crème de menthe
1 tablespoon fresh lemon juice
2 dashes Angostura bitters

Pour all of the ingredients into a shaker two-thirds full of ice cubes. Shake well. Strain into a chilled cocktail glass.

FANCY BRANDY

2½ fl oz (75 ml) brandy
1 tablespoon triple sec
½ teaspoon simple syrup (page 23)
2 dashes Angostura bitters
1 lemon twist, for garnish

Pour the brandy, triple sec, simple syrup, and bitters into a mixing glass two-thirds full of ice cubes. Stir well. Strain into a chilled cocktail glass. Add the lemon twist.

FANCY IRISH

2½ fl oz (75 ml) Irish whiskey
1 tablespoon triple sec
½ teaspoon simple syrup (page 23)
2 dashes Angostura bitters
1 lemon twist, for garnish

Pour the whiskey, triple sec, simple syrup, and bitters into a mixing glass two-thirds full of ice cubes. Stir well. Strain into a chilled cocktail glass. Add the lemon twist.

FANCY SCOTCH

2 fl oz (60 ml) Scotch
1 tablespoon triple sec
½ teaspoon simple syrup (page 23)
2 dashes Angostura bitters
1 lemon twist, for garnish

Pour the Scotch, triple sec, simple syrup, and bitters into a mixing glass two-thirds full of ice cubes. Stir well. Strain into a chilled cocktail glass. Add the lemon twist.

FANCY WHISKY

2½ fl oz (75 ml) blended Canadian whisky
1 tablespoon triple sec
½ teaspoon simple syrup (page 23)
2 dashes Angostura bitters
1 lemon twist, for garnish

Pour the whisky, triple sec, simple syrup, and bitters into a mixing glass two-thirds full of ice cubes. Stir well. Strain into a chilled cocktail glass. Add the lemon twist.

⃠ FAUX BELLINI

A nonalcoholic version of the Bellini (page 100).

Makes 4 drinks.

1 ripe white peach, pitted but not peeled, and cut into 1-inch (2.5-cm) cubes
1 teaspoon fresh lemon juice
1 teaspoon simple syrup (page 23)
2 cups (16 fl oz/500 ml) nonalcoholic sparkling wine

Combine the peach cubes, lemon juice, and simple syrup in a blender. Blend well. Divide the peach puree among four chilled Champagne flutes. Gently pour in the sparkling wine. Stir lightly to combine.

FINE AND DANDY

2 fl oz (60 ml) blended Canadian whisky
1 tablespoon Dubonnet Rouge
1 tablespoon triple sec
1 lemon twist, for garnish

Pour the whisky, Dubonnet, and triple sec into a mixing glass two-thirds full of ice cubes. Stir well. Strain into a chilled cocktail glass. Garnish with the lemon twist.

FINO MARTINI

2½ fl oz (75 ml) gin
1½ teaspoons fino sherry

Pour both ingredients into a mixing glass two-thirds full of ice cubes. Stir well. Strain into a chilled cocktail glass.

FISH HOUSE PUNCH

A once-secret recipe from Philadelphia's venerable Fish House Club.

Makes 20 6-fl-oz (180-ml) servings.

1 cup (8 fl oz/250 ml) simple syrup (page 23)
2 fl oz (60 ml) cold water
1¼ cups (10 fl oz/310 ml) fresh lime juice
1¼ cups (10 fl oz/310 ml) fresh lemon juice
2 750-ml bottles dark rum
2¼ cups (18 fl oz/560 ml) brandy
1 cup (8 fl oz/250 ml) peach brandy
1 large block of ice, for serving

Pour all of the ingredients into a large container made of stainless steel or other nonreactive material. Stir well. Cover and refrigerate until chilled, at least 4 hours.

Place the ice block in the center of a large punch bowl. Pour in the punch. Serve in punch cups.

FLAMINGO COCKTAIL

A dash of grenadine lends a flamingo-pink coloring to this drink.

2 fl oz (60 ml) gin
1 tablespoon apricot brandy
1 tablespoon fresh lime juice
Dash of grenadine

Pour all of the ingredients into a shaker two-thirds full of ice cubes. Shake well. Strain into a chilled cocktail glass.

FLYING DUTCHMAN

London Dry Gin actually works far better in this drink than the Dutch-style Genever gin used originally (see Gin, page 160).

2 fl oz (60 ml) gin
1 tablespoon triple sec

Pour all of the ingredients into a mixing glass two-thirds full of ice cubes. Stir well. Strain into an ice-filled Old-Fashioned glass.

FRENCH CHAMPAGNE COCKTAIL

1 sugar cube
2 dashes Angostura bitters
1 tablespoon crème de cassis
5 fl oz (150 ml) chilled Champagne

Drop the sugar cube into the bottom of a chilled Champagne flute. Add the bitters and the crème de cassis. Gently pour in the Champagne.

FRENCH KISS

Although the French Kiss is traditionally served on the rocks, it also works well stirred over ice and strained into a chilled cocktail glass.

2 tablespoons sweet vermouth
2 tablespoons dry vermouth
1 lemon twist, for garnish

Pour both vermouths into an ice-filled Old-Fashioned glass. Stir briefly. Add the lemon twist.

French 75

THIS DRINK SUPPOSEDLY took its name from a 75-mm artillery piece Allied soldiers used during World War I. Although the French 75 boasts Champagne, a French invention, it also quite fittingly depends on British gin.

Many people make the French 75 with brandy instead of gin, but the recipe using brandy is actually the French 76, a later variation that calls for lemon juice instead of lime.

2 fl oz (60 ml) gin
1 tablespoon fresh lime juice
2 teaspoons simple syrup (page 23)
4 fl oz (120 ml) chilled Champagne

Pour the gin, lime juice, and simple syrup into a shaker two-thirds full of ice cubes. Shake well. Strain the mixture into a wineglass filled with crushed ice. Top with the Champagne.

FRENCH ROSE COCKTAIL

1½ fl oz (45 ml) gin
1½ teaspoons dry vermouth
1 tablespoon cherry brandy

Pour all of the ingredients into a mixing glass two-thirds full of ice cubes. Stir well. Strain into a chilled cocktail glass.

FROZEN BANANA DAIQUIRI

A favorite drink in the Caribbean. To add body and flavor, try substituting dark rum for the light.

2 fl oz (60 ml) light rum
2 tablespoons fresh lime juice
1 ripe banana, cut into 1-inch (2.5-cm) pieces

Place all of the ingredients into a blender containing 1 cup (8 fl oz/250 ml) of ice cubes. Blend well. Pour into a chilled wineglass.

FROZEN DAIQUIRI

2½ fl oz (75 ml) light rum
2 tablespoons fresh lime juice
1 tablespoon simple syrup (page 23)

Pour all of the ingredients into a blender containing 1 cup (8 fl oz/250 ml) of ice cubes. Blend well. Pour into a chilled wineglass.

FROZEN MARGARITA

2 fl oz (60 ml) white tequila
2 tablespoons triple sec
2 tablespoons fresh lime juice
1 teaspoon simple syrup (page 23)

Pour all of the ingredients into a blender containing 1 cup (8 fl oz/250 ml) of ice cubes. Blend well. Pour into a chilled wineglass.

FROZEN PEACH DAIQUIRI

2 fl oz (60 ml) light rum
2 tablespoons fresh lime juice
1 ripe peach, stoned and cut into 8 wedges

Put all of the ingredients in a blender containing 1 cup (8 fl oz/250 ml) of ice cubes. Blend well. Pour into a chilled wineglass.

FROZEN PEACH MARGARITA

Tangy, sweet peach and sharp, peppery tequila—what a combination!

2 fl oz (60 ml) white tequila
2 tablespoons fresh lime juice
1 ripe peach, stoned and cut into 8 wedges

Put all of the ingredients in a blender containing 1 cup (8 fl oz/250 ml) of ice cubes. Blend well. Pour into a chilled wineglass.

FROZEN STRAWBERRY DAIQUIRI

2 fl oz (60 ml) light rum
2 tablespoons fresh lime juice
8 ripe strawberries, hulled and halved

Put all of the ingredients in a blender containing 1 cup (8 fl oz/250 ml) of ice cubes. Blend well. Pour into a chilled wineglass.

FROZEN STRAWBERRY MARGARITA

2 fl oz (60 ml) white tequila
2 tablespoons fresh lime juice
8 ripe strawberries, hulled and halved

Put all of the ingredients in a blender containing 1 cup (8 fl oz/250 ml) of ice cubes. Blend well. Pour into a chilled wineglass.

⊘ FRUIT PUNCH

Makes 20 6-fl-oz (180-ml) servings.

2 quarts (64 fl oz/2 l) fresh grapefruit juice
1 quart (32 fl oz/1 l) fresh orange juice
1½ cups (12 fl oz/375 ml) cranberry juice cocktail
4 fl oz (120 ml) fresh lime juice
4 fl oz (120 ml) fresh lemon juice
6 fl oz (180 ml) simple syrup (page 23)
2 fl oz (60 ml) grenadine
2 tablespoons orgeat syrup
1 large block of ice, for serving

Pour all of the liquid ingredients into a large pan or bowl made of stainless steel or other nonreactive material. Stir well. Cover and refrigerate until chilled, at least 4 hours. Place the ice in the center of a large punch bowl. Pour in the punch. Serve in punch cups.

FUZZY NAVEL

A fruit of the 1970s debut of peach schnapps in the United States.

2 fl oz (60 ml) vodka
2 tablespoons peach schnapps
3 to 4 fl oz (90 to 120 ml) fresh orange juice

Pour all of the ingredients into an ice-filled highball glass. Stir briefly.

Gibson

THE GIBSON WAS CREATED for Charles Dana Gibson (1867–1944), the famous magazine illustrator whose drawings of turn-of-the-century women became known as "Gibson Girls." The story of the cocktail's birth varies from source to source. Some say that the bartender, Charlie (or Charley) Connolly, at New York's The Players decided to put two pearl onions into Mr. Gibson's Martini because he requested something a little different; others say that poor Mr. Connolly was fresh out of olives. Whatever is true, there's no difference between this drink and a Dry Martini (page 209) save for the garnish, and you should feel free to use any of the Martini recipes to make your Gibson.

3 fl oz (90 ml) gin
1 tablespoon dry vermouth
1 or 2 pearl onion(s), for garnish

Pour the gin and vermouth into a mixing glass two-thirds full of ice cubes. Stir well. Strain into a chilled cocktail glass. Add the garnish.

GIMLET—See Gin Gimlet, page 169.

Gin

Usually 40–50% alcohol by volume

An ingredient in many of the world's most popular drinks, gin is a flavored spirit generally made from pure grain alcohol that has been redistilled with juniper and a group of other botanical ingredients. These include angelica, caraway, cardamom, cassia, cinnamon, coriander, fennel, ginger, lemon zest, licorice, and orange zest.

Old American bottling of London Dry Gin

HOW GIN IS MADE

Although the grain alcohol used in the production of gin is normally made in a cost-efficient continuous still, its redistillation with botanicals is usually done by the slower, old-fashioned pot-still method. Inferior bottlings called compound gins are often made with the addition of flavored oils to what is essentially vodka.

STYLES OF GIN

Gin can be divided into two principal types—British-style London Dry Gin, and Dutch-style Genever (or Hollands)—plus several more obscure variants. (Not covered here is sloe gin, which usually contains no gin at all; see Sloe Gin, page 263.)

LONDON DRY GIN This crisp, very dry British-type gin is the world's most popular style of gin; recipes calling for gin are usually referring to it. London Dry Gins are made throughout the world, but most bottlings sold in the United States are produced domestically or imported from England. By U.S. law, all London Dry Gins must bear strong juniper flavors, and the botanicals used to make them must be distilled into the product rather than added. If it's labeled *London Dry Gin* or *distilled gin,* you can be sure the spirit was made in the preferred way.

Soldiers returning home introduced gin to England in the late 1500s, after fighting alongside the Dutch in the conflict leading to the Thirty Years' War. At that time the name was *genièvre* (juniper, in French), which the British shortened to *gin.*

LONDON DRY GIN

This style of gin is strongly flavored with juniper and other botanicals that have been distilled with pure grain alcohol. London Dry Gin, such as the Beefeater label, is the gin of choice for mixing.

Early English gins were comparatively sweet, with sweeteners probably added to mask the off flavors of inefficient distilling. The nineteenth-century invention of the continuous still made possible the creation of purer gin at lower cost. This drier gin became known as London Dry.

Bar coaster advertising gin

PLYMOUTH GIN This gin is made by the same methods as London Dry Gin and is very similar in style. But unlike London Dry, which can be made anywhere, under British law Plymouth Gin must be made in the city of Plymouth. Since only one distillery is located there—Blackfriar's, which issues Coates Plymouth Gin—there is only one Plymouth Gin on the market. It is extremely dry, very herbal in nature, and well suited to Martinis (page 208) and the Pink Gin (page 226).

GENEVER OR HOLLANDS Fruit-based spirits flavored with juniper were made in Holland in the late sixteenth century. It wasn't until the mid-seventeenth century that gin was made from a grain base, and the style of gin we now call Genever came into being. Today's Genever gins, especially those labeled *oude* (old), begin as a mash of malted barley and other grains that is distilled twice in an old-fashioned pot still. During the secondary distillation, juniper is distilled into the spirit. The result is mixed with neutral grain spirits made in a modern continuous still.

Jonge (young) Genever gins contain more flavored neutral grain spirits and are thus lighter than oude gins. Even so, they are too heavy-bodied for most cocktails and far too sweet for Martinis—

MOST POPULAR GIN DRINKS

(according to U.S. bartenders)

1. Gin and Tonic, page 164
2. Martini (Dry), page 209
3. Gibson, page 159
4. Gin Gimlet, page 169
5. Bronx Cocktail, page 127

which is why both are usually sipped neat. Most Genever gins are aged for less than a year, whereas most other gins are not aged at all.

COMPOUND If the words *London Dry, distilled,* or *Genever* do not appear on the label, the bottle likely contains a compound gin made by adding botanical flavorings to neutral grain spirits rather than by distilling botanicals into the liquor. Usually inexpensive, compound gins are inferior to London Dry gins in complexity.

OLD TOM The original Old Tom or liqueur gin mimicked the flavor of early gins, which were made in pot stills and sweetened to disguise any off taste. The Old Tom now on the market is a compound gin that tastes nothing like previous bottlings. Use it as you would a compound gin.

FLAVORED GIN

Gins flavored with lime, grapefruit, or other essences have recently appeared on the market. Although they have not been around long enough for much experimentation, they will no doubt become more popular as time goes by.

Serving Gin

ALTHOUGH GIN IS SOMETIMES served neat, at room temperature, London Dry and Plymouth Gins are far more palatable chilled and/or diluted. Pour the gin over ice, stir for up to 30 seconds, and strain the diluted spirit into a chilled cocktail glass. Better still, use your gin to make a Dry Martini (page 209). The drier, more herbal bottlings, such as Beefeater and Tanqueray, are preferable for this over fruitier gins, such as Seagrams, which are better for recipes containing fruit juices.

Genever gin is best served well chilled in a small vessel such as a sherry copita glass (page 41). Compound gins can be successfully mixed in drinks calling for fruit juices or other sweet ingredients such as liqueurs.

GIN AND IT

The sweet vermouth—often referred to as Italian vermouth regardless of its place of origin—is the "It" in this cocktail.

3 fl oz (90 ml) gin
1 tablespoon sweet vermouth

Pour the gin and vermouth into a mixing glass two-thirds full of ice cubes. Stir well. Strain into a chilled cocktail glass.

GIN AND TONIC

A refreshing drink that's popular around the world. Be sure to use as much ice as will fit into the glass—a Gin and Tonic should be ice cold.

2½ fl oz (75 ml) gin
4 fl oz (120 ml) tonic water
1 lime wedge, for garnish

Pour the gin and tonic water into an ice-filled highball glass. Stir briefly. Add the lime wedge.

GIN BLOODY MARY

2 fl oz (60 ml) gin
4 fl oz (120 ml) tomato juice
1 tablespoon fresh lemon juice
¼ teaspoon black pepper
Generous pinch of salt
¼ teaspoon ground cinnamon
2 dashes Worcestershire sauce
1 lemon wedge, for garnish

Pour the gin, tomato juice, and lemon juice into a shaker two-thirds full of ice cubes. Add the pepper, salt, cinnamon, and Worcestershire sauce. Shake well. Strain into an ice-filled highball glass. Add the lemon wedge.

Gin Buck

DRINKS MADE WITH A BASE SPIRIT such as gin, whisk(e)y, or rum; a squeezed wedge of lemon; and ginger ale are known as Bucks. The Gin Buck is considered to be the original member of this category.

1 lemon wedge
2 fl oz (60 ml) gin
5 fl oz (150 ml) ginger ale

Squeeze the lemon wedge into a highball glass and drop it into the glass. Fill the glass with ice cubes. Add the gin and ginger ale. Stir briefly.

SEE ALSO *Bourbon Buck, Brandy Buck, Irish Buck, Rum Buck, Scotch Buck, Whisky Buck.*

GIN COBBLER

The simple syrup added to London Dry Gin creates a taste reminiscent of the old-fashioned sweetened gin known as Old Tom (page 163).

2½ fl oz (75 ml) gin
1 tablespoon simple syrup (page 23)
1 lemon wedge, for garnish

Pour the gin and simple syrup into a wineglass filled with crushed ice. Stir briefly. Add the lemon wedge.

GIN CRUSTA

Granulated sugar, to coat rim of glass
Lemon peel spiral (see technique, page 53)
2 fl oz (60 ml) gin
1 tablespoon maraschino liqueur
1 tablespoon fresh lemon juice

Coat the rim of a Sour glass with sugar (see technique, page 49). Place the lemon peel spiral into the glass so that it uncoils to almost fill the interior.

Pour the gin, maraschino liqueur, and lemon juice into a shaker two-thirds full of crushed ice. Shake well. Strain into the glass.

Gin Daisy

THE GIN DAISY IS THE representative member of the Daisy family. Daisies are prepared using a range of spirits and are ideal for those who want something a bit sweeter than a Sour.

2½ fl oz (75 ml) gin
2 tablespoons fresh lemon juice
1 tablespoon grenadine
1 lemon twist, for garnish

Pour the gin, lemon juice, and grenadine into a shaker two-thirds full of crushed ice. Shake well. Strain into a highball glass filled with crushed ice. Add the lemon twist.

SEE ALSO *Brandy Daisy, Irish Daisy, Rum Daisy, Scotch Daisy.*

Gin Fix

LEMON JUICE AND PINEAPPLE JUICE are the basis for the Fix family, of which the Gin Fix is prototypical.

2½ fl oz (75 ml) gin
2 tablespoons fresh lemon juice
1 tablespoon pineapple juice
1 pineapple spear, for garnish

Pour the gin, lemon juice, and pineapple juice into a shaker two-thirds full of crushed ice. Shake well. Strain into a highball glass filled with crushed ice. Add the pineapple spear.

SEE ALSO *Bourbon Fix, Brandy Fix, Rum Fix, Scotch Fix, Tequila Fix, Vodka Fix, Whisky Fix.*

GIN FIZZ—See page 168.

GIN FLIP

2½ fl oz (75 ml) gin
1½ tablespoons simple syrup (page 23)
1 egg (see caution, page 22)
Ground or freshly grated nutmeg, for garnish

Pour the gin and simple syrup into a shaker two-thirds full of ice cubes. Add the egg. Shake very well. Strain into a chilled wineglass. Sprinkle with nutmeg.

GIN RICKEY—See page 170.

Gin Fizz

ALTHOUGH THE RAMOS GIN FIZZ (page 235) may be better known, the Gin Fizz is said to be the classic.

- 2 fl oz (60 ml) gin
- 2 tablespoons fresh lime juice
- 1 tablespoon simple syrup (page 23)
- 5 to 6 fl oz (150 to 180 ml) club soda
- 1 lime wedge, for garnish

Pour the gin, lime juice, and simple syrup into a shaker two-thirds full of ice cubes. Shake well. Strain into a chilled wineglass. Add the club soda. Stir briefly. Add the lime wedge.

SEE ALSO *Applejack Fizz, Apricot Fizz, Bourbon Fizz, Brandy Fizz, Champagne Fizz, Irish Fizz, Ramos Gin Fizz, Rum Fizz, Scotch Fizz, Sloe Gin Fizz, Tequila Fizz, Whisky Fizz.*

GIN SLING

- 2½ fl oz (75 ml) gin
- 1 tablespoon triple sec
- 1 tablespoon fresh lemon juice
- 5 to 6 fl oz (150 to 180 ml) club soda
- 1 lemon wedge, for garnish

Pour the gin, triple sec, and lemon juice into a shaker two-thirds full of ice cubes. Shake well. Strain the drink into an ice-filled Collins glass. Add the club soda. Stir briefly. Garnish with the lemon wedge.

Gin Gimlet

LIKE THE DAIQUIRI (page 146), the Gin Gimlet was invented as a medicinal potion. Presumably the gin, with supposed diuretic properties, added to the scurvy-preventative lime juice, made a great deal of sense to Sir T.O. Gimlette, the nineteenth-century British naval physician for whom the drink was named.

2½ fl oz (75 ml) gin
1 tablespoon sweetened lime juice (such as Rose's)
1 lime wedge, for garnish

Pour the gin and sweetened lime juice into an ice-filled Old-Fashioned glass. Stir briefly. Garnish with the lime wedge.

SEE ALSO *Vodka Gimlet.*

GIN SOUR

2 fl oz (60 ml) gin
1½ tablespoons fresh lemon juice
1 tablespoon simple syrup (page 23)
1 orange wheel, for garnish
1 maraschino cherry, for garnish

Pour the gin, lemon juice, and simple syrup into a shaker two-thirds full of ice cubes. Shake well. Strain into a chilled Sour glass. Add the orange wheel and cherry.

Gin Rickey

RICKEYS ARE MADE WITH a base spirit, fresh lime juice, and club soda, garnished with a wedge of lime. The Gin Rickey is the most popular drink in this category, and it makes a very refreshing quaff on a hot summer day.

2½ fl oz (75 ml) gin
2 tablespoons fresh lime juice
5 to 6 fl oz (150 to 180 ml) club soda
1 lime wedge, for garnish

Pour the gin and lime juice into an ice-filled highball glass. Add the club soda. Stir briefly. Add the lime wedge.

SEE ALSO *Applejack Rickey, Apricot Rickey, Cherry Brandy Rickey, Rum Rickey, Vodka Rickey.*

GIN SWIZZLE

2 fl oz (60 ml) gin
1 tablespoon fresh lime juice
1 tablespoon triple sec
5 to 6 fl oz (150 to 180 ml) ginger ale
1 lemon wheel, for garnish

Pour the gin, lime juice, and triple sec into a shaker two-thirds full of ice cubes. Shake well. Strain the mixture into an ice-filled Collins glass. Add the ginger ale. Stir briefly. Add the lemon wheel and a swizzle stick.

⦸ GINGERED PEACH

3 fl oz (90 ml) peach nectar
1 cup (8 fl oz/250 ml) ginger beer

Pour both ingredients into a large ice-filled wineglass.

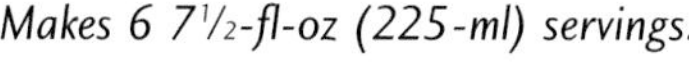

GLOGG

This Swedish flaming drink is traditional during the winter holidays. Please read the cautions about flaming, page 63.

Makes 6 7½-fl-oz (225-ml) servings.

1 750-ml bottle brandy
4 fl oz (120 ml) simple syrup (page 23)
8 whole cloves
½ cup (4 fl oz/120 ml) raisins
½ cup (4 fl oz/120 ml) blanched slivered almonds
1 cup (8 fl oz/250 ml) ruby port

Place all of the ingredients but the port into a large saucepan made of stainless steel or other nonreactive material. Cook over medium-low heat until warm. Ignite the liquid with a match and allow it to flame for about 15 seconds. Add the port and stir constantly with a long-handled wooden spoon until the flames subside. Ladle into Irish Coffee glasses, including some of the raisins and almonds.

GODFATHER

A drink that became popular in the 1970s, when amaretto first caught on in the United States and the film *The Godfather* was released.

2 fl oz (60 ml) Scotch
2 tablespoons amaretto

Pour both ingredients into an ice-filled Old-Fashioned glass. Stir briefly.

GODMOTHER

2 fl oz (60 ml) vodka
2 tablespoons amaretto

Pour both ingredients into an ice-filled Old-Fashioned glass. Stir briefly.

GOLDEN CADILLAC

Both this and the Golden Dream became fashionable in the swinging sixties, when American bartenders first came to appreciate the vanilla-orange flavor of Galliano (page 199).

2 fl oz (60 ml) white crème de cacao
1 ½ tablespoons Galliano
2 tablespoons light cream

Pour all of the ingredients into a shaker two-thirds full of ice cubes. Shake well. Strain into a chilled cocktail glass.

GOLDEN DREAM

2 fl oz (60 ml) Galliano
1 tablespoon triple sec
2 tablespoons fresh orange juice
2 tablespoons light cream

Pour all of the ingredients into a shaker two-thirds full of ice cubes. Shake well. Strain into a chilled cocktail glass.

⦸ GRAPEFRUIT FIZZ

Omit the bitters if you can't tolerate even a tiny amount of alcohol.

6 fl oz (180 ml) fresh grapefruit juice
3 fl oz (90 ml) lemon-lime soda
Dash of Angostura bitters

Pour all of the ingredients into an ice-filled Collins glass. Stir briefly.

GRASSHOPPER

3 tablespoons green crème de menthe
3 tablespoons white crème de cacao
1½ tablespoons light cream

Pour all of the ingredients into a shaker two-thirds full of ice cubes. Shake well. Strain into a chilled cocktail glass.

GREYHOUND

2½ fl oz (75 ml) vodka
4 fl oz (120 ml) grapefruit juice

Pour both ingredients into an ice-filled highball glass. Stir briefly.

Local whiskey labels from America's past

HARVEY WALLBANGER

Legend has it that a California surfer named Harvey became too fond of this drink (originally called the Italian Screwdriver) and would bang into walls on his way home from the bar—hence the new name.

2 fl oz (60 ml) vodka
6 fl oz (180 ml) orange juice
1 tablespoon Galliano

Pour the vodka and orange juice into an ice-filled highball glass. Stir briefly. Carefully pour the Galliano over the back of a spoon so that it floats on top of the drink and the ice.

HAVANA COCKTAIL

2 fl oz (60 ml) light rum
2 tablespoons pineapple juice
2 tablespoons fresh lemon juice

Pour all of the ingredients into a shaker two-thirds full of ice cubes. Shake well. Strain into a chilled cocktail glass.

HIGHLAND FLING

This is a variation on the Rob Roy (page 237), differing only in the addition of orange bitters.

2½ fl oz (75 ml) Scotch
1½ tablespoons sweet vermouth
2 dashes orange bitters

Pour all of the ingredients into a mixing glass two-thirds full of ice cubes. Stir well. Strain into a chilled cocktail glass.

HORSE'S NECK

Many people make the Horse's Neck with brandy, but bourbon was in the original version created prior to Prohibition.

Lemon peel spiral (see technique, page 53)
2½ fl oz (75 ml) bourbon
4 to 5 fl oz (120 to 150 ml) ginger ale

Place the lemon peel spiral into a Collins glass so that it uncoils to almost fill the interior. Fill the glass with ice cubes. Pour the bourbon and ginger ale into the glass. Stir briefly.

HOT BUTTERED RUM

Don't stir the melted butter into the drink. It should float on top.

2 fl oz (60 ml) dark rum
1 tablespoon simple syrup (page 23)
3 whole cloves
1 cinnamon stick (about 3 inches/7.5 cm long)
4 to 5 fl oz (120 to 150 ml) boiling water
2 teaspoons unsalted butter
Ground or freshly grated nutmeg, for garnish

Pour the rum and simple syrup into an Irish Coffee glass. Add the cloves and the cinnamon stick. Add the boiling water to almost fill the glass. Add the butter and stir briefly to help it melt. Sprinkle with nutmeg.

Old Kentucky bourbons

HOT MULLED WINE

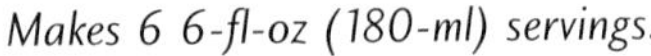

Makes 6 6-fl-oz (180-ml) servings.

8 whole cloves
1 teaspoon ground or freshly grated nutmeg
1 teaspoon ground allspice
1 cinnamon stick (about 3 inches/7.5 cm long)
2 fl oz (60 ml) simple syrup (page 23)
1 ½ cups (12 fl oz/375 ml) hot water
1 750-ml bottle dry red wine
6 lemon twists

Put the cloves, nutmeg, allspice, and cinnamon stick in a large pot made of stainless steel or other nonreactive material. Add the simple syrup and hot water. Bring the mixture to a boil over high heat. Reduce the heat to low and simmer for 10 minutes.

Strain the mixture through a double layer of dampened cheesecloth and return it to the pan. Pour in the wine and cook over medium heat until hot. Divide among six Irish Coffee glasses. Add a lemon twist to each serving.

HOT SPICED CIDER

Make a nonalcoholic version of this drink by substituting nonalcoholic apple cider for the hard cider.

Makes 8 6-fl-oz (180-ml) servings.

4 whole cloves
1 teaspoon ground or freshly grated nutmeg
1 teaspoon ground allspice
½ teaspoon ground mace
2 cinnamon sticks (each 3 inches/7.5 cm long)
1 ½ cups (12 fl oz/375 ml) hot water
4½ cups (36 fl oz/1.1 l) hard cider
8 apple slices, for garnish

Put the cloves, nutmeg, allspice, mace, and cinnamon sticks in a large pot made of stainless steel or other non-reactive material. Add the hot water. Bring the mixture to a boil over high heat. Reduce the heat to low and simmer for 10 minutes.

Strain the mixture through a double layer of dampened cheesecloth and return it to the pot. Pour in the hard cider; cook over medium heat until hot. Divide among eight Irish Coffee glasses. Add an apple slice to each serving.

HOT SPIKED CHOCOLATE

For adults only.

6 fl oz (180 ml) prepared hot chocolate
2 tablespoons brandy
1 tablespoon dark crème de cacao
Ground or freshly grated nutmeg, for garnish

Pour the hot chocolate into an Irish Coffee glass. Add the brandy and the crème de cacao. Stir briefly. Sprinkle with nutmeg.

HOT TODDY

Feel free to substitute rum, brandy, or any whisk(e)y for the bourbon.

3 tablespoons bourbon
2 whole cloves
Pinch of ground mace
Pinch of ground cinnamon
4 to 5 fl oz (120 to 150 ml) boiling water
1 lemon twist, for garnish
1 cinnamon stick, for garnish

Pour the bourbon into an Irish Coffee glass. Stir in the cloves, mace, and cinnamon. Add boiling water to almost fill the glass. Add the garnishes.

IRISH BUCK

1 lemon wedge
2 fl oz (60 ml) Irish whiskey
5 fl oz (150 ml) ginger ale

Squeeze the lemon wedge into a highball glass and drop it into the glass. Fill the glass with ice cubes. Add the whiskey and ginger ale. Stir briefly.

IRISH CHAMPAGNE COCKTAIL

1 sugar cube
2 to 3 dashes Angostura bitters
2 tablespoons Irish whiskey
5 fl oz (150 ml) Champagne or sparkling wine
1 lemon twist, for garnish

Drop the sugar cube into the bottom of a Champagne flute. Add the bitters and whiskey. Carefully pour in the Champagne. Garnish with the lemon twist.

IRISH COBBLER

2½ fl oz (75 ml) Irish whiskey
1 tablespoon simple syrup (page 23)
1 lemon wedge, for garnish

Pour the whiskey and simple syrup into a wineglass filled with crushed ice. Stir briefly. Add the lemon wedge.

Irish Coffee

IRISH COFFEE WAS CREATED in the 1940s at the Shannon Airport in Ireland. When an American newspaper reporter, Stanton Delaplane, first sampled one of these delicious drinks, he decided to pass on the recipe to his local bar, the Buena Vista in San Francisco. Word of Irish Coffee quickly spread throughout the nation, and since then it has become a classic drink.

The original Irish Coffee didn't include the green crème de menthe this recipe calls for, but it does add a colorful touch, especially if you will be serving the drink on Saint Patrick's Day.

3 tablespoons Irish whiskey
1 tablespoon simple syrup (page 23)
4 fl oz (120 ml) hot coffee
2 tablespoons whipped cream
1 teaspoon green crème de menthe

Pour the whiskey, simple syrup, and coffee into an Irish Coffee glass. Stir briefly. Carefully spoon the whipped cream onto the coffee so that it floats on top. Drizzle the crème de menthe over the cream.

SEE ALSO *Italian Coffee, Jamaican Coffee, Keoki Coffee, Mexican Coffee, Monk's Coffee.*

IRISH COLLINS

2 fl oz (60 ml) Irish whiskey
1 tablespoon fresh lemon juice
1 tablespoon simple syrup (page 23)
5 to 6 fl oz (150 to 180 ml) club soda
1 lemon wedge, for garnish

Pour the whiskey, lemon juice, and simple syrup into a shaker two-thirds full of ice cubes. Shake well. Strain into an ice-filled Collins glass. Add the club soda. Stir briefly. Garnish with the lemon wedge.

IRISH COOLER

2½ fl oz (75 ml) Irish whiskey
6 to 7 fl oz (180 to 210 ml) ginger ale
1 lemon twist, for garnish

Pour the whiskey and ginger ale into an ice-filled Collins glass. Stir briefly. Add the lemon twist.

IRISH CRUSTA

Granulated sugar, to coat rim of glass
Lemon peel spiral (see technique, page 53)
2 fl oz (60 ml) Irish whiskey
1 tablespoon maraschino liqueur
1 tablespoon fresh lemon juice

Coat the rim of a Sour glass with sugar (see technique, page 49). Place the lemon peel spiral into the glass so that it uncoils to almost fill the interior. Pour the whiskey, maraschino liqueur, and lemon juice into a shaker two-thirds full of crushed ice. Shake well. Strain into the glass.

IRISH DAISY

2½ fl oz (75 ml) Irish whiskey
2 tablespoons fresh lemon juice
1 tablespoon grenadine
1 lemon twist, for garnish

Pour the whiskey, lemon juice, and grenadine into a shaker two-thirds full of crushed ice. Shake well. Strain into a highball glass filled with crushed ice. Add the lemon twist.

IRISH EGGNOG

If you are hesitant to use the raw eggs this recipe calls for, just substitute 5 cups (40 fl oz/1.25 l) of store-bought unspiced, pasteurized eggnog for the eggs and milk.

Makes 8 6-fl-oz (180-ml) servings.

4 eggs (see caution, page 22)
6 fl oz (180 ml) Irish whiskey
2 fl oz (60 ml) Irish Mist liqueur
1 teaspoon vanilla extract
½ teaspoon ground cinnamon
½ teaspoon ground allspice
1 quart (32 fl oz/1 l) milk
Ground or freshly grated nutmeg, for garnish

Break the eggs into a large bowl and whisk until frothy. Add the whiskey, Irish Mist, vanilla extract, cinnamon, and allspice. Whisk to combine. Slowly add the milk, whisking all the time, until thoroughly mixed. Ladle into Irish Coffee glasses. Sprinkle nutmeg on each serving.

IRISH FIZZ

2 fl oz (60 ml) Irish whiskey
2 tablespoons fresh lemon juice
1 tablespoon simple syrup (page 23)
5 to 6 fl oz (150 to 180 ml) club soda
1 lemon twist, for garnish

Pour the whiskey, lemon juice, and simple syrup into a shaker two-thirds full of ice cubes. Shake well. Strain into a chilled wineglass. Add the club soda. Stir briefly. Add the lemon twist.

IRISH JULEP

2 tablespoons simple syrup (page 23)
3 fl oz (90 ml) Irish whiskey
3 large mint sprigs, for garnish

Pour the simple syrup into a Julep cup filled with crushed ice. Stir well. Add the whiskey. Stir until a film of ice forms on the exterior of the Julep cup. Garnish with the mint sprigs.

IRISH OLD-FASHIONED

3 dashes Angostura bitters
1 orange slice
1 lemon wedge
1 maraschino cherry
1 sugar cube
2½ fl oz (75 ml) Irish whiskey

Put the bitters, orange slice, lemon wedge, maraschino cherry, and sugar cube in a double Old-Fashioned glass and muddle well (see technique, page 64). Fill the glass with ice cubes and add the whiskey. Stir well.

IRISH SANGAREE

The Irish Mist in this recipe adds a hint of honey that makes the Irish Sangaree very special.

2 fl oz (60 ml) Irish whiskey
1 tablespoon ruby port
1 tablespoon Irish Mist
Ground or freshly grated nutmeg, for garnish

Pour the whiskey, port, and Irish Mist into a mixing glass two-thirds full of ice cubes. Stir well. Strain into a chilled small wineglass. Sprinkle with nutmeg.

IRISH SLING

2½ fl oz (75 ml) Irish whiskey
1 tablespoon cherry brandy
1 tablespoon fresh lemon juice
5 to 6 fl oz (150 to 180 ml) club soda
1 lemon wedge, for garnish

Pour the whiskey, cherry brandy, and lemon juice into a shaker two-thirds full of ice cubes. Shake well. Strain the drink into an ice-filled Collins glass. Add the club soda. Stir briefly. Add the lemon wedge.

IRISH SMASH

6 fresh mint leaves
1½ tablespoons simple syrup (page 23)
2½ fl oz (75 ml) Irish whiskey
1 mint sprig, for garnish

Place the mint leaves in the bottom of an Old-Fashioned glass. Add the simple syrup and muddle well (see technique, page 64). Fill the glass with crushed ice. Add the whiskey. Stir briefly. Garnish with the mint sprig.

IRISH SOUR

2 fl oz (60 ml) Irish whiskey
1 ½ tablespoons fresh lemon juice
1 tablespoon simple syrup (page 23)
1 orange wheel, for garnish
1 maraschino cherry, for garnish

Pour the whiskey, lemon juice, and simple syrup into a shaker two-thirds full of ice cubes. Shake well. Strain the drink into a chilled Sour glass. Add the garnishes.

IRISH SWIZZLE

2 fl oz (60 ml) Irish whiskey
1 tablespoon fresh lemon juice
1 tablespoon curaçao
5 to 6 fl oz (150 to 180 ml) ginger ale
1 lemon wheel, for garnish

Pour the whiskey, lemon juice, and curaçao into a shaker two-thirds full of ice cubes. Shake well. Strain the mixture into an ice-filled Collins glass. Add the ginger ale. Stir briefly. Add the lemon wheel and a swizzle stick.

IRISH WHISKEY—See Whisk(e)y, page 300.

ITALIAN COFFEE

3 tablespoons hazelnut liqueur (such as Frangelico)
4 fl oz (120 ml) hot coffee
2 tablespoons whipped cream

Pour the hazelnut liqueur and coffee into an Irish Coffee glass. Stir briefly. Carefully spoon the whipped cream onto the coffee so that it floats on top.

JACK ROSE

The classic Jack Rose is served straight up in a cocktail glass, but it makes an equally refreshing tall drink when strained into an ice-filled Collins glass and topped with club soda.

2½ fl oz (75 ml) applejack
1 tablespoon fresh lemon juice
2 teaspoons grenadine

Pour all of the ingredients into a shaker two-thirds full of ice cubes. Shake well. Strain into a chilled cocktail glass.

JAMAICAN COFFEE

If you happen to have Blue Mountain coffee from Jamaica, use it to make this drink—it's fairly strong and marries well with the Tia Maria.

3 tablespoons Tia Maria
4 fl oz (120 ml) hot coffee
2 tablespoons whipped cream

Pour the Tia Maria and coffee into an Irish Coffee glass. Stir briefly. Carefully spoon the whipped cream onto the coffee so that it floats on top.

JAMAICAN MARTINI

2 fl oz (60 ml) dark rum
1 tablespoon Tia Maria

Pour the ingredients into a mixing glass two-thirds full of ice cubes. Stir well. Strain into a chilled cocktail glass.

JAPANESE COCKTAIL

3 tablespoons brandy
1 tablespoon orgeat syrup
1 tablespoon fresh lime juice
1 lime wheel, for garnish

Pour the brandy, orgeat syrup, and lime juice into a shaker two-thirds full of ice cubes. Shake well. Strain into a chilled cocktail glass. Add the lime wheel.

JOCK COLLINS

Although it goes by the name of Jock, this drink is more properly called the Scotch Collins.

2 fl oz (60 ml) Scotch
1 tablespoon fresh lemon juice
1 tablespoon simple syrup (page 23)
5 to 6 fl oz (150 to 180 ml) club soda
1 lemon wedge, for garnish

Pour the Scotch, lemon juice, and simple syrup into a shaker two-thirds full of ice cubes. Shake well. Strain into an ice-filled Collins glass. Add the club soda. Stir briefly. Add the lemon wedge.

JOCKEY CLUB COCKTAIL

2 fl oz (60 ml) gin
1½ teaspoons white crème de cacao
1 tablespoon fresh lemon juice

Pour all of the ingredients into a shaker two-thirds full of ice cubes. Shake well. Strain into a chilled cocktail glass.

JOHN COLLINS

Most people call it John Collins, but it's officially Bourbon Collins.

2 fl oz (60 ml) bourbon
1 tablespoon fresh lemon juice
1 tablespoon simple syrup (page 23)
5 to 6 fl oz (150 to 180 ml) club soda
1 orange wheel, for garnish

Pour the bourbon, lemon juice, and simple syrup into a shaker two-thirds full of ice cubes. Shake well. Strain into an ice-filled Collins glass. Add the club soda. Stir briefly. Add the orange wheel.

KAMIKAZE

The Kamikaze was created in the 1970s and fostered considerable overindulgence, since many people insisted on drinking it as a shooter. Some early versions didn't include the triple sec.

2 fl oz (60 ml) vodka
1 tablespoon triple sec
1½ teaspoons fresh lime juice

Pour all of the ingredients into a shaker two-thirds full of ice cubes. Shake well. Strain into a chilled cocktail glass.

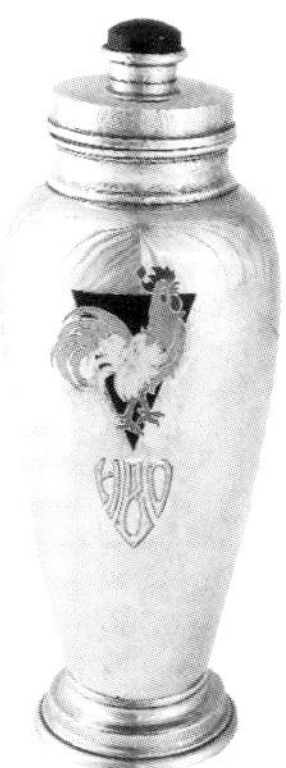

ENAMELED SHAKER

Monogrammed silver shaker from 1929 is enameled with an Art Deco rooster motif.

KENTUCKY CHAMPAGNE COCKTAIL

The sweet-tangy flavors of the Peychaud bitters in this recipe marry marvelously with the bourbon.

1 sugar cube
2 to 3 dashes Peychaud bitters
2 tablespoons bourbon
5 fl oz (150 ml) Champagne or sparkling wine
1 lemon twist, for garnish

Drop the sugar cube into the bottom of a Champagne flute. Add the bitters and bourbon. Carefully pour in the Champagne. Add the lemon twist.

KENTUCKY COLONEL

It's likely this drink was named for the Honorable Order of Kentucky Colonels, a philanthropic society based in Louisville, Kentucky.

2½ fl oz (75 ml) bourbon
1 tablespoon Bénédictine
1 lemon twist, for garnish

Pour the bourbon and Bénédictine into a mixing glass two-thirds full of ice cubes. Stir well. Strain into a chilled cocktail glass. Garnish with the lemon twist.

KENTUCKY COWHAND

2½ fl oz (75 ml) bourbon
1½ teaspoons Southern Comfort
1½ teaspoons light cream

Pour all of the ingredients into a shaker two-thirds full of ice cubes. Shake well. Strain into a chilled cocktail glass.

KENTUCKY PUNCH

A very strong punch that should be served—and drunk—judiciously.

Makes 20 6-fl-oz (180-ml) servings.

1 750-ml bottle bourbon
1 750-ml bottle dark rum
1 750-ml bottle brandy
6 fl oz (180 ml) simple syrup (page 23)
1 cup (8 fl oz/250 ml) fresh lemon juice
2 fl oz (60 ml) grenadine
1 large block of ice
2 cups (16 fl oz/500 ml) club soda

Pour the bourbon, rum, brandy, simple syrup, lemon juice, and grenadine into a large pan or bowl made of stainless steel or other nonreactive material. Stir well. Cover and refrigerate until chilled, at least 4 hours.

Place the ice in the center of a large punch bowl. Add the punch. Pour in the club soda. Serve in punch cups.

KENTUCKY STINGER

This is the only Stinger with more than two ingredients. The addition of Southern Comfort makes this drink quite sweet.

3 tablespoons bourbon
1½ teaspoons Southern Comfort
1½ teaspoons white crème de menthe

Pour all of the ingredients into a shaker two-thirds full of ice cubes. Shake well. Strain into a wineglass filled with crushed ice.

KEOKI COFFEE

2 tablespoons brandy
2 tablespoons coffee liqueur (such as Kahlúa)
4 fl oz (120 ml) hot coffee
2 tablespoons whipped cream

Pour the brandy, coffee liqueur, and coffee into an Irish Coffee glass. Stir briefly. Carefully spoon the whipped cream onto the coffee so that it floats on top.

KING ALPHONSE

2 fl oz (60 ml) coffee liqueur (such as Kahlúa)
2 tablespoons whipped cream

Pour the coffee liqueur into an ice-filled Old-Fashioned glass. Carefully spoon the cream onto the drink so that it floats on top.

KIR

Kir was named for a certain Canon Kir, once mayor of Dijon, France, a town that produces crème de cassis from local blackcurrants.

5 fl oz (150 ml) chilled dry white wine
2 teaspoons crème de cassis
1 lemon twist, for garnish

Pour the wine and cassis into a wineglass. Stir briefly. Add the lemon twist.

KIR ROYALE

5 fl oz (150 ml) chilled Champagne or sparkling wine
2 teaspoons crème de cassis
1 lemon twist, for garnish

Pour the Champagne and cassis into a Champagne flute. Stir briefly. Garnish with the lemon twist.

KNICKERBOCKER COCKTAIL

2 fl oz (60 ml) gin
1 tablespoon dry vermouth
2 teaspoons sweet vermouth
1 lemon twist, for garnish

Pour the gin and both vermouths into a mixing glass two-thirds full of ice cubes. Stir well. Strain into a chilled cocktail glass. Add the lemon twist.

LAGER—See Beer, page 98.

LAGER AND LIME

1 to 2 fl oz (30 to 60 ml) sweetened lime juice (such as Rose's)
1½ cups (12 fl oz/375 ml) chilled lager

Pour the sweetened lime juice and the lager into a 16-fl-oz (500-ml) beer glass.

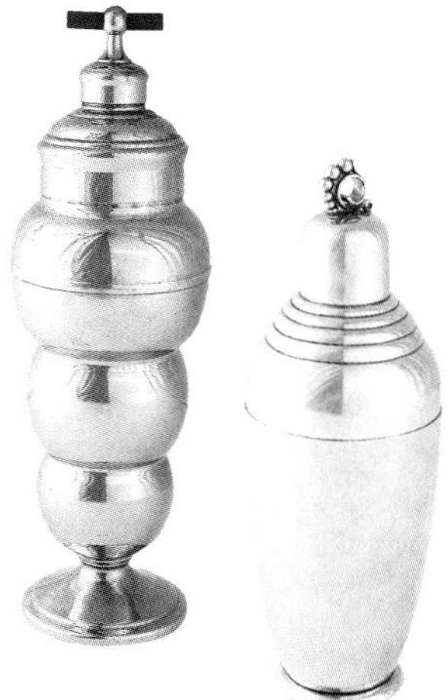

ART DECO SHAKERS

Chrome-plated "bubble" shaker, left, was popular in 1937. Elegant silver shaker, right, dates from the 1920s or early 1930s.

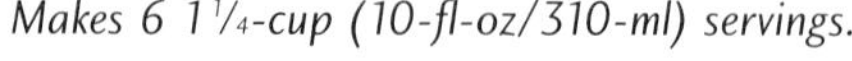

LAMB'S WOOL

Lamb's Wool is actually a variation on Wassail, differentiated mainly by the roasted apples in the recipe. It is so named because of the froth that forms on top.

Makes 6 1¼-cup (10-fl-oz/310-ml) servings.

6 apples, peeled and cored, each cut into 6 wedges
2 tablespoons unsalted butter
1 cup (8 fl oz/250 ml) hot water
1 cup (8 fl oz/250 ml) firmly packed brown sugar
3 tablespoons grated fresh ginger
2 teaspoons ground or freshly grated nutmeg
1 quart (32 fl oz/1 l) brown ale
1½ cups (12 fl oz/375 ml) stout

Preheat the oven to 375°F (190°C). Arrange the apple wedges on an oiled baking sheet. Dot with small pieces of butter. Bake until soft, about 30 minutes.

Put the roasted apples in a blender and puree. Scrape the puree into a large saucepan made of stainless steel or other nonreactive material. Add the water, sugar, ginger, and nutmeg. Stirring constantly over medium heat, cook until hot, about 10 minutes.

Add the ale and stir constantly until the mixture almost boils. Add the stout, pouring it from about 10 inches (25 cm) above the pan, ensuring a lot of foam. Stir briefly. Ladle into beer mugs for serving.

LEMON DROP

This relatively new drink came to light around the same time as citrus-flavored vodkas. Though it's generally served straight up in a cocktail glass, it also works well strained into an ice-filled Old-Fashioned glass.

Granulated sugar, to coat rim of glass
2 fl oz (60 ml) citrus vodka
1 tablespoon triple sec

Coat the rim of a cocktail glass with sugar (see technique, page 49) and chill it. Pour the remaining ingredients into a mixing glass two-thirds full of ice cubes. Stir well. Strain into the glass.

⃠ LEMON-LIME FIZZ

The ginger beer gives this drink a marvelous spiciness that makes it perfect for children and adults alike.

2 tablespoons fresh lemon juice
2 tablespoons fresh lime juice
2 fl oz (60 ml) ginger beer
4 fl oz (120 ml) club soda

Pour all the ingredients into an ice-filled Collins glass. Stir briefly.

⃠ LEMONADE

2 fl oz (60 ml) fresh lemon juice
1 tablespoon simple syrup
6 to 8 fl oz (180 to 250 ml) cold water

Pour the lemon juice and simple syrup into an ice-filled Collins glass. Add the cold water. Stir briefly.

⃠ LIMEADE

2 fl oz (60 ml) fresh lime juice
1 tablespoon simple syrup
6 to 8 fl oz (180 to 250 ml) cold water

Pour the lime juice and simple syrup into an ice-filled Collins glass. Add the cold water. Stir briefly.

LONG ISLAND ICED TEA

This odd mixture of ingredients comes together as a well-balanced potion that tastes remarkably like regular iced tea. But beware! This "tea" is strong.

1 tablespoon gin
1 tablespoon light rum
1 tablespoon white tequila
1 tablespoon vodka
1 tablespoon triple sec
2 tablespoons fresh lemon juice
1 tablespoon simple syrup (page 23)
5 fl oz (150 ml) cola
1 lemon wedge, for garnish

Pour all of the liquids except the cola into a shaker two-thirds full of ice cubes. Shake well. Strain into an ice-filled Collins glass. Add the cola. Stir briefly. Add the lemon wedge.

Liqueurs

15–55% alcohol by volume

Sometimes referred to as cordials, liqueurs are distilled beverages flavored with fruits, herbs, spices, or other botanicals, and sweetened with sugar, honey, or other ingredients. First produced by religious orders during the Middle Ages, they are indispensable to today's mixologists, adding a range of distinctive flavors that belie the modest quantities in which they are often used. A few are also enjoyed neat in cordial glasses (see page 41) or on the rocks.

French monks first made Bénédictine in 1510.

The best liqueurs on the market, such as Chartreuse or Drambuie, are intricate in flavor as well as manufacture, and these top-of-the-line products usually have herbs, fruits, and spices distilled into them—an expensive and time-consuming process. Many of these bottlings are savored neat as an after-dinner drink, but they can also be essential in preparing first-class cocktails and mixed drinks. With other, simpler liqueurs, such as generic crème de bananes, the producers often simply add artificial flavorings to a neutral spirit made from fruits or grains.

The following are descriptions of some of the best-known liqueurs. For a list of essential ones for the bar, see page 19.

AMARETTO An almond-flavored liqueur made with apricot pits; see page 81.

ANISE A generic name for aniseed-flavored liqueurs, such as anisette and sambuca. Most can be sipped neat and are also used in cocktails and mixed drinks.

ANISETTE A white, somewhat syrupy style of liqueur with a strong aniseed flavor. It's usually consumed neat, but is often included in cocktails and mixed drinks.

APRICOT BRANDY An apricot-flavored liqueur used in many cocktails and mixed drinks; rarely consumed neat.

B&B A French brand of Bénédictine mixed with brandy. It can be sipped neat, and is also often used as an ingredient in cocktails and mixed drinks.

BÉNÉDICTINE A very complex French brand of herbal liqueur with a somewhat sweet medicinal flavor.

BÉNÉDICTINE

Honoring its monastic origin, the Bénédictine label bears the letters "D.O.M.," for the Latin Deo Optimo Maximo *("To God, Most Good, Most Great").*

BLACKBERRY BRANDY A blackberry-flavored liqueur used principally in cocktails and mixed drinks.

CHAMBORD A brand-name French liqueur flavored with black raspberries, honey, and herbs. Often served neat as an after-dinner drink, it is also an ingredient in cocktails and mixed drinks.

CHARTREUSE A French brand of herbal liqueur, tasting somewhat sweet and medicinal. The two types (green and yellow) use different recipes but taste quite similar. Chartreuse is often served neat after dinner, but it is also a distinctive flavoring in cocktails and mixed drinks.

CHERRY BRANDY A type of cherry-flavored liqueur used in many cocktails and mixed drinks; seldom served neat.

COINTREAU A highly regarded French brand of triple sec, far drier than most less-expensive triple secs. Cointreau is most often used as a flavoring ingredient, but it is also a very pleasant postprandial potion, served neat or on the rocks.

CRÈME DE BANANES The generic term for a banana-flavored liqueur used in many cocktails and mixed drinks.

CRÈME DE CACAO A chocolate-flavored liqueur used in many cocktails and mixed drinks; seldom served neat. It is available in white and dark types, the dark bearing more vanilla notes.

CRÈME DE CASSIS This blackcurrant-flavored liqueur is used in many cocktails and mixed drinks. It is seldom served neat. The best bottlings of crème de cassis are produced in France.

CHAMBORD

According to legend, Chambord originated in France during the reign of Louis XIV.

CHARTREUSE

Carthusian monks first made Chartreuse in 1737 and still make it today.

CRÈME DE MENTHE Peppermint-flavored liqueur used mainly as a flavoring ingredient. Green and white types are available, but their tastes are very similar.

CRÈME DE NOYAUX An almond-flavored liqueur made from peach, apricot, or other fruit kernels. It is an integral ingredient in some popular cocktails, such as the Pink Squirrel, page 227.

CURAÇAO A generic style of orange-flavored liqueur, somewhat sweeter than most triple secs. Available in white, blue, and a few orange bottlings, which differ only in color, curaçao is used most frequently as a mixing ingredient and is seldom served neat.

Display card from the 1920s advertises an Italian brand of curaçao.

DRAMBUIE A Scottish brand of Scotch-based liqueur flavored with honey, herbs, and spices, whose name comes from the Gaelic *an dram buidheach* ("the drink that satisfies"). Drambuie is a delightful after-dinner drink served neat or even on the rocks, and is also often employed as an ingredient in cocktails and mixed drinks.

FRANGELICO An Italian brand-name liqueur flavored predominantly with hazelnuts. Frangelico makes a good after-dinner drink served neat, and is often an ingredient in cocktails and mixed drinks.

DRAMBUIE

Bonnie Prince Charlie is said to have passed the recipe for Drambuie to Captain John Mackinnon, who sheltered the prince from the English after his 1748 defeat at the Battle of Culloden.

GALLIANO A brand of Italian liqueur that tastes of vanilla and orange, with hints of herbs, roots, and spices. It is most often an ingredient in cocktails and mixed drinks.

GRAND MARNIER A French brand of intricate, orange-flavored liqueur made with cognac. Although it sometimes substitutes for triple sec, its cognac renders it somewhat sweeter than the best triple secs, such as Cointreau.

IRISH CREAM A liqueur made with Irish whiskey and heavy cream, bearing a vanilla-cocoa flavor. Often used in cocktails and mixed drinks, it is also served neat or on the rocks.

IRISH MIST A brand-name liqueur based on Irish whiskey and flavored with herbs and honey. Usually used in drinks with an Irish whiskey base, it can also be served neat after dinner.

JÄGERMEISTER A German brand of liqueur tasting somewhat medicinal; often served chilled from the freezer as a shooter.

KAHLÚA A brand-name Mexican coffee-flavored liqueur made from a sugar-based spirit and Mexican coffee beans. It is used primarily as a mixing ingredient.

MARASCHINO A liqueur distilled in Europe from whole Dalmatian cherries, complete with their crushed kernels. It is an integral ingredient in crustas such as the Brandy Crusta, page 122.

MIDORI A Japanese brand of green, melon-flavored liqueur used in many cocktails and mixed drinks.

OUZO The generic term for an anise-flavored liqueur made in Greece and

GALLIANO

Galliano was named for Major Giuseppe Galliano, a hero of the Italian-Abyssinian war of 1895–96.

IRISH CREAM

Baileys was the original Irish cream liqueur.

LIQUEUR OR BRANDY?

A number of fruit-flavored liqueurs are labeled as brandy, but don't let that confuse you. Unlike true brandy (page 114), they contain only a small percentage of spirits distilled from the specific fruits; the bulk of their flavor comes from fruit essences sweetened with sugar.

TRIPLE SEC

Orange peels flavor this liqueur used mainly for mixing.

Cyprus. Ouzo is usually drier than anise-based liqueurs from France and Italy.

PEACH BRANDY Sweet peach-flavored liqueur commonly used for mixing. Some enjoy it neat as an after-dinner potion.

PEAR BRANDY Pear-flavored liqueur used primarily as a mixed-drink ingredient.

SAMBUCA A generic type of anise-based liqueur from Italy, traditionally consumed neat after dinner. It is available in its original white form and in a black bottling that bears distinctive lemon-zest notes.

SCHNAPPS, FLAVORED A genre of often sweet liqueurs in a wide range of flavors including peach, peppermint, even butterscotch and root beer. Most function solely as mixing ingredients; some, such as peach schnapps, are also served neat.

SLOE GIN An infusion of sloe berries into gin or neutral spirits; see page 263.

SOUTHERN COMFORT An American brand of fruit-flavored liqueur, often erroneously thought to have a whiskey base. Used frequently in cocktails and mixed drinks, and sometimes served on the rocks.

STRAWBERRY BRANDY A strawberry-flavored liqueur normally used for mixing.

TIA MARIA A Jamaican brand of coffee-flavored rum-based liqueur. It is more complex and has stronger coffee notes than Kahlúa, so the two are not usually interchangeable. It is usually served neat or on the rocks as an after-dinner drink.

TRIPLE SEC A drier version of curaçao, flavored with orange peels. Some inexpensive bottlings are quite sweet, however. Triple sec is used primarily as an ingredient in cocktails and mixed drinks.

MADEIRA—See page 202.

MADRAS

2 fl oz (60 ml) vodka
2 fl oz (60 ml) fresh orange juice
3 tablespoons cranberry juice cocktail

Pour all of the ingredients into an ice-filled highball glass. Stir briefly.

MAI TAI

Legend attributes the Mai Tai to the late Victor Bergeron, founder of the Trader Vic's chain of Polynesian-themed restaurants.

3 tablespoons dark rum
2 tablespoons light rum
2 tablespoons triple sec
1 tablespoon apricot brandy
2 tablespoons fresh lime juice
2 tablespoons simple syrup (page 23)
Dash of orgeat syrup

Pour all of the ingredients into a shaker two-thirds full of ice cubes. Shake well. Strain into a large, ice-filled wineglass.

MAIDEN'S PRAYER

For a sweeter Maiden's Prayer, use curaçao instead of triple sec.

2 fl oz (60 ml) gin
1 tablespoon triple sec
1 tablespoon fresh lemon juice

Pour all of the ingredients into a shaker two-thirds full of ice cubes. Shake well. Strain into a chilled cocktail glass.

Madeira

15–20% alcohol by volume

This wine fortified with grape spirit is named for the island of its origin, Madeira, situated in the Atlantic Ocean west of Morocco but belonging to Portugal. The fortified wine was very popular in Colonial America, and although it has fallen from favor somewhat, it is still beloved by some aficionados.

Portugal's Madeira Islands

HOW MADEIRA IS MADE

Madeira is the only wine purposefully matured for a short period at high temperatures—typically 104 to 122°F (40 to 50°C). It is fortified with grape spirit and moved to cooler cellars to rest for at least 18 months. Finally, it matures in a complex *solera* system like that used for sherry (page 258). The rigors of Madeira's heat-aging process make even an opened bottle almost impervious to spoilage.

RAINWATER

The style originated by accident in the eighteenth century, when casks left out in the rain absorbed water, changing the taste of the wine.

STYLES OF MADEIRA

The best Madeiras are made in five distinct styles with varying degrees of sweetness. Each (except Rainwater) is named after the grape variety used in its production.

SERCIAL The driest style of Madeira, delightful as an aperitif.

VERDELHO A medium-dry bottling with high acidity, served before or after dinner.

RAINWATER A blend of Madeira that is pale, medium-dry, and versatile.

BUAL Medium sweet, this Madeira is a perfect after-dinner libation.

MALMSEY The sweetest style; generally rich and full bodied, with a huge bouquet. Serve it after dinner.

Serving Madeira

SAVOR MADEIRA in 2-fl-oz (60-ml) portions poured into small wineglasses. Bual and Malmsey, the sweetest types, are best at room temperature. Serve Sercial and Verdelho slightly chilled, and Rainwater straight from the refrigerator.

Manhattan

THIS COCKTAIL made its debut at New York's Manhattan Club, at a banquet given by Lady Jenny Churchill for Samuel Tilden, the lawyer who prosecuted the infamous Tweed Ring in the 1870s.

Unlike the Dry Martini (page 209), which will be a success if you simply combine a decent amount of a good London Dry Gin with a splash of your favorite dry vermouth, the Manhattan is a challenge to mix because its ratio of whisk(e)y to vermouth is absolutely critical. Results also depend on the type of whisk(e)y you use: Although blended Canadian whisky works fairly well, using straight rye or bourbon whiskey will produce a superior beverage.

2½ fl oz (75 ml) rye, bourbon, or blended Canadian whisk(e)y
1½ tablespoons sweet vermouth
2 dashes Angostura bitters
1 maraschino cherry, for garnish

Pour the whisk(e)y, vermouth, and bitters into a mixing glass two-thirds full of ice cubes. Stir well. Strain into a chilled cocktail glass. Garnish with the cherry.

SEE ALSO *Dubonnet Manhattan, Martinez, Southern Comfort Manhattan.*

MANHATTAN (DRY)

2½ fl oz (75 ml) rye, bourbon, or blended Canadian whisk(e)y
1½ tablespoons dry vermouth
2 dashes Angostura bitters
1 lemon twist, for garnish

Pour the whisk(e)y, vermouth, and bitters into a mixing glass two-thirds full of ice cubes. Stir well. Strain into a chilled cocktail glass. Add the lemon twist.

MANHATTAN (PERFECT)

The term "perfect" refers to the use of both sweet and dry vermouths in a cocktail recipe.

2½ fl oz (75 ml) rye, bourbon, or blended Canadian whisk(e)y
1 tablespoon sweet vermouth
1 tablespoon dry vermouth
2 dashes Angostura bitters
1 maraschino cherry, for garnish
1 lemon twist, for garnish

Pour the whisk(e)y, both vermouths, and the bitters into a mixing glass two-thirds full of ice cubes. Stir well. Strain into a chilled cocktail glass. Add the garnishes.

CHICKEN SHAKER

Cocktail ingredients enter through the neck and exit from the beak of this fanciful silver-plated shaker from the 1930s.

Margarita

TEQUILA ONCE HAD a limited audience because it was regarded as a tough man's drink. That all changed in 1945, when businessman Vernon Underwood gained exclusive rights to distribute Jose Cuervo tequila in the United States. Seeking ways to broaden its appeal, he took out magazine ads that pictured himself toasting a goddess who held a Margarita in her hand. The caption read: "Margarita, more than a girl's name."

Although white tequila is the norm, substituting reposado or añejo tequila (page 274) can make for a much better cocktail. Many recipes call for Cointreau (page 197), which does indeed make a marvelous Margarita. But if you don't have Cointreau, use a very dry triple sec—never a sweet one.

The proportions in the recipe below are classic, but feel free to alter the ratio of tequila to triple sec as you like.

Salt, to coat rim of glass
2 fl oz (60 ml) white tequila
3 tablespoons triple sec
2 tablespoons fresh lime juice

Coat the rim of a cocktail glass with salt (see technique, page 49) and chill it. Pour all of the remaining ingredients into a shaker two-thirds full of ice cubes. Shake well. Strain into the glass.

SEE ALSO *Frozen Margarita, Frozen Peach Margarita, Frozen Strawberry Margarita.*

MANILA FIZZ

It's not a true Fizz (see Gin Fizz, page 168), but the root beer complements the gin in this recipe to produce a wonderful drink.

2 fl oz (60 ml) gin
1 teaspoon simple syrup (page 23)
1 egg (see caution, page 22)
3 fl oz (90 ml) root beer

Pour the gin and simple syrup into a shaker two-thirds full of ice cubes. Add the egg. Shake very well. Strain into a Collins glass three-quarters full of crushed ice. Add the root beer. Stir briefly.

MARTINEZ

This dates back to the 1800s. For a drier cocktail, use less simple syrup.

2 fl oz (60 ml) gin
1 tablespoon sweet vermouth
2 teaspoons maraschino liqueur
1 tablespoon simple syrup (page 23)

Pour all of the ingredients into a mixing glass two-thirds full of ice cubes. Stir well. Strain into a chilled cocktail glass.

MARTINI (DRY)—See page 209.

MARTINI (EXTRA DRY)

3 fl oz (90 ml) gin
1 ½ teaspoons dry vermouth
1 green cocktail olive or 1 lemon twist, for garnish

Pour the gin and vermouth into a mixing glass two-thirds full of ice cubes. Stir well. Strain into a chilled cocktail glass. Add the desired garnish.

Martini

THIS QUINTESSENTIAL COCKTAIL is the model of sophistication, yet its marriage of gin and vermouth is the ultimate in simplicity. The recipe, first detailed in cocktail books around 1900, has undergone many changes since its creation, the most prevalent being the ratio of gin to vermouth. Early recipes called for as much dry vermouth as dry gin, making a Martini that would hardly be acceptable today. And as late as the 1940s, many Martinis even contained a few dashes of bitters.

Beginning in the 1950s, the proportion of vermouth began shrinking toward the vanishing point. Today in some bars and restaurants, bartenders merely glance at the bottle of vermouth and proceed to pour a Martini that is 100 percent gin. This drink, more accurately known as a Naked Martini (page 217), is of course just chilled gin, and it misses the mark by not allowing the wonderful herbal notes of a good dry vermouth to mingle with the gin's aromatic botanicals.

An Extra Dry Martini (page 207) should contain no less

than 1 part vermouth to 12 parts gin, and many who use less vermouth would probably marvel at a properly constructed Martini. Some Martini aficionados prechill their gin in the refrigerator or freezer, and this too is a mistake. Room-temperature gin melts just enough ice to make a Martini palatable, whereas if chilled gin is used, the drink will be far too strong.

Martinis these days are preferably stirred, not shaken. In the past, experts have differed on this point, so although the recipe below calls for stirring the drink, you might want to experiment with shaking it.

Garnishes are another area of contention. Olives and lemon twists are commonly seen, usually separately but sometimes together. Yet it isn't uncommon to see caperberries, tiny tomatoes, and even dill pickles in Martinis, and this choice should be left to the individual. Of course, if a cocktail onion is used, the drink becomes a Gibson (page 159).

Here is the classic Dry Martini:

3 fl oz (90 ml) gin
1 tablespoon dry vermouth
1 green cocktail olive or 1 lemon twist, for garnish

Pour the gin and vermouth into a mixing glass two-thirds full of ice cubes. Stir well. Strain into a chilled cocktail glass. Add the desired garnish.

SEE ALSO *Banana Rum Martini, Cajun Martini, Chocolate Martini, Dirty Martini, Fino Martini, Jamaican Martini, Martini (Extra Dry, Medium, Sweet), Naked Martini, Spiced Rum and Chocolate Martini, Tequila Martini (Dry, Extra Dry, Medium, Sweet), Vesper Martini, Vodka Martini (Dry, Extra Dry, Medium, Sweet).*

MARTINI (MEDIUM)

2½ fl oz (75 ml) gin

1½ teaspoons dry vermouth

1 green cocktail olive or 1 lemon twist, for garnish

Pour the gin and vermouth into a mixing glass two-thirds full of ice cubes. Stir well. Strain into a chilled cocktail glass. Add the desired garnish.

MARTINI (SWEET)

2½ fl oz (75 ml) gin

1½ teaspoons sweet vermouth

1 lemon twist, for garnish

Pour the gin and vermouth into a mixing glass two-thirds full of ice cubes. Stir well. Strain into a chilled cocktail glass. Add the lemon twist.

MARY PICKFORD

The spiciness of rum and maraschino liqueur admirably offsets the sweetness of pineapple juice in this drink named for the popular silent-screen star known as "America's Sweetheart."

2 fl oz (60 ml) light rum

2 tablespoons pineapple juice

1 teaspoon maraschino liqueur

Dash of grenadine

Pour all of the ingredients into a shaker two-thirds full of ice cubes. Shake well. Strain into a chilled cocktail glass.

MELON BALL

Popular since the 1970s when melon-flavored liqueur first arrived in the United States from Japan, this very sweet drink can be made drier with less melon liqueur and more vodka.

3 tablespoons melon liqueur (such as Midori)
2 tablespoons vodka
2 fl oz (60 ml) pineapple juice

Pour all of the ingredients into a shaker two-thirds full of ice cubes. Shake well. Strain into an ice-filled Old-Fashioned glass.

MERRY WIDOW

2 fl oz (60 ml) gin
1 tablespoon dry vermouth
2 dashes Bénédictine
2 dashes absinthe substitute (such as Pernod or Ricard)

Pour all of the ingredients into a mixing glass two-thirds full of ice cubes. Stir well. Strain into a chilled cocktail glass.

METROPOLITAN—See page 212.

MEXICAN COFFEE

3 tablespoons Kahlúa
4 fl oz (120 ml) hot coffee
2 tablespoons whipped cream

Pour the Kahlúa and coffee into an Irish Coffee glass. Stir briefly. Carefully spoon the whipped cream onto the coffee so that it floats on top.

MEZCAL—See page 272.

Metropolitan

CHUCK COGGINS, a bartender at Marion's Continental Restaurant and Lounge in downtown Manhattan, reportedly created this drink. It is merely a variation on the popular Cosmopolitan (page 143), but the use of currant-flavored vodka makes it a drink unto itself. The inclusion of sweetened lime juice in addition to fresh lime juice makes this drink overpoweringly sweet for some. If you prefer a drier taste, cut the sweetened lime juice back to 1½ teaspoons—but don't omit it entirely, because this drink does require some sweetness.

- 2½ fl oz (75 ml) Absolut Kurant vodka
- 1 tablespoon sweetened lime juice (such as Rose's)
- 1 tablespoon fresh lime juice
- 1 tablespoon cranberry juice cocktail
- 1 lime wedge, for garnish

Pour all of the liquids into a shaker two-thirds full of ice cubes. Shake well. Strain into a chilled cocktail glass. Add the lime wedge.

MILLIONAIRE

1 fl oz (60 ml) blended Canadian whisky
1 tablespoon triple sec
2 dashes grenadine
1 egg white (see caution, page 22)

Pour all of the ingredients into a shaker two-thirds full of ice cubes. Shake well. Strain into a chilled cocktail glass.

MIMOSA

Ubiquitous on brunch menus, this Champagne cocktail is lower in alcohol than most other mixed drinks.

1 tablespoon triple sec
2 tablespoons fresh orange juice
4 fl oz (120 ml) Champagne or sparkling wine
1 orange wheel, for garnish

Pour the triple sec, orange juice, and Champagne into a Champagne flute. Stir briefly. Add the orange wheel.

MIND ERASER

To clear your mind with this relatively new Pousse-Café–style drink, use the straw to consume it from the bottom up in one go.

1½ tablespoons coffee liqueur (such as Kahlúa)
1½ tablespoons vodka
1½ tablespoons club soda
1 short straw

Pour the ingredients, in the order given, over the back of a spoon into a Pousse-Café glass, floating one on top of the other (see technique, page 60). Add a short straw.

Mint Julep

THE MINT JULEP IS traditionally served in Kentucky during Kentucky Derby Week, which culminates after the race is run on the first Saturday in May. But you can serve this quintessentially American drink at any time when the sun is shining and fresh mint is close at hand.

Some people like to muddle mint leaves in the bottom of the Julep cup prior to building the drink, but ideally the only mint is the aromatic garnish one inhales as one sips the sweetened bourbon. Apart from mint, the other hallmark of this drink is the silvery Julep cup, which is always coated with a thin film of ice—achieved by stirring the ice-filled cup long enough for the condensation on the outside to freeze.

Juleps can be made with spirits other than bourbon. In fact, peach brandy was the earlier basis for the drink. But straight Kentucky bourbon is now the liquor of choice.

2 tablespoons simple syrup (page 23)
3 fl oz (90 ml) bourbon
3 large mint sprigs, for garnish

Pour the simple syrup into a Julep cup filled with crushed ice. Stir well. Add the bourbon. Stir until a film of ice forms on the exterior of the cup. Garnish with the mint sprigs.

SEE ALSO *Brandy Julep, Champagne Julep, Irish Julep, Peach Brandy Julep.*

MOJITO

The Mojito originated in the Caribbean, probably in Cuba. It is more or less a Rum Smash (page 246) with the addition of club soda, which makes for a long, thirst-quenching drink.

6 fresh mint leaves

1 ½ tablespoons simple syrup (page 23)

1 tablespoon fresh lime juice

2 fl oz (60 ml) light rum

2 fl oz (60 ml) club soda

1 lime wedge, for garnish

Put the mint leaves in the bottom of a highball glass. Add the simple syrup and lime juice and muddle well (see technique, page 64). Fill the glass with crushed ice. Add the rum and club soda. Stir briefly. Add the garnish.

MONKEY GLAND COCKTAIL

2 fl oz (60 ml) gin

1 tablespoon Bénédictine

2 tablespoons fresh orange juice

Dash of grenadine

Pour all of the ingredients into a shaker two-thirds full of ice cubes. Shake well. Strain into a chilled cocktail glass.

MONK'S COFFEE

Named for the monks who have made Chartreuse since the eighteenth century, this is an interesting variation on the Irish Coffee (page 179), but suitable only for those who appreciate the sweet-herbal, somewhat medicinal tones of Chartreuse.

3 tablespoons green Chartreuse
4 fl oz (120 ml) hot coffee
2 tablespoons whipped cream

Pour the Chartreuse and coffee into an Irish Coffee glass. Stir briefly. Carefully spoon the whipped cream onto the coffee so that it floats on top.

MORNING GLORY FIZZ

2 fl oz (60 ml) vodka
1 tablespoon white crème de cacao
2 tablespoons light cream
4 fl oz (120 ml) club soda
Ground or freshly grated nutmeg, for garnish

Pour the vodka, crème de cacao, and cream into a shaker two-thirds full of ice cubes. Shake well. Strain into an ice-filled Collins glass. Add the club soda. Stir well. Sprinkle with nutmeg.

MOSCOW MULE

This was one of the first vodka-based drinks to catch on in the United States. Note that the recipe calls for ginger beer, not ginger ale.

2 fl oz (60 ml) vodka
2 tablespoons fresh lime juice
4 to 6 fl oz (120 to 180 ml) ginger beer
1 lime wedge, for garnish

Pour the vodka, lime juice, and ginger beer into an ice-filled highball glass. Stir briefly. Add the lime wedge.

MUDSLIDE

2 tablespoons coffee liqueur (such as Kahlúa)
2 tablespoons vodka
2 tablespoons Irish cream liqueur

Pour all of the ingredients into a shaker two-thirds full of ice cubes. Shake well. Strain into a chilled cocktail glass.

NAKED MARTINI

It's not a true Martini (page 208) since it contains no vermouth, but those who love straight, chilled gin favor this drink.

3 fl oz (90 ml) gin
1 green cocktail olive or 1 lemon twist, for garnish

Pour the gin into a mixing glass two-thirds full of ice cubes. Stir well. Strain into a chilled cocktail glass. Add the desired garnish.

NEGRONI—See page 218.

NEW ORLEANS COCKTAIL

2 fl oz (60 ml) bourbon
1 tablespoon absinthe substitute (such as Pernod or Ricard)
1 tablespoon simple syrup (page 23)
1 tablespoon fresh lemon juice

Pour all of the ingredients into a shaker two-thirds full of ice cubes. Shake well. Strain into a chilled cocktail glass.

Negroni

THE NEGRONI IS A VARIATION on the Americano (page 82) and its creation is credited to a certain Count Negroni, an Italian aristocrat who lived in Florence during the late nineteenth century when the Americano became popular in Italy. The story goes that Negroni felt the Americano was far too commonplace for someone of his standing, so he instructed his local bartender to add a tot of gin to the drink. And since he felt it imperative to distinguish his glass from everyone else's, he demanded that a slice of orange be added for garnish. These days, orange wheels are also used in the Americano, but the addition of gin was truly an inspired act.

This is a fairly bitter drink, but the vermouth nicely quells the harsher aspects of the Campari, while the gin adds an aromatic quality to the experience.

2 tablespoons gin
2 tablespoons sweet vermouth
2 tablespoons Campari
1 orange wheel, for garnish

Pour the gin, vermouth, and Campari into an ice-filled Old-Fashioned glass. Stir briefly. Add the orange wheel.

Old-Fashioned

THE OLD-FASHIONED WAS reportedly created at the Pendennis Club in Louisville, Kentucky, where in the late 1880s a regular customer requested that the bartender make him a special drink. Instead of naming the drink after the customer, as was the practice, the bartender called it the Old-Fashioned in honor of the bitters (a centuries-old ingredient) deemed to give it an antique flavor. Although the original was probably made with straight Kentucky bourbon, blended Canadian whisky is now the more usual choice.

Some people don't muddle the fruits in an Old-Fashioned; however, the juices produced by mashing the fruits together make an astonishing difference in this drink.

3 dashes Angostura bitters
1 orange slice
1 lemon wedge
1 maraschino cherry
1 sugar cube
2½ fl oz (75 ml) blended Canadian whisky

Put the bitters, orange slice, lemon wedge, maraschino cherry, and sugar cube in an Old-Fashioned glass and muddle well (see technique, page 64). Fill the glass with ice cubes. Add the whisky. Stir well.

SEE ALSO *Bourbon Old-Fashioned, Irish Old-Fashioned, Scotch Old-Fashioned.*

OLYMPIC COCKTAIL

3 tablespoons brandy
1 tablespoon triple sec
1 tablespoon fresh orange juice

Pour all of the ingredients into a shaker two-thirds full of ice cubes. Shake well. Strain into a chilled cocktail glass.

OPERA COCKTAIL

2 fl oz (60 ml) gin
1 tablespoon Dubonnet Rouge
1 tablespoon maraschino liqueur

Pour all of the ingredients into a mixing glass two-thirds full of ice cubes. Stir well. Strain into a chilled cocktail glass.

ORANGE BLOSSOM COCKTAIL

This cocktail appeared in American bars prior to Prohibition and is still popular among gin lovers today. Use just a teaspoon of simple syrup for a drier version.

2½ fl oz (75 ml) gin
2 tablespoons fresh orange juice
1½ teaspoons simple syrup (page 23)
1 orange wheel, for garnish

Pour the gin, orange juice, and simple syrup into a shaker two-thirds full of ice cubes. Shake well. Strain into a chilled cocktail glass. Add the orange wheel.

⊘ ORANGEADE

4 fl oz (120 ml) fresh orange juice
1 ½ teaspoons grenadine
2 fl oz (60 ml) club soda

Pour all the ingredients into an ice-filled Collins glass. Stir briefly.

PANAMA COCKTAIL

Based loosely on the Brandy Alexander (page 113), the Panama Cocktail calls for white, not dark, crème de cacao.

2 tablespoons brandy
2 tablespoons white crème de cacao
2 tablespoons light cream

Pour all of the ingredients into a shaker two-thirds full of ice cubes. Shake well. Strain into a chilled cocktail glass.

PARADISE COCKTAIL

2 fl oz (60 ml) gin
2 tablespoons dry vermouth
1 teaspoon absinthe substitute (such as Pernod or Ricard)
2 dashes orange bitters

Pour all of the ingredients into a mixing glass two-thirds full of ice cubes. Stir well. Strain into a chilled cocktail glass.

PEACH BRANDY—See Liqueurs, page 200.

PEACH BRANDY JULEP

A predecessor of the bourbon-based Mint Julep (page 214).

3 fl oz (90 ml) peach brandy
2 dashes Angostura bitters
3 large mint sprigs, for garnish

Pour the peach brandy and bitters into a Julep cup filled with crushed ice. Stir until a film of ice forms on the exterior of the cup. Garnish with the mint sprigs.

PEG O' MY HEART

This pre-Prohibition drink was named for a Broadway play.

2 fl oz (60 ml) dark rum
2 tablespoons fresh lime juice
1 tablespoon grenadine

Pour all of the ingredients into a shaker two-thirds full of ice cubes. Shake well. Strain into a chilled cocktail glass.

PERFECTION COCKTAIL

A drink is called "perfect" when it contains both the sweet and dry styles of vermouth.

2 fl oz (60 ml) brandy
1½ teaspoons sweet vermouth
1½ teaspoons dry vermouth
1½ teaspoons triple sec

Pour all of the ingredients into a mixing glass two-thirds full of ice cubes. Stir well. Strain into a chilled cocktail glass.

Pernod

40% alcohol by volume

PERNOD IS AN absinthe substitute (see page 78) made by Pernod et Fils in France—a company that produced true absinthe before France banned it in 1914. Although far sweeter than absinthe, Pernod shares its predominant flavor of anise. Used in small quantities, Pernod can modify all the flavors of a drink without making its own presence overbearing. However, few mixed drinks call for it as a main ingredient. It is classically served by itself, in a tall ice-filled glass with about twice as much water as spirit. This drink makes a good aperitif. The similar product pastis, also made by the Pernod firm and others, is based on licorice instead of anise.

PERNOD FRAPPÉ

2 fl oz (60 ml) Pernod
3 straws, each cut to measure about 3 inches (7.5 cm) long

Fill a chilled cocktail glass with crushed ice until it forms a dome that rises in the center of the glass. Drizzle the Pernod into the glass. Add the straws.

PIERCED NAVEL

A variation on the Fuzzy Navel (page 158), this version has less alcohol.

2 fl oz (60 ml) peach schnapps
4 fl oz (120 ml) cranberry juice cocktail

Pour both ingredients into an ice-filled highball glass. Stir briefly.

Pimm's Cup

IT ISN'T TOO WELL KNOWN in the United States, but Pimm's Cup is a marvelously refreshing long drink that is not too high in alcohol. Pimm's was created by Londoner James Pimm, who opened a restaurant in the 1840s and eventually concocted this gin-based drink, flavored with fruit liqueurs and herbs and traditionally served in tankards. Pimm's became so successful that its fruit-and-liquor base was bottled and sold throughout the British Empire. A total of six varieties of Pimm's—based on gin, Scotch, brandy, rum, rye, and vodka—were eventually introduced. Of these, only No. 1 is still available, at least in the United States.

The gin-based Pimm's Cup is typically served with an unusual garnish—a sliver of cucumber rind, which adds a refreshing aroma to the moderately heavy herbal notes of this drink. But some people enjoy their Pimm's Cup garnished with a variety of fruit, so you should feel free to add orange wheels, pineapple spears, lemon twists, or whatever you have on hand. You can also replace the ginger ale with ginger beer, lemon-lime soda, or club soda if you wish.

4 fl oz (120 ml) Pimm's No. 1
1 cup (8 fl oz/250 ml) ginger ale
1 sliver of cucumber rind, for garnish

Pour the Pimm's and ginger ale into an ice-filled 20-fl-oz (625-ml) beer tankard. Stir briefly. Garnish with the cucumber rind.

Piña Colada

BARTENDER RAMÓN (Monchito) Marrero created this classic in 1954, at the Caribe Hilton Hotel in San Juan, Puerto Rico—and it has since become what may just be the world's most popular rum drink. Marrero, of course, called for Puerto Rican rum in his Piña Colada, and the recipe below employs the light rum with which Puerto Rico is often associated. If you want a drink with a little more body, use a dark rum instead.

The ratio of pineapple juice to coconut cream here is classic, but if you love the coconut aspect you can add up to 1 tablespoon more of canned coconut cream. Don't overdo it or the coconut will take over completely.

2 fl oz (60 ml) light rum
6 fl oz (180 ml) pineapple juice
2 fl oz (60 ml) canned coconut cream (such as Coco López)
1 pineapple spear, for garnish

· Pour the rum, pineapple juice, and coconut cream into a shaker two-thirds full of ice cubes. Shake well. Strain into an ice-filled wineglass. Add the pineapple spear.

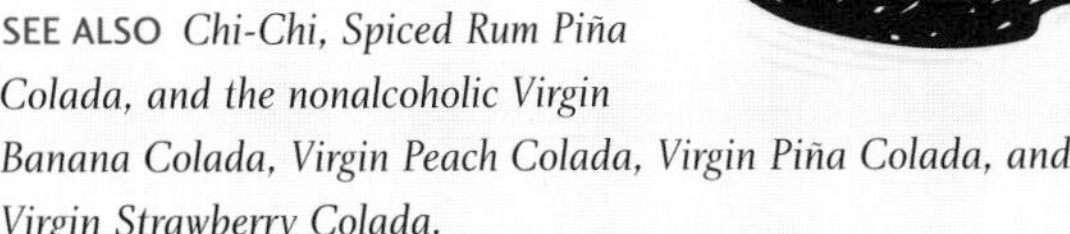

SEE ALSO *Chi-Chi, Spiced Rum Piña Colada, and the nonalcoholic Virgin Banana Colada, Virgin Peach Colada, Virgin Piña Colada, and Virgin Strawberry Colada.*

PINEAPPLE-CHERRY COOLER

2 fl oz (60 ml) gin
1 tablespoon cherry brandy
4 fl oz (120 ml) pineapple juice

Pour all the ingredients into an ice-filled highball glass. Stir briefly.

Pink Gin

IT IS SAID THAT the Pink Gin originated in Plymouth, England, and was first made with gin from the Coates Plymouth Gin distillery. The story goes that bitters, often used as a cure for stomach ailments, was prescribed for sailors leaving Plymouth Harbor, but since bitters is far too concentrated to drink on its own, the seafarers simply added it to their favorite spirit—gin.

In England, the Pink Gin is served at room temperature. If you wish to sample it this way, first coat the glass with the bitters (see technique, page 50), then simply pour the gin into the glass. However, most Americans prefer this drink chilled.

2 fl oz (60 ml) Plymouth Gin
3 dashes Angostura bitters

Pour both ingredients into a mixing glass two-thirds full of ice cubes. Stir well. Strain into a chilled cocktail glass.

⦸ PINK GRAPEFRUIT

Since the bitters does add a trace of alcohol, those who must avoid alcohol completely should forgo this drink.

6 fl oz (180 ml) fresh grapefruit juice
1 tablespoon grenadine
2 dashes Peychaud bitters

Pour all of the ingredients into an ice-filled Collins glass. Stir briefly.

PINK LADY

If you are cautious about using raw egg white, you can omit it from this recipe. The texture will be quite different, but the cocktail remains a pleasing after-dinner drink.

2 fl oz (60 ml) gin
1 tablespoon heavy cream
2 dashes grenadine
1 egg white (see caution, page 22)

Pour all of the ingredients into a shaker two-thirds full of ice cubes. Shake very well. Strain into a chilled cocktail glass.

PINK SQUIRREL

Crème de noyaux (page 198) can sometimes be hard to find. If you can't locate it, substitute amaretto (page 81).

2 tablespoons crème de noyaux
2 tablespoons white crème de cacao
2 tablespoons light cream

Pour all of the ingredients into a shaker two-thirds full of ice cubes. Shake well. Strain into a chilled cocktail glass.

Pisco Brandy

45% alcohol by volume

A GRAPE BRANDY from Peru and a few other South American countries, Pisco is distilled from Muscat grapes and usually is aged for only a few months in clay containers. Although this is not a smooth spirit, it does bear more fruit flavors than other briefly aged brandies. It takes its name from the Peruvian seaport town of Pisco, located near the region where the grapes are grown.

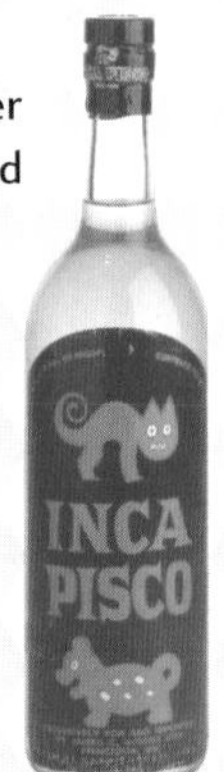

Peruvian Pisco brandy

PISCO SOUR

There is no substitute for the Pisco brandy, which a liquor store can order for you if it has none in stock. Some bartenders sprinkle the bitters on top instead of blending it in.

- 2 fl oz (60 ml) Pisco brandy
- 1 ½ tablespoons fresh lemon juice
- 1 tablespoon simple syrup (page 23)
- 1 egg white (see caution, page 22)
- 2 dashes Angostura bitters

Pour all of the ingredients into a shaker two-thirds full of ice cubes. Shake very well. Strain into a chilled cocktail glass.

PLANTER'S PUNCH

Jamaica is the home of this thirst quencher. No two recipes are alike.

- 2 fl oz (60 ml) dark rum
- 2 fl oz (60 ml) fresh grapefruit juice
- 2 tablespoons pineapple juice
- 2 tablespoons fresh lime juice
- 1 tablespoon simple syrup (page 23)
- 2 tablespoons club soda
- 1 pineapple spear, for garnish

Pour the rum, fruit juices, and simple syrup into a shaker two-thirds full of ice cubes. Shake well. Pour into an ice-filled Collins glass. Pour in the club soda. Stir briefly. Garnish with the pineapple spear.

⃠ PONY'S NECK

The dash of bitters does add a trace of alcohol—omit it if you like.

- 1 lemon peel spiral (see technique, page 53)
- 6 to 8 fl oz (180 to 250 ml) ginger ale
- Dash of Angostura bitters

Put the lemon peel spiral in a Collins glass. Fill the glass with ice cubes. Pour the ginger ale and bitters into the glass. Stir briefly.

PORT—See page 230.

PORT AND BRANDY

- 3 tablespoons ruby port
- 3 tablespoons brandy

Pour the port and brandy into a small wineglass. Stir briefly.

Port

17%–20% alcohol by volume

A wine fortified with grape brandy, port is made in most countries that produce table wine. Porto, the original port from the demarcated Douro region of Portugal, is the benchmark, considered by many to be the only true port. However, many good ports now emanate from California, Australia, and South Africa.

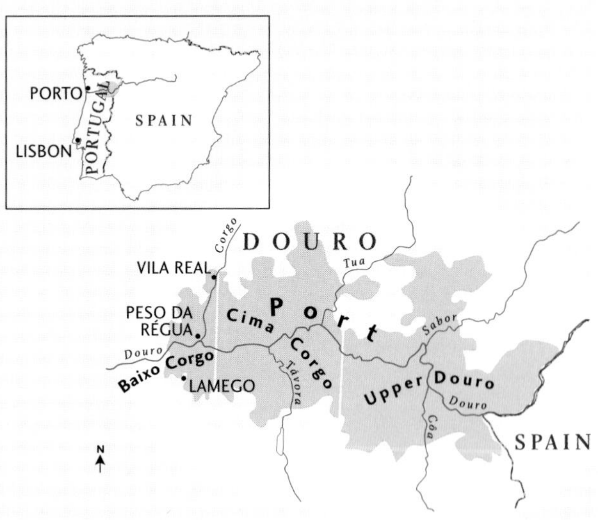

Portugal's Douro region, where port is made

HOW PORT IS MADE

The brandy added to fortify the young wine halts fermentation, leaving some grape sugars unfermented and thus sweetening the port. The port is then aged in oak casks and (with vintage ports) also in the bottle.

STYLES OF PORT

Ports are made in a variety of styles, from both red and white grapes.

WHITE Sometimes light and dry but more often sweet and medium-bodied, this port is usually offered as an aperitif.

RUBY Wines from a variety of casks are blended to produce a sweet, medium-to-full-bodied port. Sip ruby port on its own or use it for mixing.

TAWNY Inexpensive tawny port is a blend of white and ruby ports. Aged tawny port is ruby port aged until its color turns to a tawny brown and its sweetness mellows to a complex, fruity nuttiness.

VINTAGE Bottled after two years in casks, this product of an esteemed vintage continues to improve in the bottle and should be kept at least ten years before opening.

LATE BOTTLED VINTAGE Aged four to six years in casks, this port doesn't improve after bottling. It can be drunk immediately.

DECANTING VINTAGE PORT

Because vintage ports usually contain a crust or sediment, they must be decanted before serving. To do this, stand the bottle upright for several hours, then remove the cork carefully. (With very old bottles, whose corks crumble, red-hot port tongs are used to snap off a portion of the neck.) Place a cheesecloth-lined funnel into a decanter and hold a candle behind the bottle's neck as you pour the port through. Stop pouring when the candlelight reveals the first sediment.

Serving Port

SAVOR 2-FL-OZ (60-ml) portions in small wineglasses after dinner or at any other time. Chill white port in the refrigerator before serving; serve other types at room temperature.

PORT WINE COBBLER

2½ fl oz (75 ml) ruby port
1 tablespoon simple syrup (page 23)
1 orange wheel, for garnish

Pour the port and simple syrup into a wineglass filled with crushed ice. Stir briefly. Add the orange wheel.

PORT WINE FLIP

2½ fl oz (75 ml) ruby port
1½ tablespoons simple syrup (page 23)
1 egg (see caution, page 22)
Ground or freshly grated nutmeg, for garnish

Pour the port and simple syrup into a shaker two-thirds full of ice cubes. Add the egg. Shake very well. Strain into a chilled wineglass. Sprinkle with nutmeg.

PORT WINE SANGAREE

2 fl oz (60 ml) ruby port
1 tablespoon simple syrup (page 23)
Ground or freshly grated nutmeg, for garnish

Pour the port and simple syrup into a mixing glass two-thirds full of ice cubes. Stir well. Strain into a chilled wineglass. Sprinkle with nutmeg.

POUSSE-CAFÉ

A classic version of this classic layered drink.

1 ½ tablespoons grenadine

1 ½ tablespoons green crème de menthe

1 ½ tablespoons light rum

Pour the ingredients, in the order given, over the back of a spoon into a Pousse-Café glass, floating one on top of the other (see technique, page 60).

⃠ PRAIRIE OYSTER

Often used as a hangover cure, but usually to no avail, this drink mimics the flavor, if not the texture, of a raw oyster. Drink it in one go.

1 egg (see caution, page 22)

1 teaspoon fresh lemon juice

Dash of hot sauce

Salt and pepper

Break the egg into an Old-Fashioned glass. Add the lemon juice, hot sauce, and salt and pepper to taste.

PREAKNESS COCKTAIL

Named for the racetrack that hosts the Preakness Stakes—the second leg of the annual Triple Crown.

2 fl oz (60 ml) blended Canadian whisky

1 tablespoon sweet vermouth

2 dashes Bénédictine

Dash of Angostura bitters

1 lemon twist, for garnish

Pour the whisky, vermouth, Bénédictine, and bitters into a mixing glass two-thirds full of ice cubes. Stir well. Strain into a chilled cocktail glass. Add the garnish.

PRINCETON COCKTAIL

One of several drinks named for Ivy League colleges, this cocktail is a tart one, since it contains no sweetener to counteract the lime juice.

3 tablespoons gin
1 tablespoon dry vermouth
1 tablespoon fresh lime juice

Pour all of the ingredients into a shaker two-thirds full of ice cubes. Shake well. Strain into a chilled cocktail glass.

⃠ PUSSYFOOT

6 fl oz (180 ml) fresh orange juice
2 tablespoons fresh lime juice
2 tablespoons fresh lemon juice
1 egg yolk (see caution, page 22)

Pour all of the ingredients into a shaker two-thirds full of ice cubes. Shake very well. Strain into an ice-filled wineglass.

RED WINE—**See Wine, page 309.**

RED WINE COOLER

4 fl oz (120 ml) dry red wine
4 fl oz (120 ml) lemon-lime soda
1 lemon twist, for garnish

Pour the wine and soda into an ice-filled Collins glass. Stir briefly. Add the lemon twist.

Ramos Gin Fizz

ALTHOUGH THIS IS the most famous Fizz, it is actually not a true Fizz at all because it varies from the classic ingredients and construction method (see Gin Fizz, page 168). The secret of this drink, created in the late nineteenth century by New Orleans restaurateur Henry Ramos, lies in the shaking: a full 3 minutes is required. Though this may seem like a very long time, especially as the metal part of the shaker grows colder and colder during the process, it is necessary in order to achieve the silky mouthfeel that denotes the correct consistency. Some people add a couple of drops of vanilla extract to this drink. Feel free to experiment with that ingredient if you so desire.

- 2 fl oz (60 ml) gin
- 1 tablespoon fresh lime juice
- 1 tablespoon fresh lemon juice
- 1 tablespoon simple syrup (page 23)
- 4 drops orange flower water
- 1 egg white (see caution, page 22)
- 2 tablespoons light cream
- 2 fl oz (60 ml) club soda

Pour the gin, citrus juices, simple syrup, orange flower water, egg white, and cream into a shaker two-thirds full of crushed ice. Shake very well for at least 3 minutes. Strain into a chilled wineglass. Add the club soda. Stir briefly.

Remsen Cooler

COOLERS TYPICALLY consist of a base spirit or liqueur topped with any carbonated beverage, served in a Collins glass and garnished with a lemon twist. The Remsen Cooler is said to have been the first drink in the Cooler category, and some say it was originally made with Scotch instead of gin.

- 2½ fl oz (75 ml) gin
- 6 to 7 fl oz (180 to 210 ml) club soda
- 1 lemon twist, for garnish

Pour the gin and club soda into an ice-filled Collins glass. Stir briefly. Add the lemon twist.

SEE ALSO *Applejack Cooler, Apricot Cooler, Brandy Cooler, Irish Cooler, Pineapple-Cherry Cooler, Red Wine Cooler, Rum Cooler, Scotch Cooler, Tequila Cooler, Whisky Cooler.*

ROB ROY (DRY)

- 2½ fl oz (75 ml) Scotch
- 1½ teaspoons dry vermouth
- 1 lemon twist, for garnish

Pour the Scotch and vermouth into a mixing glass two-thirds full of ice cubes. Stir well. Strain into a chilled cocktail glass. Garnish with the lemon twist.

Rob Roy

IT COULD BE SAID that the Rob Roy (named for a Scottish outlaw of the eighteenth century) is a variation on the Manhattan. However, its absence of bitters and substitution of Scotch for rye or bourbon make it a much different drink.

The ratio of Scotch to sweet vermouth in this recipe works well, but you can use as little as 1 ½ teaspoons of vermouth.

2 ½ fl oz (75 ml) Scotch
1 tablespoon sweet vermouth
1 maraschino cherry, for garnish

Pour the Scotch and vermouth into a mixing glass two-thirds full of ice cubes. Stir well. Strain into a chilled cocktail glass. Add the cherry.

SEE ALSO *Affinity Cocktail, Beadlestone Cocktail, Bobby Burns, Highland Fling, Rob Roy (Dry), Rob Roy (Perfect).*

ROB ROY (PERFECT)

2 ½ fl oz (75 ml) Scotch
1 ½ teaspoons sweet vermouth
1 ½ teaspoons dry vermouth
1 lemon twist, for garnish

Pour the Scotch and both vermouths into a mixing glass two-thirds full of ice cubes. Stir well. Strain into a chilled cocktail glass. Add the lemon twist.

ROYAL CHAMPAGNE COCKTAIL

1 tablespoon brandy
1 tablespoon Grand Marnier
5 fl oz (150 ml) Champagne or sparkling wine
1 orange twist, for garnish

Pour the brandy and Grand Marnier into a Champagne flute. Carefully add the Champagne. Garnish with the orange twist.

ROYAL MIMOSA

1½ teaspoons brandy
1½ teaspoons Grand Marnier
2 tablespoons fresh orange juice
4 fl oz (120 ml) Champagne or sparkling wine
1 orange wheel, for garnish

Pour the brandy, Grand Marnier, orange juice, and Champagne into a Champagne flute. Stir briefly. Add the orange wheel.

RUM—See page 240.

RUM BUCK

You can replace the ginger ale with spicier ginger beer, although the result will not be a true Buck.

1 lemon wedge
2 fl oz (60 ml) light rum
5 fl oz (150 ml) ginger ale

Squeeze the lemon wedge into a highball glass and drop it into the glass. Fill the glass with ice cubes. Add the rum and ginger ale. Stir briefly.

RUM COBBLER

2½ fl oz (75 ml) dark rum
1 tablespoon simple syrup (page 23)
1 pineapple spear, for garnish

Pour the rum and simple syrup into a wineglass filled with crushed ice. Stir briefly. Add the pineapple spear.

RUM COLLINS

2 fl oz (60 ml) dark rum
1 tablespoon fresh lemon juice
1 tablespoon simple syrup (page 23)
5 to 6 fl oz (150 to 180 ml) club soda
1 lemon wedge, for garnish

Pour the rum, lemon juice, and simple syrup into a shaker two-thirds full of ice cubes. Shake well. Strain into an ice-filled Collins glass. Add the club soda. Stir briefly. Add the lemon wedge.

RUM COOLER

2½ fl oz (75 ml) dark rum
6 to 7 fl oz (180 to 210 ml) ginger ale
1 lemon twist, for garnish

Pour the rum and ginger ale into an ice-filled Collins glass. Stir briefly. Garnish with the lemon twist.

Rum

Usually 40–50% alcohol by volume

Rum is a distilled spirit made from molasses or sugarcane juice that is fermented before distillation. Although molasses is a less expensive base ingredient than sugarcane juice, its use does not necessarily denote an inferior product. Though most rums come from the Caribbean, almost every country that cultivates sugar also produces a rum. There is a popular misconception that rums from certain countries are better than those from others. Actually, most countries produce both good and bad rums.

The Barcardi logo features a bat, a symbol of good fortune in old Cuba.

HOW RUM IS MADE

Rum can be made in old-fashioned pot stills, or in the more modern, more economical continuous stills; either method can produce both great rums and poor ones. Most rums are aged in oak casks for at least a year. It can be tempting to think that darker rums are older, but many rums have had caramel coloring added, so a deeper hue isn't always a sign of age.

Brugal, from the Dominican Republic, is one of many fine Caribbean rums.

PUERTO RICO

Puerto Rico has produced rum for more than 400 years, and three-quarters of the rum consumed in the United States is made there. All rums from Puerto Rico are made at one of three plants: Bacardi, Barrilito, and Serrallés. Because all Puerto Rican rums must be aged for at least one year before bottling and therefore gain color from the wood, Puerto Rican white rum is filtered before bottling to remove all traces of color.

BACARDI Originally based in Cuba, Puerto Rico's leading producer issues many bottlings of its signature rum. White Bacardi is well liked in cocktails and mixed drinks, especially the Bacardi Cocktail (page 91). The distillery also makes some fine aged rums, suitable for sipping neat, as well as a 151-proof bottling. Rum such as the latter is commonly used as a "floater" on flamed drinks (see Flaming, page 63).

BARRILITO The smallest Puerto Rican producer, Barrilito issues just two bottlings: a two-star rum, aged for two to three years, and a three-star rum that spends six to ten

MOST POPULAR RUM DRINKS

(according to U.S. bartenders)

1. Daiquiri, page 146
2. Piña Colada, page 225
3. Cuba Libre, page 145
4. Bay Breeze, page 93
5. Caipirinha, page 130

FLAVORED AND SPICED RUMS

Rums have recently become available in a range of flavors—coconut, pineapple, citrus, and spiced types among them. These products offer excellent opportunities for experimentation. For example, coconut-flavored rum in a Daiquiri produces a very different drink than white rum would.

HAITIAN RUM

Made in small pot stills, Haiti's Rhum Barbancourt is aged for long periods in oak casks.

years in the wood. Barrilito rum, before entering the casks, is infused with a host of secret ingredients. This, combined with its years in oak, is what makes Barrilito rum so intricate in flavor.

SERRALLÉS This producer's Don Q rums, named for Don Quixote, are very popular with natives of Puerto Rico. They are well-made products, ideal for use in cocktails and mixed drinks.

BARBADOS

The Mount Gay distillery on the island of Barbados issues many bottlings, all of high quality. Most of them are versatile enough for either sipping or mixing.

BRAZIL

One style of rum that has become popular of late, especially in drinks such as the Caipirinha (page 130), is cachaça. This Brazilian rum, usually made in pot stills, is not aged and can be very spicy.

DOMINICAN REPUBLIC

Brugal rums from this country are of very high quality, especially Brugal Añejo, best served neat.

GUADELOUPE

Kaniche Guadeloupe, a ten-year-old rum, is, like Kaniche Martinique, a high-quality sipping rum that performs admirably in mixed drinks as well.

HAITI

The best-known Haitian rum is Rhum Barbancourt, best reserved for sipping neat.

JAMAICA

Myers's Original dark rum is probably the more popular for cocktail-making, but the Jamaican distillery also produces a spicy white rum that is catching on. Appleton Estate's "gold" bottlings are of high quality and can be used behind the bar. Appleton also produces C.J. Wray, a dry white rum, and Wray & Nephew White Overproof rum, which at 126 proof should be well diluted before consumption.

MARTINIQUE

Kaniche Martinique is a high-quality rum distilled in pot stills and aged in French oak barrels for 12 years. It is of sipping quality, but can also be used in the construction of cocktails and mixed drinks.

VENEZUELA

Two very good labels are made in Venezuela: Pampero, usually considered a sipping rum; and Ocumare, available in white and añejo (aged) bottlings. Both can be used for mixing, though the añejo bottling is worthy of sipping neat.

VENEZUELAN RUM

Pampero's Ron Añejo Aniversario, from Venezuela, is esteemed as a fine sipping rum. It is aged in casks for six to eight years.

Serving Rum

HIGH-QUALITY SIPPING RUMS should be served at room temperature in either brandy snifters or sherry copita glasses (page 41). Pour 1½-fl-oz (45-ml) portions. Rum makes a good accompaniment to a fine cigar, and some Caribbean residents are known to dip the cigar's end into their rum.

RUM CRUSTA

Granulated sugar, to coat rim of glass
Lemon peel spiral (see technique, page 53)
2 fl oz (60 ml) dark rum
1 tablespoon maraschino liqueur
1 tablespoon fresh lemon juice

Coat the rim of a Sour glass with sugar (see technique, page 49). Place the lemon peel spiral into the glass so that it uncoils to almost fill the interior. Pour the rum, maraschino liqueur, and lemon juice into a shaker two-thirds full of crushed ice. Shake well. Strain into the glass.

RUM DAISY

2½ fl oz (75 ml) light rum
2 tablespoons fresh lemon juice
1 tablespoon grenadine
1 lemon twist, for garnish

Pour the rum, lemon juice, and grenadine into a shaker two-thirds full of crushed ice. Shake well. Strain into a highball glass filled with crushed ice. Add the garnish.

RUM FIX

2½ fl oz (75 ml) light rum
2 tablespoons fresh lemon juice
1 tablespoon pineapple juice
1 pineapple spear, for garnish

Pour the rum, lemon juice, and pineapple juice into a shaker two-thirds full of crushed ice. Shake well. Strain into a highball glass filled with crushed ice. Garnish with the pineapple spear.

RUM FIZZ

Feel free to replace the lime juice in this recipe with lemon juice.

2 fl oz (60 ml) dark rum
2 tablespoons fresh lime juice
1 tablespoon simple syrup (page 23)
5 to 6 fl oz (150 to 180 ml) club soda
1 lime wedge, for garnish

Pour the rum, lime juice, and simple syrup into a shaker two-thirds full of ice cubes. Shake well. Strain into a chilled wineglass. Add the club soda. Stir briefly. Add the lime wedge.

RUM FLIP

2½ fl oz (75 ml) dark rum
1½ tablespoons simple syrup (page 23)
1 egg (see caution, page 22)
Ground or freshly grated nutmeg, for garnish

Pour the rum and simple syrup into a shaker two-thirds full of ice cubes. Add the egg. Shake very well. Strain into a chilled wineglass. Sprinkle with nutmeg.

RUM RICKEY

2½ fl oz (75 ml) light rum
2 tablespoons fresh lime juice
5 to 6 fl oz (150 to 180 ml) club soda
1 lime wedge, for garnish

Pour the rum and lime juice into an ice-filled highball glass. Add the club soda. Stir briefly. Garnish with the lime wedge.

RUM SANGAREE

Do not be tempted to use light rum in this drink. The ruby port will overpower it.

2 fl oz (60 ml) dark rum
1 tablespoon ruby port
1 tablespoon triple sec
Ground or freshly grated nutmeg, for garnish

Pour the rum, port, and triple sec into a mixing glass two-thirds full of ice cubes. Stir well. Strain into a wineglass filled with crushed ice. Sprinkle with nutmeg.

RUM SLING

Lime juice may be substituted for the lemon juice.

2½ fl oz (75 ml) light rum
1 tablespoon simple syrup (page 23)
1 tablespoon fresh lemon juice
5 to 6 fl oz (150 to 180 ml) club soda
1 lemon wedge, for garnish

Pour the rum, simple syrup, and lemon juice into a shaker two-thirds full of ice cubes. Shake well. Strain the drink into an ice-filled Collins glass. Add the club soda. Stir briefly. Add the lemon wedge.

RUM SMASH

6 fresh mint leaves
1½ tablespoons simple syrup (page 23)
2½ fl oz (75 ml) dark rum
1 mint sprig, for garnish

Place the mint leaves in the bottom of an Old-Fashioned glass. Add the simple syrup and muddle well (see technique, page 64). Fill the glass with crushed ice. Add the rum. Stir briefly. Garnish with the mint sprig.

RUM SOUR

2 fl oz (60 ml) light rum
1 ½ tablespoons fresh lemon juice
1 tablespoon simple syrup (page 23)
1 orange wheel, for garnish
1 maraschino cherry, for garnish

Pour the rum, lemon juice, and simple syrup into a shaker two-thirds full of ice cubes. Shake well. Strain the drink into a chilled Sour glass. Add the garnishes.

Rum Swizzle

THE HALLMARK OF ALL Swizzles is the swizzle stick. It's for decoration only, since overstirring makes the drink go flat.

2 fl oz (60 ml) dark rum
1 tablespoon fresh lemon juice
1 tablespoon triple sec
5 to 6 fl oz (150 to 180 ml) ginger ale
1 lemon wheel, for garnish

Pour the rum, lemon juice, and triple sec into a shaker two-thirds full of ice cubes. Shake well. Strain the mixture into an ice-filled Collins glass. Add the ginger ale. Stir briefly. Add the garnish and a swizzle stick.

SEE ALSO *Applejack Swizzle, Bourbon Swizzle, Brandy Swizzle, Gin Swizzle, Irish Swizzle, Scotch Swizzle, Whisky Swizzle.*

RUSTY NAIL

This drink has been around since the 1960s. For a drier version, try using only 1 ½ teaspoons of Drambuie.

2 fl oz (60 ml) Scotch
1 tablespoon Drambuie
1 lemon twist, for garnish

Pour the Scotch and Drambuie into an ice-filled Old-Fashioned glass. Stir briefly. Add the lemon twist.

RYE WHISKEY—See Whisk(e)y, page 302.

SALTY DOG

This is essentially a Greyhound (page 173) in a salt-rimmed glass. Strange as it sounds, the salt works very well with the grapefruit juice.

Salt, to coat rim of glass
2½ fl oz (75 ml) vodka
4 fl oz (120 ml) fresh grapefruit juice

Coat the rim of a highball glass with salt (see technique, page 49) and fill the glass with ice. Pour in the vodka and grapefruit juice. Stir briefly.

ART DECO SHAKERS

Trio of silver-plated shakers from the 1930s embodies the elegant Art Deco style.

SANGRIA

For a less potent Sangria, add more orange and cranberry juice.

Makes 6 to 8 6-fl-oz (180-ml) servings.

1 750-ml bottle dry red wine
4 fl oz (120 ml) brandy
4 fl oz (120 ml) triple sec
4 fl oz (120 ml) simple syrup (page 23)
4 fl oz (120 ml) fresh orange juice
4 fl oz (120 ml) cranberry juice cocktail
Orange wheels, for garnish
Lemon wheels, for garnish

Pour all of the liquids into a large pan or bowl made of stainless steel or other nonreactive material. Stir well. Cover and refrigerate until chilled, at least 4 hours. Pour the punch into a large pitcher. Add the garnishes and stir to mix in. Serve in wineglasses.

SAZERAC—**See page 250.**

SCORPION

The Scorpion, probably the drink of choice in most Polynesian restaurants, enjoyed its heyday in the 1950s and 1960s.

2 fl oz (60 ml) dark rum
1 tablespoon brandy
1 tablespoon dry vermouth
2 tablespoons fresh orange juice
2 tablespoons fresh lemon juice
1 teaspoon orgeat syrup
1 mint sprig, for garnish

Pour all of the liquids into a shaker two-thirds full of ice cubes. Shake well. Strain into a large, ice-filled wineglass. Garnish with the mint sprig.

Sazerac

THIS DRINK REPORTEDLY originated in nineteenth-century New Orleans. The first versions were made with brandy rather than bourbon. Try it as an interesting variation.

½ teaspoon absinthe substitute (such as Pernod or Ricard)
2 fl oz (60 ml) bourbon
1 tablespoon simple syrup (page 23)
2 dashes Peychaud bitters
1 lemon twist, for garnish

Coat the interior of an Old-Fashioned glass with the absinthe substitute (see technique, page 50). Fill the glass with crushed ice. Pour the bourbon, simple syrup, and bitters into a mixing glass two-thirds full of ice cubes. Stir well. Strain into the glass. Add the garnish.

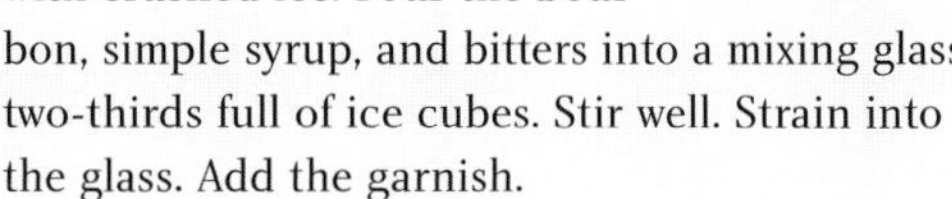

SCOTCH—See Whisk(e)y, page 299.

SCOTCH AND SODA

2½ fl oz (75 ml) Scotch
5 fl oz (150 ml) club soda

Pour the Scotch and club soda into an ice-filled highball glass. Stir briefly.

SCOTCH BUCK

1 lemon wedge
2 fl oz (60 ml) Scotch
5 fl oz (150 ml) ginger ale

Squeeze the lemon wedge into a highball glass and drop it into the glass. Fill the glass with ice cubes. Add the Scotch and ginger ale. Stir briefly.

SCOTCH COBBLER

2½ fl oz (75 ml) Scotch
1 tablespoon simple syrup (page 23)
1 lemon twist, for garnish

Pour the Scotch and simple syrup into a wineglass filled with crushed ice. Stir briefly. Add the lemon twist.

SCOTCH COLLINS—See Jock Collins, page 186.

SCOTCH COOLER

If you like, replace the ginger ale with spicier ginger beer or milder lemon-lime soda.

2½ fl oz (75 ml) Scotch
6 to 7 fl oz (180 to 210 ml) ginger ale
1 lemon twist, for garnish

Pour the Scotch and ginger ale into an ice-filled Collins glass. Stir briefly. Add the lemon twist.

SCOTCH CRUSTA

Granulated sugar, to coat rim of glass
Lemon peel spiral (see technique, page 53)
2 fl oz (60 ml) Scotch
1 tablespoon maraschino liqueur
1 tablespoon fresh lemon juice

Coat the rim of a Sour glass with sugar (see technique, page 49). Place the lemon peel spiral inside the glass so that it uncoils to almost fill the interior. Pour the Scotch, maraschino liqueur, and lemon juice into a shaker two-thirds full of crushed ice. Shake well. Strain into the glass.

SCOTCH DAISY

2½ fl oz (75 ml) Scotch
2 tablespoons fresh lemon juice
1 tablespoon grenadine
1 lemon twist, for garnish

Pour the Scotch, lemon juice, and grenadine into a shaker two-thirds full of crushed ice. Shake well. Strain into a highball glass filled with crushed ice. Garnish with the lemon twist.

SCOTCH FIX

2½ fl oz (75 ml) Scotch
2 tablespoons fresh lemon juice
1 tablespoon pineapple juice
1 lemon twist, for garnish

Pour the Scotch, lemon juice, and pineapple juice into a shaker two-thirds full of crushed ice. Shake well. Strain into a highball glass filled with crushed ice. Add the lemon twist.

SCOTCH FIZZ

2 fl oz (60 ml) Scotch
2 tablespoons fresh lemon juice
1 tablespoon simple syrup (page 23)
5 to 6 fl oz (150 to 180 ml) club soda
1 lemon twist, for garnish

Pour the Scotch, lemon juice, and simple syrup into a shaker two-thirds full of ice cubes. Shake well. Strain into a chilled wineglass. Add the club soda. Stir briefly. Garnish with the lemon twist.

SCOTCH FLIP

2½ fl oz (75 ml) Scotch
1½ tablespoons simple syrup (page 23)
1 egg (see caution, page 22)
Ground or freshly grated nutmeg, for garnish

Pour the Scotch and simple syrup into a shaker two-thirds full of ice cubes. Add the egg. Shake very well. Strain into a chilled wineglass. Sprinkle with nutmeg.

SCOTCH MIST

Scotch Mist was originally made without the Drambuie, but this version is now far more popular.

2 fl oz (60 ml) Scotch
1 tablespoon Drambuie

Fill a Sour glass with crushed ice. Add the Scotch and Drambuie.

SCOTCH OLD-FASHIONED

3 dashes Angostura bitters
1 orange slice
1 lemon wedge
1 maraschino cherry
1 sugar cube
2½ fl oz (75 ml) Scotch

In a double Old-Fashioned glass, muddle the bitters, orange slice, lemon wedge, and maraschino cherry into the sugar cube (see technique, page 64). Fill the glass with ice cubes. Add the Scotch. Stir well.

SCOTCH SANGAREE

The combination of Scotch, port, and Drambuie produces a very complex drink.

2 fl oz (60 ml) Scotch
1 tablespoon ruby port
1 tablespoon Drambuie
Ground or freshly grated nutmeg, for garnish

Pour the Scotch, port, and Drambuie into a mixing glass two-thirds full of ice cubes. Stir well. Strain into a chilled small wineglass. Sprinkle with nutmeg.

PENGUIN SHAKER

The beak of this silver-plated whimsy from the 1930s opens automatically as the shaker tips to pour.

SCOTCH SLING

The apricot brandy in this Sling adds a sweet fruitiness that is very pleasing.

2½ fl oz (75 ml) Scotch
1 tablespoon apricot brandy
1 tablespoon fresh lemon juice
5 to 6 fl oz club soda
1 lemon wedge, for garnish

Pour the Scotch, apricot brandy, and lemon juice into a shaker two-thirds full of ice cubes. Shake well. Strain the drink into an ice-filled Collins glass. Add the club soda. Stir briefly. Add the lemon wedge.

SCOTCH SMASH

6 fresh mint leaves
1½ tablespoons simple syrup (page 23)
2½ fl oz (75 ml) Scotch
1 mint sprig, for garnish

Place the mint leaves in the bottom of an Old-Fashioned glass. Add the simple syrup and muddle well (see technique, page 64). Fill the glass with crushed ice. Add the Scotch. Stir briefly. Add the mint sprig.

SCOTCH SOUR

2 fl oz (60 ml) Scotch
1½ tablespoons fresh lemon juice
1 tablespoon simple syrup (page 23)
1 orange wheel, for garnish
1 maraschino cherry, for garnish

Pour the Scotch, lemon juice, and simple syrup into a shaker two-thirds full of ice cubes. Shake well. Strain the drink into a chilled Sour glass. Add the garnishes.

SCOTCH SWIZZLE

You can substitute lime juice for the lemon juice.

2 fl oz (60 ml) Scotch
1 tablespoon fresh lemon juice
1 tablespoon triple sec
5 to 6 fl oz (150 to 180 ml) ginger ale
1 lemon wheel, for garnish

Pour the Scotch, lemon juice, and triple sec into a shaker two-thirds full of ice cubes. Shake well. Strain the mixture into an ice-filled Collins glass. Add the ginger ale. Stir briefly. Add the lemon wheel and a swizzle stick.

SCREWDRIVER

This drink supposedly got its name when a group of workmen used a screwdriver to stir their vodka-and-orange-juice highballs.

2½ fl oz (75 ml) vodka
4 fl oz (120 ml) fresh orange juice

Pour the vodka and orange juice into an ice-filled highball glass. Stir briefly.

SEA BREEZE

Created in the 1980s, the Sea Breeze is very refreshing in hot weather. For a variation, try the Bay Breeze, page 93.

2 fl oz (60 ml) vodka
2 fl oz (60 ml) fresh grapefruit juice
3 tablespoons cranberry juice cocktail
1 lime wedge, for garnish

Pour the vodka and both juices into an ice-filled highball glass. Stir briefly. Add the lime wedge.

SEVEN AND SEVEN

2½ fl oz (75 ml) Seagram's 7 Crown whisky
4 fl oz (120 ml) 7-Up soda
1 lemon twist, for garnish

Pour the whiskey and 7-Up into an ice-filled highball glass. Stir briefly. Add the lemon twist.

SHANDYGAFF

1 cup (8 fl oz/250 ml) lemon-lime soda
1 cup (8 fl oz/250 ml) amber ale

Carefully pour the lemon-lime soda and the ale into a 16-fl-oz (500-ml) beer glass.

SHERRY—See page 258.

SHERRY FLIP

2½ fl oz (75 ml) dry sherry
1½ tablespoons simple syrup (page 23)
1 egg (see caution, page 22)
Ground or freshly grated nutmeg, for garnish

Pour the sherry and simple syrup into a shaker two-thirds full of ice cubes. Add the egg. Shake very well. Strain into a chilled wineglass. Sprinkle with nutmeg.

SHERRY SANGAREE

2 fl oz (60 ml) dry sherry
1 tablespoon simple syrup (page 23)
Ground or freshly grated nutmeg, for garnish

Pour the sherry and simple syrup into a mixing glass two-thirds full of ice cubes. Stir well. Strain into a chilled small wineglass. Sprinkle with nutmeg.

Sherry

15–20% alcohol by volume

A Spanish wine fortified with grape spirit, sherry is produced in a demarcated region of southern Andalucía that encompasses the towns of Sanlúcar de Barrameda, Puerto de Santa María, and Jerez de la Frontera. The word sherry *is probably a corruption of* Jerez *(pronounced HAIR-eth), the center of the sherry trade. Although many other countries produce sherry styles, Spanish sherry is the benchmark.*

The sherry region of Spain

HOW SHERRY IS MADE

Once its fermentation is complete, the wine that will become sherry is pumped into casks that are filled only partway. The hope is that a white film, known as *flor* ("flower"), will form on its surface.

The flor, an airborne yeast, can occur as a thick layer on top of the sherry, in which case the sherry will be of the Fino style. A fino sherry with a thinner layer of flor may develop into an amontillado with age. If no film appears, an Oloroso results. It is not known why some wines attract quantities of flor and some none at all, but the flor is closely monitored over the next 12 to 24 months. During this time, the wines are fortified with grape spirit according to their style: Finos are fortified to a slightly lower alcohol level than those that will become Olorosos. Finally, the wine is transferred to smaller casks, known as *butts*, and taken to warehouses to undergo the solera system of aging.

This system is peculiar to sherries, Spanish brandies (page 117), and Madeira (page 202). It involves arranging the barrels in tiers, sometimes ten butts high, each tier containing a younger sherry than the one below. When the bottom tier is ready for bottling, no more than half of the wine is removed. That tier is then replenished with wine from the tier above, and the process is repeated for each tier. The half-empty top tier of barrels is filled with younger sherries that are deemed to refresh the older ones. Before bottling, the alcohol level is adjusted and, for some styles, sweetening wine is added.

FINO SHERRY

A layer of yeast called flor *transforms young sherry into the Fino style.*

MANZANILLA SHERRY

A pleasant saltiness is the hallmark of this Fino style.

STYLES OF SHERRY

Sherries are made in a variety of styles, most of them based on the Palomino grape.

FINO Pale, dry, and medium-bodied, Fino sherries are often served as an aperitif.

MANZANILLA A light-bodied subcategory of the Finos, Manzanilla sherries are aged in the coastal town of Sanlúcar de Barrameda, where they attain a pleasant saltiness not typical of regular Finos.

AMONTILLADO Another Fino type, Amontillados are darker in color and have a pleasant, crisp nuttiness. Inexpensive blends are usually slightly sweetened.

OLOROSO Deep golden in color, Olorosos are mostly nutty, full-bodied, and sweet. There is also a dry style.

CREAM SHERRY This term refers to a style of Oloroso sherry that is sweet and has a somewhat creamy texture.

PEDRO XIMÉNEZ The sweetest of all sherries, these are made solely from the Pedro Ximénez grape.

Serving Sherry

Sherries should be served in sherry copita glasses (page 41). Pour 2 fl oz (60 ml) per serving. Finos and Manzanillas are classic accompaniments to Spanish tapas; serve them chilled, from the refrigerator or on the rocks. Amontillado sherries are also served chilled, usually between meals or with cheeses. Sweeter Oloroso, Cream, and Pedro Ximénez sherries are best savored at room temperature, with dessert or with blue or strong cheeses.

SHIRLEY TEMPLE—See page 263.

Sidecar

A BARTENDER AT HARRY'S New York Bar in Paris is said to have created this drink during World War I. The customer for whom it was invented reportedly drove into the bar on his motorbike, and the bartender gave him a Sidecar to complement it.

Don't use an inexpensive triple sec to make the Sidecar—most of these bottlings are far too sweet. Some recipes call specifically for Cointreau; this brand-name triple sec is very dry and very complex. You should also stay away from the prepared sour mixes some bartenders use to make mixed drinks such as the Sidecar—fresh lemon juice makes a huge difference in this recipe.

Granulated sugar, to coat rim of glass
2½ fl oz (75 ml) brandy
1 tablespoon triple sec
1 tablespoon fresh lemon juice

Coat the rim of a cocktail glass with sugar (see technique, page 49) and chill it. Pour the remaining ingredients into a shaker two-thirds full of ice cubes. Shake well. Strain into the glass.

SEE ALSO *Between the Sheets, Classic Cocktail, Olympic Cocktail.*

Singapore Sling

THE SINGAPORE SLING was created at Singapore's famous colonial-era Raffles Hotel and is the most popular drink in the Sling category. Like other Slings, it is made of a base spirit, citrus juice, simple syrup or a liqueur, and club soda, served over ice in a Collins glass and typically garnished with fresh fruit.

Many people use grenadine instead of the cherry brandy in this recipe, but it results in an inferior imitation of the classic drink. If you are not enamored of Bénédictine, make the Singapore Sling without it, although the resultant drink will not be as complex. You can also substitute B&B (page 196) if you desire.

2 fl oz (60 ml) gin
1 tablespoon Bénédictine
1 tablespoon cherry brandy
2 tablespoons fresh lemon juice
1 tablespoon simple syrup (page 23)
2 to 3 fl oz (60 to 90 ml) club soda
1 lemon twist, for garnish

Pour all of the liquids except the club soda into a shaker two-thirds full of ice cubes. Shake well. Strain into an ice-filled Collins glass. Pour in the club soda. Garnish with the lemon twist.

SEE ALSO *Applejack Sling, Bourbon Sling, Brandy Sling, Gin Sling, Irish Sling, Rum Sling, Scotch Sling, Whisky Sling.*

⃠ SHIRLEY TEMPLE

Named for the child star of the 1930s and 1940s, this is an ever-popular drink for the young at heart. Ironically, the grown-up Shirley Temple once admitted to disliking this drink.

2 tablespoons fresh orange juice
1 tablespoon fresh lemon juice
1 teaspoon fresh lime juice
6 fl oz (180 ml) lemon-lime soda
Dash of grenadine
1 maraschino cherry, for garnish

Pour the citrus juices into a shaker two-thirds full of ice cubes. Shake well. Strain into an ice-filled Collins glass. Add the lemon-lime soda and the grenadine. Stir briefly. Garnish with the cherry.

Sloe Gin

15–30% alcohol by volume

ALTHOUGH IT USED TO BE common to make sloe gin by infusing sloe berries (the fruit of the blackthorn, a relative of the plum) into gin, most bottlings of this red-hued liqueur now contain no gin at all—they are merely sloe-flavored neutral spirits.

Not many cocktails or mixed drinks call for sloe gin, but the Sloe Gin Fizz (page 264) is a popular potion that is truly refreshing.

SLOE GIN FIZZ

2 fl oz (60 ml) sloe gin
2 tablespoons fresh lemon juice
1 tablespoon simple syrup (page 23)
5 to 6 fl oz (150 to 180 ml) club soda
1 orange wheel, for garnish

Pour the sloe gin, lemon juice, and simple syrup into a shaker two-thirds full of ice cubes. Shake well. Strain into a chilled wineglass. Add the club soda. Stir briefly. Add the orange wheel.

SOMBRERO

2 fl oz (60 ml) coffee liqueur (such as Kahlúa)
3 tablespoons light cream

Pour both ingredients into a shaker two-thirds full of ice cubes. Shake well. Strain into an ice-filled Old-Fashioned glass.

SOUL KISS COCKTAIL

This complex drink can be made with bourbon instead of Canadian whisky if desired.

2 fl oz (60 ml) blended Canadian whisky
1 ½ teaspoons dry vermouth
1 ½ teaspoons Dubonnet Rouge
1 tablespoon fresh orange juice

Pour all of the ingredients into a shaker two-thirds full of ice cubes. Shake well. Strain into a chilled cocktail glass.

SOUTHERN COMFORT MANHATTAN

An extremely sweet variation on the Manhattan that can be made a little drier with less Southern Comfort.

2½ fl oz (75 ml) Southern Comfort
1 tablespoon sweet vermouth
2 dashes Angostura bitters
1 maraschino cherry, for garnish

Pour the Southern Comfort, vermouth, and bitters into a mixing glass two-thirds full of ice cubes. Stir well. Strain into a chilled cocktail glass. Garnish with the cherry.

SOUTHERN COMFORT SOUR

The lemon juice in this drink provides a good counterpoint to the sweetness of the Southern Comfort.

2 fl oz (60 ml) Southern Comfort
1½ tablespoons fresh lemon juice
1 orange wheel, for garnish
1 maraschino cherry, for garnish

Pour the Southern Comfort and lemon juice into a shaker two-thirds full of ice cubes. Shake well. Strain the drink into a chilled Sour glass. Add the garnishes.

SOUTHSIDE COCKTAIL

2½ fl oz (75 ml) bourbon
1 tablespoon sweet vermouth
1 teaspoon Bénédictine
1 teaspoon brandy

Pour all of the ingredients into a shaker two-thirds full of ice cubes. Shake well. Strain into a chilled cocktail glass.

⦸ SPICED CIDER

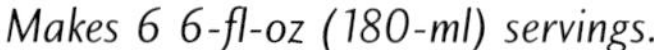

Makes 6 6-fl-oz (180-ml) servings.

1 quart (32 fl oz/1 l) unsweetened apple cider
4 fl oz (120 ml) water
2 whole cloves
1 cinnamon stick (about 3 inches/7.5 cm long)
½ teaspoon freshly grated or ground nutmeg
1 large block of ice, for serving
6 apple slices, for garnish

Pour the apple cider and water into a large pot made of stainless steel or other nonreactive material; set over high heat. Add the cloves, cinnamon, and nutmeg and bring the mixture to a boil. Reduce the heat to low, cover, and simmer for 20 minutes.

Strain the mixture through a double layer of dampened cheesecloth. Set aside to cool to room temperature, about 1½ hours. Cover and refrigerate for at least 2 hours and up to 5 days.

Put the block of ice in a punch bowl. Add the chilled punch. Add the garnish. Serve in punch cups, adding an apple slice to each cup.

⦸ SPICED CRANBERRY-ORANGE CUP

Makes 10 6-fl-oz (180-ml) servings.

1 quart (32 fl oz/1 l) fresh orange juice
1 quart (32 fl oz/1 l) cranberry juice cocktail
5 whole cloves
2 cinnamon sticks (each about 3 inches/7.5 cm long)
1 teaspoon freshly grated or ground nutmeg
1 large block of ice, for serving
10 orange wheels, for garnish

Pour the orange juice and cranberry juice cocktail into a large pot made of stainless steel or other nonreactive material; set over high heat. Add the cloves, cinnamon sticks, and nutmeg and bring the mixture to a boil. Reduce the heat to low, cover the pot, and simmer for 20 minutes.

Strain the mixture through a double layer of dampened cheesecloth. Set aside to cool to room temperature, about 1½ hours. Cover and refrigerate for at least 2 hours and up to 5 days.

Put the block of ice in a punch bowl. Add the chilled punch. Add the orange wheels. Serve in punch cups.

SPICED HARD CIDER PUNCH

You can omit the applejack by doubling the amount of brandy.

Makes 8 6-fl-oz (180-ml) servings.

5 whole cloves
2 cinnamon sticks (each about 3 inches/7.5 cm long)
1 teaspoon freshly grated or ground nutmeg
1 cup (8 fl oz/250 ml) hot water
1 quart (32 fl oz/1 l) hard cider
4 fl oz (120 ml) applejack
4 fl oz (120 ml) brandy
1 large block of ice, for serving
8 apple slices, for garnish

Place the cloves, cinnamon sticks, nutmeg, and hot water in a large pot made of stainless steel or other nonreactive material Set over high heat and bring the mixture to a boil. Reduce the heat to low, cover the pot, and simmer for 20 minutes.

Strain the mixture through a double layer of dampened cheesecloth. Set aside to cool to room temperature, about 1½ hours.

Pour in the cider, applejack, and brandy and stir well. Cover and refrigerate for at least 4 hours and up to 5 days.

Put the block of ice in a punch bowl. Add the chilled punch. Add the apple slices. Serve in punch cups.

SPICED RUM AND CHOCOLATE MARTINI

The unusual combination of rich, spiced rum and chocolate liqueur comes together wonderfully as a sophisticated after-dinner cocktail.

2 fl oz (60 ml) spiced rum (such as Captain Morgan)
1 tablespoon chocolate liqueur (such as Godiva)
1 maraschino cherry, for garnish

Pour the rum and chocolate liqueur into a mixing glass two-thirds full of ice cubes. Stir well. Strain into a chilled cocktail glass. Garnish with the cherry.

SPICED RUM PIÑA COLADA

2 fl oz (60 ml) spiced rum (such as Captain Morgan)
6 fl oz (180 ml) pineapple juice
3 tablespoons canned coconut cream (such as Coco López)
1 pineapple spear, for garnish

Pour the rum, pineapple juice, and coconut cream into a shaker two-thirds full of ice cubes. Shake well. Strain into an ice-filled wineglass. Add the pineapple spear.

⃠ SPICED TEA PUNCH

The fresh ginger in this recipe adds extra spiciness to a soothing and refreshing punch.

Makes 6 6-fl-oz (180-ml) servings.

½ teaspoon grated fresh ginger
½ teaspoon ground allspice
6 fl oz (180 ml) fresh orange juice
1 cup (8 fl oz/250 ml) hot water
3 cups (24 fl oz/750 ml) brewed strong, hot tea

Combine the ginger, allspice, orange juice, and hot water in a large pot made of stainless steel or other nonreactive material. Set over high heat and bring the mixture to a boil. Reduce the heat to low, cover, and simmer for 10 minutes.

Strain the mixture through a double layer of dampened cheesecloth. Divide the hot tea among 6 teacups. Add 2 tablespoons of the spiced orange juice to each.

SPIKED TEA PUNCH

Makes 8 6-fl-oz (180-ml) servings.

5 whole cloves
2 cinnamon sticks (each about 3 inches/7.5 cm long), broken
1 teaspoon ground or freshly grated nutmeg
1 teaspoon grated fresh ginger
1 cup (8 fl oz/250 ml) hot water
1 quart (32 fl oz/1 l) strong tea, chilled
4 fl oz (120 ml) Drambuie
4 fl oz (120 ml) Scotch
1 large block of ice, for serving

Combine the cloves, cinnamon sticks, nutmeg, ginger, and hot water in a large pot made of stainless steel or other nonreactive material. Set over high heat and bring the mixture to a boil. Reduce the heat to low, cover, and simmer for 20 minutes.

Strain the mixture through a double layer of dampened cheesecloth. Set aside to cool to room temperature, about 1½ hours.

Pour in the tea, Drambuie, and Scotch and stir well. Cover and refrigerate for a minimum of 4 hours and a maximum of 5 days.

Put the block of ice in a punch bowl. Add the chilled punch.

Stinger

THE STINGER IS A CLASSIC drink of unknown origins. It and the Vesper Martini (page 285) are the only two clear drinks that are traditionally shaken rather than stirred.

2½ fl oz (75 ml) brandy
1 tablespoon white crème de menthe

Pour the ingredients into a shaker two-thirds full of ice cubes. Shake well. Strain into a wineglass filled with crushed ice.

SEE ALSO *Kentucky Stinger, White Spider.*

ROOSTER SHAKER

The rooster shape of this 1928 silver-plated shaker is a visual play on the word "cocktail."

Stout Sangaree

THE STOUT SANGAREE is a bold and hearty drink, ideal to serve on a cold winter evening. It is the most popular drink in the large and varied Sangaree category, whose members are all made with a base wine, spirit, or beer and a sweetening agent such as simple syrup (or a liqueur such as Drambuie or triple sec). The result is garnished with a grating of nutmeg. Sangarees (whose name is a variant of Sangria in honor of the wine that's sometimes used) can be served over ice, neat, or straight up in a wineglass or beer glass.

1 ¼ cups (10 fl oz/310 ml) stout
2 fl oz (60 ml) ruby port
Ground or freshly grated nutmeg, for garnish

Pour the stout and port into a large wineglass. Sprinkle with nutmeg.

SEE ALSO *Applejack Sangaree, Brandy Sangaree, Irish Sangaree, Port Wine Sangaree, Rum Sangaree, Scotch Sangaree, Sherry Sangaree.*

STOUT—See Beer, page 97.

Tequila & Mezcal

Usually 40% alcohol by volume

All tequilas are distilled spirits made in demarcated regions of Mexico from a fermented mash of cooked blue agave, a member of the amaryllis family. By law, tequila must be made from just one variety of blue agave, 'Weber Tequilana Azul'. The related spirit known as mezcal is often made from other agaves as well.

The tequila production areas of Mexico

HOW TEQUILA IS MADE

Field workers known as *jimadores* (hee-mah-DOR-ace) harvest the mature agave plants by removing their spiky outer leaves and cutting off the remaining cores at the base. Workers then take these to be cooked, usually in steam ovens. The cooked and cooled agaves are crushed to release their sugary juices. These are then fermented, sometimes by wild yeast, otherwise by commercial yeast strains.

Once fermentation is complete, usually within three days, the mash is then distilled twice. Most producers now use modern continuous stills, though a few still employ the old pot stills, which are far more labor intensive and therefore more expensive to operate. Some tequilas are aged in casks before bottling.

The major difference among tequilas lies in the amount of blue agave distillate used in each bottling. *Mixto* (MEES-toh), a form of tequila that can be made with as little as 51 percent blue agave, with the rest of the distillate usually coming from sugarcane, is to all intents and purposes a blended tequila. Mixto is also the most popular form of tequila, often used in the preparation of cocktails, such as the Margarita, and mixed drinks.

If the phrase "100 percent agave" appears on the label, then that bottling is the best that can be had. These words denote that the bottle contains tequila made only from blue agave, with no other substances added. Bottlings of this caliber are usually savored neat.

100% AGAVE TEQUILA

Tequilas made entirely from blue agave have emerged in recent years as spirits worthy of appreciative sipping. The producer of the El Tesoro ("The Treasure") label offers several fine bottlings.

MOST POPULAR TEQUILA DRINKS

(according to U.S. bartenders)

1. Margarita, page 206
2. Tequila Sunrise, page 279
3. Frozen Margarita, page 156
4. Brave Bull, page 127
5. Long Island Iced Tea, page 194

REPOSADO TEQUILA

Barrel aging lends this style an intricate flavor.

STYLES OF TEQUILA

A number of brands of the following styles of tequila are readily available in the United States. They are listed below in order of age.

If you visit Mexico, look for other brands that aren't exported—just ask the locals for recommendations.

BLANCO Known as white or silver tequilas in English, these are unaged and bring sharp, tangy, peppery notes to the palate.

GOLD Also called *joven abocado* (young and smoothed) tequilas, these must by law contain a small percentage of tequila that has been aged in oak for at least two months. Gold tequilas are called so because they are usually somewhat smoother than white tequilas.

REPOSADO Aged in oak for a minimum of two months, *reposado* (rested or aged) tequilas are usually more intricate than white tequilas and bear a fruitiness not usually found in unaged bottlings.

AÑEJO These extra-aged tequilas must spend at least one year in oak barrels. (Many times, used bourbon casks are employed.) Añejo tequilas can be of very high quality, and their flavors can differ greatly from one bottling to the next. Most, however, exhibit muted herbal notes and are quite soft on the palate. Some bottlings are labeled *muy añejo* and usually indicate their age on the label; many are aged for as long as five to seven years. Like regular añejo bottlings, these are very intricate spirits. Some are even reminiscent of fine Cognacs.

TEQUILA VERSUS MEZCAL

Since shortly after the Spanish arrived there in the sixteenth century, Mexico has produced a category of agave spirits called *mezcal*. Actually, all agave-based spirits—including tequila—are known collectively as mezcals, but those bearing the mezcal name are not necessarily made from the 'Weber Tequilana Azul' variety of blue agave, as all tequila must be by law.

Many mezcals come from small artisanal distilleries that cook the agaves in clay ovens, resulting in a smoky flavor, and then distill the product in primitive stills, sometimes also made of clay. Mezcals, which are somewhat oily and pungent, are to say the least an acquired taste. They are not usually used in the preparation of cocktails and mixed drinks.

THE MEZCAL WORM

Certain bottlings of mezcal include an agave-dwelling "worm" (actually a moth larva), whose pickled state is touted as proof that the product has not been watered down. The worm is by no means traditional, originating with a 1950s entrepreneur who first included it as a marketing gimmick.

Serving Tequila

ENJOY 100 PERCENT agave tequilas either at room temperature or chilled from the refrigerator or freezer. Serve them in sherry copita glasses or brandy snifters (page 41). Blanco and gold tequilas are best for cocktail-making or for serving neat with the traditional lime wedge and pinch of salt.

To drink tequila this way, pour 1½ fl oz (45 ml) into a shot glass. Rub the lime wedge on the back of your hand where the thumb meets the forefinger, allowing some lime juice to moisten the skin. Sprinkle the salt onto the damp area of your hand. Now lick the salt from your hand, drink the tequila in one go, and bite down on the lime wedge.

TEQUILA COOLER

2½ fl oz (75 ml) tequila
6 to 7 fl oz (180 to 210 ml) lemon-lime soda
1 lemon twist, for garnish

Pour the tequila and lemon-lime soda into an ice-filled Collins glass. Stir briefly. Add the lemon twist.

TEQUILA FIX

This isn't a true Fix since it calls for lime juice instead of lemon juice (see Gin Fix, page 167).

2½ fl oz (75 ml) tequila
2 tablespoons fresh lime juice
1 tablespoon pineapple juice
1 pineapple spear, for garnish

Pour the tequila, lime juice, and pineapple juice into a shaker two-thirds full of crushed ice. Shake well. Strain into a highball glass filled with crushed ice. Garnish with the pineapple spear.

TEQUILA FIZZ

2 fl oz (60 ml) tequila
2 tablespoons fresh lime juice
1 tablespoon simple syrup (page 23)
5 to 6 fl oz (150 to 180 ml) club soda
1 lime wedge, for garnish

Pour the tequila, lime juice, and simple syrup into a shaker two-thirds full of ice cubes. Shake well. Strain into a chilled wineglass. Add the club soda. Stir briefly. Add the lime wedge.

TEQUILA MARTINI (DRY)

Although tequila is an unconventional ingredient in a Martini, it creates an interesting counterpoint to the herbal notes in the vermouth.

3 fl oz (90 ml) white tequila
1 tablespoon dry vermouth
1 lemon twist or 1 green cocktail olive, for garnish

Pour the tequila and vermouth into a mixing glass two-thirds full of ice cubes. Stir well. Strain into a chilled cocktail glass. Add the desired garnish.

TEQUILA MARTINI (EXTRA DRY)

3 fl oz (90 ml) white tequila
1½ teaspoons dry vermouth
1 lime wedge, for garnish

Pour the tequila and vermouth into a mixing glass two-thirds full of ice cubes. Stir well. Strain into a chilled cocktail glass. Add the lime wedge.

TEQUILA MARTINI (MEDIUM)

2½ fl oz (75 ml) white tequila
1½ teaspoons dry vermouth
1 lime wedge, for garnish

Pour the tequila and vermouth into a mixing glass two-thirds full of ice cubes. Stir well. Strain into a chilled cocktail glass. Garnish with the lime wedge.

TEQUILA MARTINI (SWEET)

2½ fl oz (75 ml) añejo tequila
1½ teaspoons sweet vermouth
1 maraschino cherry, for garnish

Pour the tequila and vermouth into a mixing glass two-thirds full of ice cubes. Stir well. Strain into a chilled cocktail glass. Garnish with the cherry.

TEQUILA MARY

Tequila combines surprisingly well with tomato juice. For a variation, try using orange juice in place of the lime juice.

2 fl oz (60 ml) tequila
4 fl oz (120 ml) tomato juice
1 tablespoon fresh lime juice
¼ teaspoon black pepper
Generous pinch of salt
¼ teaspoon cayenne pepper
3 dashes hot sauce
1 lime wedge, for garnish

Pour the tequila, tomato juice, and lime juice into a shaker two-thirds full of ice cubes. Add the black pepper, salt, cayenne pepper, and hot sauce. Shake well. Strain into an ice-filled highball glass. Add the lime wedge.

TEQUILA MOCKINGBIRD

2½ fl oz (75 ml) white tequila
½ teaspoon white crème de menthe
1 tablespoon fresh lime juice

Pour all of the ingredients into a shaker two-thirds full of ice cubes. Shake well. Strain into a chilled cocktail glass.

TEQUILA PUNCH

This is a very refreshing drink to serve during hot weather. Make it more aromatic with a garnish of fresh mint sprigs.

2 fl oz (60 ml) white tequila
2 fl oz (60 ml) fresh orange juice
2 fl oz (60 ml) pineapple juice
1 tablespoon fresh lime juice
2 to 3 fl oz (60 to 90 ml) club soda

Pour the tequila and all of the fruit juices into a shaker two-thirds full of ice cubes. Shake well. Strain into an ice-filled Collins glass. Add the club soda.

TEQUILA SOUR

Technically only a distant cousin of the Sour (see Whisky Sour, page 307), this is nontheless a wonderfully refreshing drink.

2 fl oz (60 ml) white tequila
1 ½ tablespoons fresh lime juice
1 tablespoon simple syrup (page 23)
1 lime wedge, for garnish

Pour the tequila, lime juice, and simple syrup into a shaker two-thirds full of ice cubes. Shake well. Strain the drink into a chilled Sour glass. Add the lime wedge.

TEQUILA SUNRISE

2½ fl oz (75 ml) white tequila
4 fl oz (120 ml) fresh orange juice
1 ½ teaspoons grenadine

Pour the tequila and orange juice into an ice-filled highball glass. Stir briefly. Pour the grenadine into the top of the drink.

THAMES CHAMPAGNE COCKTAIL

The intricate herbal notes from the Pimm's eliminate the need for bitters in this drink.

1 sugar cube
1 tablespoon Pimm's No. 1
5 fl oz (150 ml) Champagne or sparkling wine

Drop the sugar cube into the bottom of a chilled Champagne flute. Add the Pimm's, then the Champagne.

THIRD-DEGREE COCKTAIL

This Prohibition-era drink was named for the unnerving interrogations for which the Chicago police were renowned.

2 fl oz (60 ml) gin
1 tablespoon dry vermouth
2 teaspoons absinthe substitute (such as Pernod or Ricard)

Pour all of the ingredients into a mixing glass two-thirds full of ice cubes. Stir well. Strain into a chilled cocktail glass.

TOASTED ALMOND

2 tablespoons amaretto
2 tablespoons coffee liqueur (such as Kahlúa)
3 tablespoons light cream

Pour all of the ingredients into a shaker two-thirds full of ice cubes. Shake well. Strain into an ice-filled Old-Fashioned glass.

Tom and Jerry

THIS WINTER DRINK is traditionally served from a Tom and Jerry bowl into Tom and Jerry cups. Although these sets are no longer made, they show up at many antique stores.

When making the base for this drink, beat the egg whites until frothy but not stiff; otherwise the texture will be too thick. You can substitute peach brandy for the brandy.

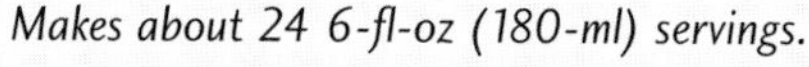

Makes about 24 6-fl-oz (180-ml) servings.

12 eggs, separated (see caution, page 22)
1½ cups (12 fl oz/375 ml) sugar
1 teaspoon baking soda
2 cups (16 fl oz/500 ml) dark rum
2 cups (16 fl oz/500 ml) brandy
2 qt plus 1 cup (72 fl oz/2.25 l) milk, scalded
Ground or freshly grated nutmeg, for garnish

In a mixing bowl, combine the egg yolks, 1¼ cups (10 fl oz/310 ml) of the sugar, and the baking soda. Whisk until the mixture is creamy and thick.

In a Tom and Jerry bowl or another mixing bowl, beat the egg whites until frothy. Sprinkle in the remaining ¼ cup (2 fl oz/65 ml) of sugar and continue beating until soft peaks form. Fold the egg whites into the egg yolk mixture to make a batter.

Gradually add the rum and brandy to the batter, whisking constantly.

Divide the batter equally among 24 Tom and Jerry cups or punch cups. Add some of the hot milk to each cup (just pour it in, don't stir). Sprinkle nutmeg over each serving.

Tom Collins

THIS DRINK WAS reportedly named for a bartender at a London restaurant called Limmer's. It was first recorded in cocktail books in the late nineteenth century, and some early recipes called for whisky rather than gin. The Collins glass (page 41) was created especially for this drink.

2 fl oz (60 ml) gin
1 tablespoon fresh lemon juice
1 tablespoon simple syrup (page 23)
5 to 6 fl oz (150 to 180 ml) club soda
1 lemon wedge, for garnish

Pour the gin, lemon juice, and simple syrup into a shaker two-thirds full of ice cubes. Shake well. Strain into an ice-filled Collins glass. Pour in the club soda. Stir briefly. Add the lemon wedge.

SEE ALSO *Applejack Collins, Brandy Collins, Irish Collins, Jock Collins, John Collins, Rum Collins, Vodka Collins, Whisky Collins.*

TRILBY COCKTAIL

2 fl oz (60 ml) blended Canadian whisky
2 tablespoons sweet vermouth
2 dashes Angostura bitters

Pour all of the ingredients into a mixing glass two-thirds full of ice cubes. Stir well. Strain into a chilled cocktail glass.

Vermouth

16–18% alcohol by volume

Vermouth is an aromatized wine—that is, a wine fortified with grape spirit, then flavored with botanicals, usually a combination of herbs, roots, seeds, fruits, and flowers. The precise recipe for the botanicals in any particular brand of vermouth is a well-protected proprietary secret.

Probably from the German Wermut, *or possibly the Old English* wermod, *vermouth means "wormwood," a bitter herb that was employed medicinally for centuries and is still an ingredient in some bottlings of vermouth.*

A 1930s advertising placard for Martini & Rossi, the major Italian maker of vermouth

SWEET VERMOUTH

Reddish in color, this style contributes bitter-herbal notes to numerous drinks.

The first commercial vermouth appeared in late-eighteenth-century Italy and resembled what we call sweet vermouth today. Dry vermouths were introduced in France in the early nineteenth century. Today vermouth is made in almost every wine-producing country, from relatively inexpensive wines.

Dry and sweet vermouth may be the most familiar types, but there are a number of other styles as well.

DRY Also known as French vermouth, this pale golden style is typically light and dry with a crisp, herbal taste.

SWEET Usually red, often labeled *Rosso,* this sweeter style (also known as Italian vermouth) has a slight bitterness, though its herbal accents are often muted.

BIANCO Like dry vermouth, bianco is clear in color and bears a medium-sweet flavor with pleasant herbal notes.

ROSÉ Similar to bianco, rosé vermouth has a pinkish hue from brief contact with grape skins, and a drier palate.

Serving Vermouth

VERMOUTHS ARE MOST familiar as ingredients in the Martini (dry vermouth) and the Manhattan (sweet vermouth), but all types are also enjoyed as aperitifs. Although they can be served neat, at room temperature, they are far more palatable over ice, preferably in a small wineglass. Dry, bianco, and rosé vermouths are also pleasant to sip tall with ice and club soda added.

VERMOUTH CASSIS

This is sometimes known as the Pompier Highball. Use a little less cassis for a drier version of the drink.

2½ fl oz (75 ml) dry vermouth
1 tablespoon crème de cassis
4 to 6 fl oz (120 to 180 ml) club soda
1 lemon twist, for garnish

Pour the vermouth and cassis into an ice-filled Collins glass. Add club soda to fill the glass. Stir briefly. Garnish with the lemon twist.

VERMOUTH COCKTAIL

An astonishingly complex drink, not too high in alcohol.

3 tablespoons sweet vermouth
3 tablespoons dry vermouth
2 dashes Angostura bitters
1 maraschino cherry, for garnish

Pour both vermouths and the bitters into a mixing glass two-thirds full of ice cubes. Stir well. Strain into a chilled cocktail glass. Add the cherry.

VESPER MARTINI

The James Bond series of books and movies made this drink popular. Note that, as Bond insisted, it is classically shaken rather than stirred.

1¼ fl oz (40 ml) gin
1¼ fl oz (40 ml) vodka
1 tablespoon Lillet Blanc
1 lemon twist, for garnish

Pour the gin, vodka, and Lillet into a shaker two-thirds full of ice cubes. Shake well. Strain into a chilled cocktail glass. Add the lemon twist.

⃠ VIRGIN BANANA COLADA

7 fl oz (210 ml) pineapple juice
$2\frac{1}{2}$ fl oz (75 ml) canned coconut cream (such as Coco Lopez)
1 ripe banana, cut into 1-inch (2.5-cm) pieces
1 pineapple spear, for garnish

Put the pineapple juice, coconut cream, and banana in a blender containing 1 cup (8 fl oz/250 ml) of ice cubes. Blend well. Pour into a chilled wineglass. Add the pineapple spear.

⃠ VIRGIN BANANA DAIQUIRI

Overripe bananas work very well in drinks such as this one; be sure to use fresh lime juice to provide a tart counterpoint.

2 fl oz (60 ml) fresh lime juice
2 tablespoons simple syrup (page 23)
1 ripe banana, cut into 1-inch (2.5-cm) pieces

Put all of the ingredients in a blender containing 1 cup (8 fl oz/250 ml) of ice cubes. Blend well. Pour into a chilled wineglass.

⃠ VIRGIN CAESAR

6 fl oz (180 ml) clam-tomato juice
1 tablespoon fresh lemon juice
Pinch of ground black pepper
Pinch of celery salt
Dash of hot sauce (optional)
1 lemon wedge, for garnish

Pour the clam-tomato juice and lemon juice into a shaker two-thirds full of ice cubes. Add the pepper, celery salt, and hot sauce. Shake well. Strain into an ice-filled highball glass. Add the lemon wedge.

⦸ VIRGIN MARY

6 fl oz (180 ml) tomato juice
1 tablespoon fresh lime juice
¼ teaspoon black pepper
Generous pinch of salt
¼ teaspoon ground cumin
2 dashes Worcestershire sauce
2 dashes hot sauce
1 lime wedge, for garnish

Pour the tomato juice and lime juice into a shaker two-thirds full of ice cubes. Add the pepper, salt, cumin, Worcestershire sauce, and hot sauce. Shake well. Strain into an ice-filled highball glass. Add the lime wedge.

⦸ VIRGIN PEACH COLADA

7 fl oz (210 ml) pineapple juice
2½ fl oz (75 ml) canned coconut cream (such as Coco López)
1 ripe peach, stoned, cut into about 6 pieces
1 pineapple spear, for garnish

Put the pineapple juice, coconut cream, and peach in a blender containing 1 cup (8 fl oz/250 ml) of ice cubes. Blend well. Pour into a chilled wineglass. Garnish with the pineapple spear.

⦸ VIRGIN PEACH DAIQUIRI

2 fl oz (60 ml) fresh lime juice
2 tablespoons simple syrup (page 23)
1 ripe peach, stoned, cut into about 6 pieces

Put all of the ingredients in a blender containing 1 cup (8 fl oz/250 ml) of ice cubes. Blend well. Pour into a chilled wineglass.

⃠ VIRGIN PIÑA COLADA

7 fl oz (210 ml) pineapple juice
2½ fl oz (75 ml) canned coconut cream (such as Coco López)
1 cup (8 fl oz/250 ml) pineapple chunks
1 pineapple spear, for garnish

Put the pineapple juice, coconut cream, and pineapple chunks in a blender containing 1 cup (8 fl oz/250 ml) of ice cubes. Blend well. Pour into a chilled wineglass. Add the pineapple spear.

⃠ VIRGIN PLANTER'S PUNCH

This is a marvelously refreshing hot-weather drink that can be made without the simple syrup if you desire a more tart rendition.

3 fl oz (90 ml) grapefruit juice
2 fl oz (60 ml) pineapple juice
2 tablespoons fresh lime juice
1 tablespoon simple syrup (page 23)
2 tablespoons club soda
1 pineapple spear, for garnish

Pour the fruit juices and simple syrup into a shaker two-thirds full of ice cubes. Shake well. Pour into an ice-filled Collins glass. Add the club soda and stir briefly. Garnish with the pineapple spear.

⊘ VIRGIN STRAWBERRY COLADA

7 fl oz (210 ml) pineapple juice
2½ fl oz (75 ml) canned coconut cream (such as Coco Lopez)
1 cup (8 fl oz/250 ml) ripe strawberries, hulled and halved
1 pineapple spear, for garnish
1 ripe strawberry, for garnish

Put the pineapple juice, coconut cream, and halved strawberries in a blender containing 1 cup (8 fl oz/250 ml) of ice cubes. Blend well. Pour into a chilled wineglass. Add the garnishes.

⊘ VIRGIN STRAWBERRY DAIQUIRI

3 tablespoons fresh lime juice
2 tablespoons simple syrup (page 23)
1 cup (8 fl oz/250 ml) ripe strawberries, hulled and halved
1 ripe strawberry, for garnish

Put the lime juice, simple syrup, and halved strawberries in a blender containing 1 cup (8 fl oz/250 ml) of ice cubes. Blend well. Pour into a chilled wineglass. Add the strawberry.

VODKA—See page 290.

VODKA AND TONIC

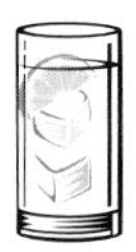

2½ fl oz (75 ml) vodka
4 fl oz (120 ml) tonic water
1 lime wedge, for garnish

Pour the vodka and tonic water into an ice-filled highball glass. Stir briefly. Add the lime wedge.

Vodka

Usually 40–50% alcohol by volume

Vodka is a clear spirit, generally distilled from a fermented mash of grains, although potatoes or beets are sometimes used. It bears no distinctive color, flavor, or aroma. This is because it is distilled to a very high proof and therefore contains few, if any, of the residual impurities that give flavor to products such as brandy or whisk(e)y. The word vodka in Russian means "small water," and the spirit originated in eastern Europe, probably in the fourteenth century. Many countries lay claim to having invented vodka, with Russia and Poland the most adamant.

Sweden, Poland, Finland, and the Netherlands are among the many producers of vodka.

FROM EUROPE TO THE UNITED STATES

An eastern European mainstay for centuries, vodka remained relatively unknown outside Europe until the 1940s. That was when John G. Martin, who was trying to get his company's Smirnoff brand off the ground, and Jack Morgan, a Los Angeles restaurateur who had a surplus of ginger beer on hand, concocted the Moscow Mule (page 216)—vodka, lime juice, and ginger beer. A decade later it was again Smirnoff who heavily promoted the Bloody Mary, making vodka even more popular. Today, American bartenders claim that Vodka Martinis outsell the gin-based original at least eight to one.

Although vodka is now distilled in many countries, the most venerated bottlings still come from vodka's traditional home in Russia, Poland, Finland, and Sweden. However, differences among vodkas are subtle because they all have so little innate flavor.

HOW VODKA IS MADE

Making vodka that has no distinctive odor or flavor requires distillation to a very high proof. Therefore, most vodkas are made in continuous stills, which can make spirits bearing as much as 96 percent alcohol in a single pass. If vodka is made in an old-fashioned pot still, it must be redistilled at least twice before it can approach this strength. Prior to bottling, all vodkas are filtered in a last attempt to remove any trace impurities. The resulting neutral spirit is bottled without aging.

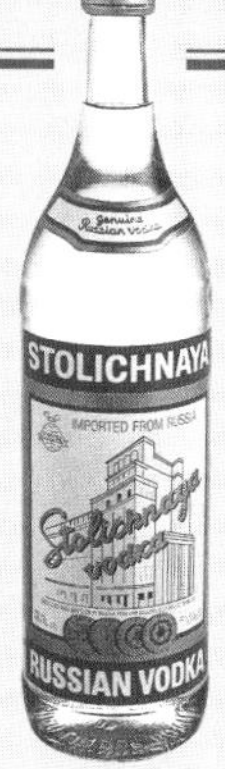

RUSSIAN VODKA

Like other quality vodkas, Stolichnaya, a premium Russian brand, is smooth and full-bodied.

PERTSOVKA VODKA

Hot peppers add zip to this Russian flavored vodka.

FLAVORED VODKAS

Flavored vodkas have found great popularity in recent years, probably because they are so handy behind the bar. Don't think that flavored vodkas are new, though. In all probability they date back just as far as vodka itself, since the poorly produced spirits of the fourteenth century were often flavored with fruits, herbs, and spices that would mask their off notes.

The flavors of most newer bottlings are usually part of the name (for example, citrus vodka, pineapple vodka), or a picture on the label indicates them. Bottles of *kafya* vodka, for instance, depict coffee beans. Labels of the fiery *pertsovka* vodka depict a bright red pepper.

Some other flavors, however, are less easy to discern. Żubrówka Bison Brand vodka, made in Poland and Russia, is flavored to resemble the bison grass formulation used traditionally and bears strong herbal notes. *Okhotnichaya* vodka, from the Russian for "hunter's vodka," gains its flavor from a host of herbs and fruit zests. It has a fruity, honeyed taste.

MOST POPULAR VODKA DRINKS

(according to U.S. bartenders)

1. Vodka and Tonic, page 289
2. Cosmopolitan, page 143
3. Bloody Mary, page 106
4. Screwdriver, page 256
5. Vodka Martini (Dry), page 294

Serving Vodka

HIGH-QUALITY VODKA should be served neat, from the freezer, in special vodka glasses (page 41), sherry copita glasses, or brandy snifters. Pour 1½ fl oz (45 ml) into each glass. Vodka is traditionally served with caviar or smoked salmon, and is downed in a single gulp.

VODKA COLLINS

2 fl oz (60 ml) vodka
1 tablespoon fresh lemon juice
1 tablespoon simple syrup (page 23)
5 to 6 fl oz (150 to 180 ml) club soda
1 lemon wedge, for garnish

Pour the vodka, lemon juice, and simple syrup into a shaker two-thirds full of ice cubes. Shake well. Strain into an ice-filled Collins glass. Add the club soda. Stir briefly. Add the lemon wedge.

VODKA FIX

2½ fl oz (75 ml) vodka
2 tablespoons fresh lemon juice
1 tablespoon pineapple juice
1 pineapple spear, for garnish

Pour the vodka, lemon juice, and pineapple juice into a shaker two-thirds full of crushed ice. Shake well. Strain into a highball glass filled with crushed ice. Add the pineapple spear.

VODKA GIBSON

Feel free to alter the proportions of vodka to vermouth to suit your taste.

3 fl oz (90 ml) vodka
1 tablespoon dry vermouth
1 pearl onion, for garnish

Pour the vodka and vermouth into a mixing glass two-thirds full of ice cubes. Stir well. Strain into a chilled cocktail glass. Add the onion.

VODKA GIMLET

2½ fl oz (75 ml) vodka
1 tablespoon sweetened lime juice (such as Rose's)
1 lime wedge, for garnish

Pour the vodka and sweetened lime juice into an ice-filled Old-Fashioned glass. Stir briefly. Add the lime wedge.

VODKA MARTINI (DRY)

3 fl oz (90 ml) vodka
1 tablespoon dry vermouth
1 lemon twist or 1 green cocktail olive, for garnish

Pour the vodka and vermouth into a mixing glass two-thirds full of ice cubes. Stir well. Strain into a chilled cocktail glass. Add the desired garnish.

VODKA MARTINI (EXTRA DRY)

3 fl oz (90 ml) vodka
1½ teaspoons dry vermouth
1 lemon twist or 1 green cocktail olive, for garnish

Pour the vodka and vermouth into a mixing glass two-thirds full of ice cubes. Stir well. Strain into a chilled cocktail glass. Add the desired garnish.

VODKA MARTINI (MEDIUM)

2½ fl oz (75 ml) vodka
1½ teaspoons dry vermouth
1 lemon twist or 1 green cocktail olive, for garnish

Pour the vodka and vermouth into a mixing glass two-thirds full of ice cubes. Stir well. Strain into a chilled cocktail glass. Add the desired garnish.

VODKA MARTINI (SWEET)

2½ fl oz (75 ml) vodka
1½ teaspoons sweet vermouth
1 lemon twist, for garnish

Pour the vodka and vermouth into a mixing glass two-thirds full of ice cubes. Stir well. Strain into a chilled cocktail glass. Garnish with the lemon twist.

VODKA RICKEY

Although the Gin Rickey (page 170) is the original drink in this category, the Vodka Rickey is probably the more popular version.

2½ fl oz (75 ml) vodka
2 tablespoons fresh lime juice
5 to 6 fl oz (150 to 180 ml) club soda
1 lime wedge, for garnish

Pour the vodka and lime juice into an ice-filled highball glass. Add the club soda. Stir briefly. Add the garnish.

VODKA SOUR

2 fl oz (60 ml) vodka
1½ tablespoons fresh lemon juice
1 tablespoon simple syrup (page 23)
1 orange wheel, for garnish
1 maraschino cherry, for garnish

Pour the vodka, lemon juice, and simple syrup into a shaker two-thirds full of ice cubes. Shake well. Strain the drink into a chilled Sour glass. Add the garnishes.

Ward Eight

THIS DRINK DATES back to 1898, when—according to William Grimes, author of *Straight Up or On the Rocks*—it was created at the Locke-Ober Café in Boston to celebrate a local politician's victory. Interestingly enough, the election was not due to be held until the day after the celebrations.

The Ward Eight is a fairly simple drink. Although you can substitute blended Canadian whisky for the bourbon in this recipe, it's important to keep the proportions of all the ingredients as listed below. The lemon juice serves as a good, tart counterpoint to the sweetness of the orange juice and the grenadine, but too much lemon juice will overpower the drink.

2 fl oz (60 ml) bourbon
2 tablespoons fresh orange juice
2 tablespoons fresh lemon juice
1 teaspoon grenadine

Pour all of the ingredients into a shaker two-thirds full of ice cubes. Shake well. Strain into a chilled cocktail glass.

These now-vanished brands of blended whiskey were produced by a Pennsylvania distillery.

Wassail

APPLE CIDER IS THE BASIS for Wassail, a traditional beverage that dates back to thirteenth-century England. At harvest time, pagan villagers would sing to the apple orchards to give thanks for a bountiful crop. Afterward, the owner of the orchard would reward the singers with a hot spiced drink containing hard cider. The word *wassail* stems from the Anglo-Saxon *wæs hæil,* which means "be thou hale" or "good health."

There are many recipes for Wassail. This one can be altered by substituting a different style of ale, such as amber, for the brown ale.

Makes 6 9-fl-oz (280-ml) servings.

1 tablespoon ground allspice
2 teaspoons ground or freshly grated nutmeg
1 cinnamon stick (about 3 inches/7.6 cm long)
4 fl oz (120 ml) simple syrup (page 23)
1 cup (8 fl oz/250 ml) hot water
1 quart (32 fl oz/1 l) brown ale
1½ cups (12 fl oz/375 ml) hard cider

Place the allspice, nutmeg, and cinnamon stick into a nonreactive large saucepan. Add the simple syrup and hot water. Cook over medium heat, stirring constantly, until hot, about 10 minutes. Add the ale and cider and cook, stirring constantly, until almost boiling. Ladle the wassail into beer mugs.

SEE ALSO *Lamb's Wool.*

Whisk(e)y

Usually 40–50% alcohol by volume

The spelling of whisk(e)y depends on where it is made: The Scots and Canadians omit the e; *the Americans and Irish include it. There are exceptions; for example, some U.S. bourbons are labeled "whisky."*

The whisky regions of Scotland

HOW WHISK(E)Y IS MADE

Production methods vary, but all whisk(e)ys are distilled from a base of fermented grains. The grain for malt whisk(e)y is sprouted before fermentation. Distillation takes place in either traditional pot stills or in modern column stills. The result is aged in casks before bottling.

SCOTLAND

Scotch whisky is the most popular style in the world, and some bottlings can be as intricate as fine Cognac. Today there are many categories and subcategories of Scotch. Here are brief descriptions of the important ones.

SINGLE-MALT SCOTCH The aficionado's favorite, single-malt Scotch is made from a fermented mash of malted barley, dried over smoldering peat to introduce the smoky flavors present in Scotch whisky. The mash is distilled at least twice—sometimes three times—in old-fashioned pot stills. To be designated a single-malt Scotch, the spirit must be the product of one distillery and must be aged for a minimum of three years in oak casks.

Where single-malt Scotch is concerned, Scotland is traditionally divided into five stylistic regions: Campbeltown, Highlands, Islay, Lowlands, and Speyside. (See map, left.)

Campbeltown, a small town on a peninsula of Scotland's southwestern coast, produces single-malt Scotches typically bearing a briny character, along with some peaty-iodine notes.

SINGLE-MALT SCOTCH

The Macallan Malt Whisky, a highly regarded single malt from the Speyside region, gets some of its flavor from the sherry casks in which it is aged.

MOST POPULAR WHISK(E)Y DRINKS

(according to U.S. bartenders)

1. Irish Coffee, page 179
2. Manhattan, page 204
3. Rob Roy, page 237
4. Whisky Sour, page 307
5. Old-Fashioned, page 219

BLENDED SCOTCH

Many drinkers prefer the milder flavor of blended Scotch, such as Dewar's.

Highland single malts, from the northern reaches of Scotland, make up the largest category. They are usually fresh, heathery, and medium-bodied, although the many bottlings can vary tremendously.

Islay (EYE-luh) Scotches, from the small island of that name just off Scotland's southwestern coast, are usually characterized by their combination of peat, seaweed, iodine, and medicinal tones.

Lowland single-malt Scotches, from southern Scotland, are usually lighter and somewhat cleaner-tasting than those from other regions of Scotland.

Speyside, a subregion of the Highlands along the Spey River, is home to more than 50 distilleries, each with its own style. Although Speyside produces light-, medium-, and heavy-bodied malts, all of these can be characterized as complex and mellow, with hints of peat.

BLENDED SCOTCH The most popular style, blended Scotch is made by combining a number of single-malt Scotches with neutral grain whisky, a flavorless, high-proof whisky similar to vodka. Blended Scotches can be intricate and very flavorful, since most higher-priced bottlings use a large percentage of single-malt Scotch.

IRELAND

The Irish claim to have started making whiskey before the Scots. It is possible that medieval Irish monks were indeed responsible for introducing the art of distillation to Scotland, although there is no written evidence of that fact.

Irish whiskey is made in much the same way as Scotch, except that peat is not used to dry the malted barley. This results in a softer spirit, full of flavor, but without the smoky notes present in Scotch.

Most bottlings of Irish whiskey are blended whiskeys—a marriage of single-malt whiskey with neutral grain whiskey. But single-malt Irish whiskeys do exist, and more bottlings are becoming available as time goes by.

UNITED STATES

Whiskey has been made in the United States since at least the early eighteenth century, when immigrant farmers from Germany, Ireland, and Scotland began distilling in Pennsylvania, Virginia, and Maryland. All American whiskeys are made in much the same manner, by distilling a fermented mash of grains in a continuous still, and then redistilling the resultant spirit in an old-fashioned pot still. The new spirit is then usually transferred to new, charred oak casks, where it ages before being bottled. American whiskeys can be very complex, although Scotch is usually regarded as superior.

BOURBON Bourbon first became known in the United States in the late eighteenth century when Kentucky distillers sent their whiskey downriver to Saint Louis and New Orleans from Bourbon County. It first became known as "whiskey from Bourbon," and eventually just as bourbon.

Bourbon must be made from a minimum of 51 percent corn. The other grains

"BOTTLED IN BOND"

Products labeled with this phrase have been government certified to contain 50 percent alcohol and to have aged at least four years.

STRAIGHT BOURBON

"Straight" means a whiskey has been barrel aged for at least two years and mixed only with water.

TENNESSEE WHISKEY

Jack Daniel's whiskey is produced at America's oldest registered distillery, in Lynchburg, Tennessee.

RYE WHISKEY

Pennsylvania, the home of this now-forgotten label, was one of the first U.S. states to produce straight rye whiskey.

are malted barley and either rye or wheat, although legally any other grains could be used. Bourbon is usually thought of as a sweet whiskey, but there are many full-bodied, complex, spicy bourbons on the market.

Small-batch bourbon is taken from a few select barrels in the aging house that the distiller who produced the bourbon has deemed superior.

Single-barrel bourbon is taken from just one barrel that the distiller has deemed superior.

TENNESSEE WHISKEY There are only two whiskey distilleries in Tennessee—George Dickel and Jack Daniel's—and these plants produce corn-based whiskeys in much the same way as bourbon distilleries do. However, before aging, Tennessee whiskey is filtered through huge vats of sugar-maple charcoal (charcoal made from sugar-maple wood).

RYE WHISKEY Straight rye whiskey is made with at least 51 percent rye and is aged in new, charred oak barrels. It is usually spicier and more fragrant than bourbon.

CANADA

Canadian whisky, very popular in mixed drinks but not considered a connoisseur's sipping whisky, has been very popular in the United States since the repeal of Prohibition in 1933. At that time, there was far more whisky in Canada than in America, and the new whiskey made in the United States still required aging before it could be bottled and sold.

Canadian whisky of the 1930s was made predominantly with rye grain, and thus became known as rye whisky. These days, however, most Canadian whisky is distilled from a fermented mash of mainly corn, aged in oak barrels, and then blended with almost flavorless, neutral grain whisky.

Under Canadian law, producers may add small amounts of wines such as sherry and prune wine; spirits such as Cognac, bourbon, malt whiskey, and rum; and other natural flavorings.

CANADIAN WHISKY

Blended Canadian whisky, such as Canadian Club, is the usual choice for mixing.

Serving Scotch and Other Whisk(e)ys

SINGLE-MALT SCOTCH and single-malt Irish whiskey should be served neat, at room temperature, in a sherry copita glass or a brandy snifter (page 41). Pour 1½ fl oz (45 ml) into each glass and add a little uncarbonated mineral water if desired.

Blended Scotch and blended Irish whiskey can also be consumed this way, but they are more often poured over ice or combined in an ice-filled highball glass with a mixer such as ginger ale. Blended Scotches are also usually the Scotch of choice when making cocktails such as the Rob Roy (page 237). Blended Irish whiskeys are typically preferred for cocktails and mixed drinks such as Irish Coffee (page 179).

High-quality American bourbons, Tennessee whiskeys, and rye whiskeys should be served neat, at room temperature, in a sherry copita glass or a brandy snifter. Although some people enjoy Canadian whisky neat at room temperature, it is best served over ice in a rocks glass or in an ice-filled highball glass with a mixer such as ginger ale.

WHISKY BUCK

1 lemon wedge
2 fl oz (60 ml) blended Canadian whisky
5 fl oz (150 ml) ginger ale

Squeeze the lemon wedge into a highball glass and drop it into the glass. Fill the glass with ice cubes. Add the whisky and ginger ale. Stir briefly.

WHISKY COLLINS

2 fl oz (60 ml) blended Canadian whisky
1 tablespoon fresh lemon juice
1 tablespoon simple syrup (page 23)
5 to 6 fl oz (150 to 180 ml) club soda
1 lemon wedge, for garnish

Pour the whisky, lemon juice, and simple syrup into a shaker two-thirds full of ice cubes. Shake well. Strain into an ice-filled Collins glass. Add the club soda. Stir briefly. Garnish with the lemon wedge.

WHISKY COOLER

The Whisky Cooler can be made with any carbonated beverage substituted for the ginger ale in this recipe, but the ginger ale adds a spiciness to the drink.

2½ fl oz (75 ml) blended Canadian whisky
6 to 7 fl oz (180 to 210 ml) ginger ale
1 lemon twist, for garnish

Pour the whisky and ginger ale into an ice-filled Collins glass. Stir briefly. Add the lemon twist.

WHISKY CRUSTA

Granulated sugar, to coat rim of glass
Lemon peel spiral (see technique, page 53)
2 fl oz (60 ml) blended Canadian whisky
1 tablespoon maraschino liqueur
1 tablespoon fresh lemon juice

Coat the rim of a Sour glass with sugar (see technique, page 49). Place the lemon peel spiral in the glass so that it uncoils to almost fill the interior. Pour the whisky, maraschino liqueur, and lemon juice into a shaker two-thirds full of crushed ice. Shake well. Strain into the glass.

WHISKY FIX

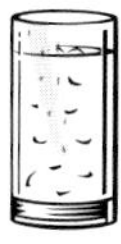

2½ fl oz (75 ml) blended Canadian whisky
2 tablespoons fresh lemon juice
1 tablespoon pineapple juice
1 pineapple spear, for garnish

Pour the whisky, lemon juice, and pineapple juice into a shaker two-thirds full of crushed ice. Shake well. Strain into a highball glass filled with crushed ice. Garnish with the pineapple spear.

WHISKY FIZZ

2 fl oz (60 ml) blended Canadian whisky
2 tablespoons fresh lemon juice
1 tablespoon simple syrup (page 23)
5 to 6 fl oz (150 to 180 ml) club soda
1 lemon wedge, for garnish

Pour the whisky, lemon juice, and simple syrup into a shaker two-thirds full of ice cubes. Shake well. Strain into a chilled wineglass. Add the club soda. Stir briefly. Add the lemon wedge.

WHISKY FLIP

2½ fl oz (75 ml) blended Canadian whisky
1½ tablespoons simple syrup (page 23)
1 egg (see caution, page 22)
Ground or freshly grated nutmeg, for garnish

Pour the whisky and simple syrup into a shaker two-thirds full of ice cubes. Add the egg. Shake very well. Strain into a chilled wineglass. Sprinkle with nutmeg.

WHISKY SLING

2½ fl oz (75 ml) blended Canadian whisky
1 tablespoon simple syrup (page 23)
1 tablespoon fresh lemon juice
5 to 6 fl oz (150 to 180 ml) club soda
1 lemon wedge, for garnish

Pour the whisky, simple syrup, and lemon juice into a shaker two-thirds full of ice cubes. Shake well. Strain the drink into an ice-filled Collins glass. Add the club soda. Stir briefly. Garnish with the lemon wedge.

WHISKY SWIZZLE

You can substitute a liqueur such as Yukon Jack for the simple syrup in this recipe.

2 fl oz (60 ml) blended Canadian whisky
1 tablespoon fresh lemon juice
1 tablespoon simple syrup (page 23)
5 to 6 fl oz (150 to 180 ml) ginger ale
1 lemon wheel, for garnish

Pour the whisky, lemon juice, and simple syrup into a shaker two-thirds full of ice cubes. Shake well. Strain the mixture into an ice-filled Collins glass. Add the ginger ale. Stir briefly. Add the lemon wheel and a swizzle stick.

Whisky Sour

DRINKS IN THE Sour category, of which the Whisky Sour is the most popular member, date back to the 1880s. Lemon juice adds the sourness, which the simple syrup tames. The drink is served in a Sour glass, created especially for it.

- 2 fl oz (60 ml) blended Canadian whisky
- 1½ tablespoons fresh lemon juice
- 1 tablespoon simple syrup (page 23)
- 1 orange wheel, for garnish
- 1 maraschino cherry, for garnish

Pour the liquids into a shaker two-thirds full of ice cubes. Shake well. Strain the drink into a chilled Sour glass. Add the garnishes.

SEE ALSO *Amaretto Sour, Apricot Sour, Bourbon Sour, Brandy Sour, Gin Sour, Irish Sour, Pisco Sour, Rum Sour, Scotch Sour, Southern Comfort Sour, Tequila Sour, Vodka Sour.*

WHITE LADY COCKTAIL

- 2½ fl oz (75 ml) gin
- 2 tablespoons light cream
- 1 egg white (see caution, page 22)
- 1 tablespoon simple syrup (page 23)

Pour all of the ingredients into a shaker two-thirds full of ice cubes. Shake very well. Strain into a chilled cocktail glass.

WHITE RUSSIAN

This was a popular drink in the 1960s and 1970s. A heavier-bodied version can be made with less vodka and more coffee liqueur.

2 fl oz (60 ml) vodka
2 tablespoons coffee liqueur (such as Kahlúa)
2 tablespoons light cream

Pour all of the ingredients into a shaker two-thirds full of ice cubes. Shake well. Strain into an ice-filled Old-Fashioned glass.

WHITE SPIDER

This drink is actually a Vodka Stinger, but is more popularly known as a White Spider.

2 fl oz (60 ml) vodka
1 tablespoon white crème de menthe

Pour the ingredients into a shaker two-thirds full of ice cubes. Shake well. Strain into a wineglass filled with crushed ice.

WHITE WINE—See Wine, opposite.

WHITE WINE SPRITZER

6 fl oz (180 ml) white wine
1 to 2 fl oz (30 to 60 ml) club soda
1 lemon twist, for garnish

Pour the wine and club soda into an ice-filled Collins glass. Stir briefly. Add the lemon twist.

Wine

Usually 9–14% alcohol by volume

Wine is the product of the natural fermentation of the sugars in the juice of ripe grapes. A wine may be red, white, or rosé (also known as blush). Wines are divided into four types: still, sparkling (see Champagne & Sparkling Wine, page 134), aromatized (see Vermouth, page 283), and fortified (see Madeira, page 202; Port, page 230; and Sherry, page 258). Still wines may be sweet, dry, or in between, depending on how much sugar remains after fermentation.

"From the vine...onto your table!" proclaims this French wine ad from the 1950s.

HOW WINE IS MADE

In simple terms, wine is produced by harvesting ripe grapes, crushing them to release their juices and to let the yeast work on the sugars in the grape juice. For white wines, the juices are separated from the skins and seeds and pumped into vats or oak casks, where the fermentation can begin. For red wines, the grape juices, skins, and seeds remain together, since the wine gains body, tannin (giving the wine texture and longevity), and color from these elements. The color of red wine comes from the skins of the black grapes, whose juice in most cases is the same clear color as that of white grapes.

Fermentation continues until all or most of the natural grape sugar is consumed, or until the yeast dies. The wine is then drawn off into vats or casks, where it will rest and precipitate solids, called *lees.* Since wines should not spend too much time in contact with lees, the wine may be moved to clean vats several times during its first year of life. Wines that will age further are moved to oak casks and taken to the cellars. Bottling takes place when the winemaker and cellar master deem the wine ready.

TASTING WINE

Start by observing the wine's clarity, and shade and depth of color. Then smell the wine: put your nose into the glass and take a deep breath. Now, swirl the wine in the glass and smell it again; note new aromas that reach your nose. Next, taste the wine: take a mouthful and swish it around against your tongue and gums, taking note of its feel, its flavor, its bite. Swallow the wine, noting how long its taste lingers. Make notes about the experience to increase your future enjoyment.

A WORLD OF WINE

Winemaking dates back to prehistoric times, and probably originated near the Black Sea. We know that wine was made in ancient Egypt, Greece, Rome, and Phoenicia, and probably anyplace else where grapevines could grow.

Who can say which country makes the best wines? Certainly, France, Italy, and the United States rank high on everyone's list, but Germany, Spain, Portugal, Chile, Argentina, Australia, New Zealand, and South Africa don't lag far behind.

Whatever their origins, the best wines are the ones that you can afford and that taste good to you. But having particular favorites should not keep you from sampling unfamiliar wines. Taste new wines whenever you can; buy a mixed case and jot down your preferences. A delicious world awaits.

FRENCH BORDEAUX

France's Bordeaux region is home to some of the world's finest wines.

Serving Wine

A GOOD BASIC WINEGLASS has a capacity of at least 8 fl oz (250 ml), and its rim is slightly smaller than the circumference of the bowl. Never fill a wineglass more than halfway full. It is necessary to leave room to swirl the wine, aerating it and opening up its aroma. Stemmed glasses are preferred, since the drinker can hold them by the stem and have a clear view of the wine. If the wine is chilled, the stem prevents the drinker from inadvertently warming the wine with his or her hands.

As a rule, red wines are served at a cool room temperature—65°F to 68°F (18°C to 20°C). A few light red wines, such as Beaujolais and Gamay, benefit from slight chilling. The ideal serving temperature for white wine is around 45°F (7°C) or slightly warmer—overchilling can mask white wine's nuances. Sweet white wines can be served slightly colder than dry white wines, but no wine should be chilled below 42°F (6°C).

WOO WOO

The Woo Woo is relatively new. If you prefer it as a shorter drink, reduce the amount of cranberry juice to 3 tablespoons, stir it over ice, and serve it in a chilled cocktail glass.

2 fl oz (60 ml) vodka
1 tablespoon peach schnapps
4 fl oz (120 ml) cranberry juice cocktail

Pour all of the ingredients into an ice-filled highball glass. Stir briefly.

XYZ COCKTAIL

2 fl oz (60 ml) dark rum
1 tablespoon triple sec
1 tablespoon fresh lemon juice

Pour all of the ingredients into a shaker two-thirds full of ice cubes. Shake well. Strain into a chilled cocktail glass.

YALE COCKTAIL

Named for the Ivy League college, this drink used to be made with crème Yvette, a violet-flavored liqueur that's no longer available.

2½ fl oz (75 ml) gin
1½ teaspoons dry vermouth
1½ teaspoons blue curaçao
Dash of Angostura bitters

Pour all of the ingredients into a mixing glass two-thirds full of ice cubes. Stir well. Strain into a chilled cocktail glass.

YELLOWBIRD

The Yellowbird is a very complex drink that's popular at a number of Caribbean resorts.

2 fl oz (60 ml) light rum
1 tablespoon Galliano
1 tablespoon triple sec
1 tablespoon fresh lime juice

Pour all of the ingredients into a shaker two-thirds full of ice cubes. Shake well. Strain into a chilled cocktail glass.

ZOMBIE

The Zombie was created in the late 1930s and was a very popular drink at Polynesian-style American restaurants such as Trader Vic's. Don't consume this potent drink through a straw, since you will not experience the delight of the 151-proof rum that floats on top.

2 fl oz (60 ml) añejo rum
2 fl oz (60 ml) dark rum
1 tablespoon fresh lime juice
2 tablespoons pineapple juice
2 teaspoons apricot brandy
2 dashes Angostura bitters
½ teaspoon 151-proof rum
1 pineapple spear, for garnish
1 mint sprig, for garnish

Pour the añejo rum, dark rum, lime juice, pineapple juice, apricot brandy, and bitters into a shaker two-thirds full of ice cubes. Shake well. Strain into an ice-filled Zombie glass. Pour the 151-proof rum over the back of a spoon on top of the drink. Add the garnishes.

Glossary

A collection of bartending terms used in this book, as defined by mixologists and beverage experts.

A

ABSINTHE SUBSTITUTE Any of several clear, aniseed-flavored liquors, such as Pernod and Ricard, that turn an opaque, pale yellow-green when diluted with water, and that replace true absinthe liquor (long banned in many countries because of its supposed toxicity).

ALE A large category of beers made with a top-fermenting yeast, including amber ale, bitter ale, India pale ale, Scotch ale, Trappist ale, porter, wheat beer, lambic, cream ale, stout, and barley wine.

ALCOHOL BY VOLUME (ABV) The percentage of alcohol in a given volume of an alcoholic beverage. Also called the Gay-Lussac scale, ABV is usually specified on beverage labels instead of or in addition to proof.

APERITIF A beverage, usually alcohol based, drunk prior to a meal to stimulate the appetite.

AROMATIZED WINES Wines, such as vermouth, slightly fortified by the addition of small amounts of spirits and flavored with an array of botanical ingredients.

ARMAGNAC A type of brandy made from fermented grape juice (wine) and produced in Gascony, France.

B

BAR SPOON A long spoon—about 11 inches (28 cm)—with a shallow bowl and a twisted shaft, usually used to stir together ingredients in cocktails and mixed drinks.

BEER An alcoholic beverage made by fermenting a mash, or soup, of cooked grains.

BITTERS An alcoholic liquid infused with various botanical ingredients, usually used in very small quantities as a flavor enhancer for cocktails and mixed drinks. Beverages such as Campari, sometimes a base in mixed drinks, contain less alcohol than do bitters such as Angostura and Peychaud, but are also known as bitters because of their bitter flavor. (They're not the same as British bitter, a type of ale.)

BLENDED CANADIAN WHISKY A spirituous liquor made in Canada from a fermented mash of grains. Natural flavorings may be added.

BLENDED WHISK(E)Y A spirituous liquor made by mixing one or more flavorful whisk(e)ys (such as single-malt Scotches) with almost flavorless neutral whisk(e)y.

BOSTON SHAKER A bar tool consisting of two tapered cylinders—one of them metal, the other glass—used to prepare shaken or stirred cocktails and mixed drinks. In the case of stirred drinks, only the glass portion of the shaker is used.

BOTANICALS A collective term describing the herbs, fruits, spices, and other ingredients used to flavor certain liquors, beers, and wines.

BOURBON A whiskey made in the United States, distilled from a fermented mash of grains composed of at least 51 percent corn.

BRANDY A spirituous liquor made from fermented grape juice (wine).

BUCK A drink made of a base spirit, a squeezed wedge of lemon, and ginger ale. Bucks are always served in highball glasses.

C

CALVADOS A spirituous liquor made in a delimited region of northern Normandy, France, typically from a fermented mash of apples.

CHAMPAGNE A sparkling wine made in a delimited region of northeastern France.

CHURCH KEY A two-headed implement for opening bottles, and also for opening cans by piercing a V-shaped hole in their lids.

COBBLER A drink consisting of a base spirit or wine and simple syrup, poured into a wine goblet full of crushed ice and stirred together.

COCKTAIL A mixed drink that is shaken or stirred with ice and strained into a chilled cocktail glass. Not all cocktails have the word *cocktail* in their name.

COLLINS A drink made with a base spirit, lime or lemon juice, simple syrup, and club soda. These drinks are always served in Collins glasses, usually garnished with fresh fruit.

COOLER A drink comprising a base spirit or liqueur topped with any carbonated beverage. Coolers are served in Collins glasses, garnished with a lemon twist.

CORDIAL An alcoholic beverage, often called a liqueur, made from a spirit, a sweetening agent such as sugar or honey (or both), and additional flavorings.

CRUSTA A drink consisting of a base spirit, lemon juice, and maraschino liqueur. Crustas are served straight up in a sugar-rimmed Sour glass lined with a spiral of lemon peel.

D

DAISY A drink composed of a base spirit, lemon juice, and grenadine. Daisies are served over crushed ice in a highball glass, garnished with a lemon twist.

DASH The amount of liquid emitted from containers with constricted openings, such as bitters bottles. Equivalent to ⅛ teaspoon.

DIGESTIF A beverage, usually with an alcohol base, that is drunk after a meal to stimulate digestion.

E

EAU-DE-VIE A type of brandy made from a fermented mash of fruit and occasionally aged in oak barrels.

F

FIX A drink composed of a base spirit, lemon juice, and pineapple juice. Fixes are served over crushed ice in a highball glass, garnished with fresh fruit.

FIZZ A drink made with a base spirit, lime or lemon juice, simple syrup, and club soda. Fizzes are served straight up in a wine goblet, garnished with fresh fruit.

FLIP A drink made with a base wine, spirit, or beer; a whole raw egg; and simple syrup. Flips are served straight up in a wine goblet or beer glass, garnished with grated nutmeg.

FORTIFIED WINE A wine that has had grape spirit added to it. The most common examples are Madeira, port, and sherry.

FRAPPÉ A drink composed solely of a base liqueur or spirit, served over crushed ice in a saucer Champagne glass or a Sour glass.

G

GARNISH A fruit or vegetable component placed into a drink mainly for visual effect. Sometimes paraphernalia such as paper parasols are also referred to as garnishes.

GIN A spirituous liquor usually made from a fermented mash of grains and flavored with various botanicals. Juniper is always the predominant botanical in this process.

H

HAWTHORN STRAINER A bar tool with a spring coil that holds it in place in a mixing glass; used to strain cocktails and mixed drinks.

HIGHBALL A simple mixed drink consisting of two ingredients (such as gin and tonic water) combined directly in the serving glass, typically a highball glass.

I

IRISH WHISKEY A spirituous liquor made in Ireland from a fermented mash of grains.

J

JIGGER A liquid measurement equal to 1½ fl oz (45 ml); a standard measurement for one portion of spirits that are served neat, such as whisk(e)y, tequila, and rum. A jigger is also a measuring device, usually metal, that doles out 1½-fl-oz

(45-ml) portions of alcohol for mixed drinks. It is usually combined with a pony measure in a device with a double-headed hourglass shape. A shot glass often has the same capacity as a jigger and is therefore sometimes used as a measuring tool; however, this practice may produce inaccurate results because a shot glass can contain up to 2 fl oz (60 ml).

L

LAGER A large category of beers made with a bottom-fermenting yeast; examples include Pilsner, Rauchbier, and the various types of Bock (Eisbock, Dopplebock, Maibock, and Märzen).

LIQUEUR An alcoholic beverage, sometimes called a cordial, made from a spirit, a sweetening agent such as sugar or honey (or both), and additional flavorings.

M

MADEIRA A wine fortified with grape spirit, produced on the Portuguese island of Madeira, situated in the Atlantic Ocean west of Morocco.

MASH Term for fruits, fruit juices, or cooked grains fermented by the introduction of yeast to produce wine (in the case of fruits and fruit juices) or beer (in the case of cooked grains), then often distilled to produce spirits.

MEZCAL A spirituous liquor made in Mexico from a fermented mash of the agave plant.

MIXED DRINK A combination of two or more liquid ingredients, at least one of them containing alcohol. A cocktail is one type of mixed drink.

MIXING GLASS The tapered glass cylinder that makes up one part of the Boston shaker; can be used alone to prepare stirred drinks rather than shaken drinks.

MUDDLING A process in which a variety of ingredients such as sugar cubes, fruit garnishes, and bitters are pressed together in the serving glass with a muddler or the back of a spoon.

N

NEAT A term referring to spirits served straight from the bottle without being chilled or mixed with any other ingredients.

P

PERFECT A term usually describing a cocktail or mixed drink that contains both sweet and dry vermouth. A few cocktails, however, contain the word *perfect* in their names but do not incorporate these ingredients.

POMACE The leftovers from the winemaking process, such as grape stems, seeds, and sometimes skins.

PONY A measure in a jigger tool, containing 1 fl oz (30 ml) of liquid. Also the name of a glass for serving spirits neat. Pony glasses vary in size, however, having a capacity of 1 to 3 fl oz (30 to 90 ml), and are therefore not reliable pony measures.

PORT A wine fortified with grape spirit, made in the Douro region of northern Portugal.

PROOF The degree of alcohol in a beverage. In the United States, proof is calculated on a scale of 200, thus 1 degree of proof equals 0.5 percent of alcohol by volume. Other countries use different scales, but almost everyone these days is discarding proof scales for the less-confusing percent alcohol by volume (ABV).

R

RICKEY A drink made with a base spirit, fresh lime juice, and club soda. Rickeys are traditionally served over ice in a highball glass, garnished with a wedge of lime.

RUM A spirituous liquor made from a fermented mash of molasses or sugarcane juice.

RYE WHISKEY A spirituous liquor made from a fermented grain mash containing a minimum of 51 percent rye grain.

S

SANGAREE A drink made with a base wine, spirit, or beer plus a sweetening agent such as simple syrup (liqueurs are sometimes used), garnished with grated nutmeg.

SCOTCH A spirituous liquor made in Scotland from a fermented mash of malted (sprouted) grains.

SHAKER A bar tool available in many different styles, used to shake together the ingredients in cocktails and mixed drinks.

SHERRY A wine fortified with grape spirit, made in a delimited region of Spain surrounding the city of Jerez.

SHOT One portion (usually 1½ fl oz/ 45 ml) of spirits served neat, typically in a shot glass, brandy snifter, or sherry copita glass. Shot glasses vary in size, however, having a capacity ranging from 1½ to 2 fl oz (45 ml to 60 ml), and are therefore not reliable shot measures.

SIMPLE SYRUP A sugar solution used to sweeten cocktails and mixed drinks because granulated sugar is hard to dissolve in cold liquids.

SINGLE-MALT SCOTCH A type of whisky produced by a single distillery in Scotland from a fermented mash of malted barley, and aged at least three years in oak casks.

SLING A drink made with a base spirit, citrus juice, simple syrup or a liqueur, and club soda. Slings are served over ice in a Collins glass, often garnished with fresh fruits.

SMASH A drink made with a base spirit, simple syrup, and crushed mint leaves. Smashes are served over crushed ice in an Old-Fashioned glass, garnished with a mint sprig.

SOUR A drink composed of a base spirit, lemon juice, and simple syrup. Sours are served straight up in a Sour glass, garnished with a maraschino cherry and an orange wheel.

SPARKLING WINE Wine containing carbon dioxide, usually produced by a secondary fermentation that takes place within the bottle. The primary fermentation takes place in vats.

SPIRIT An alcoholic beverage made by distilling a fermented mash of grains or fruits to a potency of at least 40 percent alcohol by volume. Examples include brandy, gin, rum, tequila, vodka, and whisk(e)y.

STRAIGHT WHISKEY By U.S. law, a whiskey distilled to a maximum of 80 percent alcohol by volume (ABV), aged in oak barrels to gain flavor, and diluted with water to not less than 40 percent ABV.

STRAINER A bar tool available in different styles, used to strain cocktails and mixed drinks from the ice that chills them.

SWIZZLE A drink made with a base spirit, citrus juice, simple syrup or a liqueur, and a carbonated beverage. Swizzles are served in Collins glasses with a swizzle stick and often garnished with fresh fruit.

T

TENNESSEE WHISKEY A spirituous liquor made from a fermented mash of grains. The spirit is filtered through sugar-maple charcoal prior to aging in barrels.

TEQUILA A spirituous liquor made in delimited areas of Mexico from a fermented mash of the 'Weber Tequilana Azul' variety of blue agave.

TODDY A drink made with a base spirit, hot water, and various spices. Toddies are served in Irish Coffee glasses, often garnished with a lemon twist or cinnamon stick.

V

VERMOUTH A wine slightly fortified by the addition of spirits and aromatized by the introduction of various botanicals.

VODKA A spirituous liquor made from a fermented mash, usually composed of grains but also sometimes made from vegetables and/or sugar.

W

WHISK(E)Y A spirituous liquor made from a fermented mash of grains and aged in oak barrels. Varieties include Scotch, Irish, bourbon, Tennessee, rye, and blended Canadian. As a rule, *whisky* refers to products of Scotland and Canada, *whiskey* to products of Ireland and the United States.

Z

ZEST The outer skin of citrus fruits, which contains flavored oils released by twisting the zest over the top of a cocktail or mixed drink.

Drink Index

DRINKS BY CATEGORY

BUCKS

COBBLERS

COFFEE DRINKS

COLADAS

COLLINSES

COOLERS

CRUSTAS

DAISIES

EGGNOGS

FIXES

FIZZES

⃠ *Nonalcoholic drink*

DRINKS BY LIQUOR TYPE

SCOTCH

SHERRY

SLOE GIN

SOUTHERN COMFORT

TEQUILA

TRIPLE SEC

VERMOUTH, DRY

VERMOUTH, SWEET

VODKA

DRINKS FOR SPECIAL OCCASIONS

Subject Index

C

H

I

J

K

CREDITS

PHOTOGRAPHY Scott Peterson, 4–5, 6, 8–9, 44–45, 76–77. Peter Alan Gould, 89, 123, 187, 191, 205, 248, 254, 270. Philip Griffith, photographer/collector, 240.

PHOTO STYLING Andrea Lucich

PHOTO RESEARCH Melinda Lawson Anderson, Photocentric. Lindsay Kefauver, Visual Resources.

EDITORIAL ASSISTANCE Margaret Garrou, Lisa Lee

PRODUCTION ASSISTANCE Brynn Breuner, Liz Fiorentino, Kathryn Meehan, Joan Olson

BAR TOOLS AND EPHEMERA Bacardi Rum poster, 240, reprinted from the Bacardi Museum Archives. Bacardi and the bat device are registered trademarks of Bacardi & Company Limited ©1996. Bacardi-Martini U.S.A., Inc., Miami, FL. Cocktail shakers from the collection of Robert Greenberg, 89, 123, 187, 191, 205, 248, 254, 270. Labels compliments of Vic Kroll/Kroll's Kollectibles, 96–97. Label and bottle from private collection, 200, 240. Matchbooks from the Richard I. Anderson collection, 98. Posters and promotional items from Miscellaneous Man, New Freedom, PA, 117, 134, 149, 195, 198.

PHOTO LOCATION Mecca restaurant, San Francisco, 4–5, 6, 8–9, 44–45, 76–77.

ACKNOWLEDGMENTS

The editors wish to thank Gene Tartaglian and Carl Christian, Stephen Visakay, Dale DeGroff, David Nepove, and Dr. Steve Goldenberg for their invaluable help and advice.